TRAINING THE Next Generation

ETHICAL, LEGAL, AND MANAGEMENT ISSUES IN THE WORKPLACE

D.N. McDonald
Kim F. Smith

Kendall Hunt
publishing company

Kendall Hunt
publishing company

www.kendallhunt.com
Send all inquiries to:
4050 Westmark Drive
Dubuque, IA 52004-1840

ISBN 978-1-4652-7517-2

Printed in the United States of America

BRIEF CONTENTS

Note: * indicates case studies containing sensitive content. The instructor should review the case content prior to class.

TABLE OF CONTENTS

DEDICATION

To my wonderful family, for your unconditional love and encouragement to fly;

To Dr. Quésha S. Starks, for giving me a chance in education and being the epitome of poise and professionalism under pressure;

To Dr. Edward D. Brown, for your willingness to share your wisdom;

To Rev. Lawrence Q. Barriner, for your unwavering support and prayers; and

To Sasha and Kwesiu, for the laughter in the midst of the hard work.

—D. N. McDonald

To my supportive and loving husband, Dr. Charles N. Smith, for always believing that I am capable of excelling way beyond my imagination.

To my children Joshua, Justin, Jazmyn, and Jaida and grandchildren, Leila and Mya—

Out of all of my accomplishments, none surpasses being mom and nana.

Jeremiah 29:11New International Version (NIV)

11 For I know the plans I have for you," declares the Lord, "plans to prosper you and not to harm you, plans to give you hope and a future."

—Kim F. Smith

PREFACE TO THE FIRST EDITION

One must simply examine the archives of history to find the correlation between societal issues and the law. Societal pressures, often the catalyst for legal reform, do not focus on the mundane, but target the areas that hurt, that have become so burdensome to those it enchains, that the law must respond to their cries. Part of my joy for education and passion for teaching comes from the opportunity to bring alive the voices of the silent, those who had no choice but to pursue action in courts so that their voices would be heard.

When I started teaching, I never took for granted my childhood knowledge of civil rights issues in America. Born into a family in which countless relatives participated in various civil rights events, I grew up hearing emotional accounts of how family members stopped traveling by bus and instead walked to work as participants in the Montgomery Bus Boycott. At family gatherings, stories were shared of encountering the oppressive tenets of Jim Crow as well as those of children leaving classrooms in 1963 to join classmates and others in local civil rights efforts in Birmingham. Unknowingly, through these personal experiences of my family and their friends, I was taught a solid foundation of respect for all people, an appreciation for the ultimate product of perseverance through struggle, and the awareness of the ongoing fight for equality and human rights.

The business world is reflective of the same issues. Our students exist in a post-trust era as a result of constant violations of ethics and professionalism. They will be tasked, as future business leaders, with rising above such unprincipled behavior to implement and promote sound business practices, to demonstrate cultural awareness and respect for diversity as well as to minimize liability. As an educator, I embrace the philosophy that to teach is to empower and build the whole person through knowledge, skill, character, and competence. Whatever the respective professional and personal paths my students choose, I hope that they are exposed to how the vacillating events of history have impacted us all.

On the cusp of entrance into the professional work environment, some of my students consider the oppressive weight of workforce challenges and wonder if they are ready to face them. In various classes, we have often explored a historical approach that eventually led to a road of modern day discussion. I have often heard students pose such questions as "Were work conditions so horrific that laws needed to be implemented to protect people?" and "Do we still need them now?" The goals and the title, namely *Training the Next Generation*, of this book were birthed from such classroom dialogue. Obviously, one purpose of this book is to promote skill building and growth in knowledge of business and legal concepts for the betterment of the individual and the workforce. In addition, my intent is to foster courageous conversations that will lead to a greater respect for the differences in people, a building of unbreakable bridges in culture, and an appreciation and respect for diversity.

Finally, I remind students, as I remind socially conscious faculty and myself, that the ongoing march for civil rights, in and out of the workplace, is not a singular, one-dimensional issue. It is a human issue. We should breathe and look around at all of the positive changes that have occurred. Nonetheless, we must not become complacent. I challenge students, all educators, business leaders as well as myself to continue the march, as there is much more work to be done. I hope that this engaging book encourages you to do the same.

D.N. McDonald

ACKNOWLEDGMENTS

The authors would like to thank the following individuals for their insight and support of this project. We offer a very special thank you to our copy editor, Dr. Quebe M. Bradford, for her invaluable feedback. Your assistance is greatly appreciated:

Dr. Edward D. Brown, *Alabama State University*
Dr. Charles N. Smith, *Wiley College*
Charles D. Jackson, *Auburn University at Montgomery*
Dr. Yolanda R. Cal, *Alabama State University*

The staff of Kendall Hunt Publishing Company, specifically our Senior Project Coordinator, Ryan Schrodt, and our Acquisitions Representative, Brittanie Tucker.

D.N. McDonald
Kim F. Smith

TEXT ORGANIZATION

This text explores the legal, management, and ethical issues of a fictional clothing corporation—FELIX, Inc. Each case study in this text consists of nine sections:

a. **Objectives:** Learning objectives are provided to inform instructors of specific outcomes that students may achieve through the use of case studies. At the end of the Application Activities in each case study, revisit the learning objectives to determine whether students have achieved them.

b. **Suggested Class Time:** The class time is an estimate of the time needed to read the Case Scenario, answer Discussion Questions, and complete the Self-Assessment. This section is useful for instructors to determine how to plan activities for class. The class times are flexible and may be modified to meet the needs of the instructor.

c. **Preliminary Activity:** Engaging activities designed to prepare students to learn more about key issues in the Case Scenario.

d. **Terms to Know**: Students will define the vocabulary terms that appear in this section.

e. **Who's In This Story?**: The intriguing employees of FELIX, Inc. appear throughout the 25 case studies in this text. This section will inform the reader of which employees will be showcased in each case study.

f. **Setting:** The location of where the events take place in each Case Scenario.

g. **Case Scenario:** Realistic facts concerning ethical, legal, and management issues within the workplace are featured.

h. **Discussion Questions:** Questions concerning the facts, ethical dilemmas, legal issues, and management conflicts of each case study will test student knowledge and application.

i. **Self-Assessment:** Personal exploratory assessments that lead students to evaluate themselves on a deeper level.

j. **Application Activities:** Optional extension activities that will allow instructors to incorporate additional content review for areas covered within the case study.

THE STORY OF FELIX, INC.

Phillip Fox, 64, a New York native, grew up in the New York state foster care system when both of his parents died in a car accident when he was six, leaving him with no living relatives. Though a highly intelligent youth, he engaged in delinquent behavior. While sentenced to complete community service for his offenses, Phil was mentored by a local judge, the Honorable Arthur Kines, who noted his intellect and great potential. Believing wholeheartedly in Phil and having no children of their own, Arthur and his wife Martha funded Phil's education at a prestigious fashion institute and supported him in his efforts to succeed.

Phylicia Cree, 62, heir to the multimillion dollar Cree legacy, is the only daughter of Richard and Ann Cree of *Cree Jewelers*. Foregoing a career within the family business, Phylicia followed her passion for design and attended the same fashion institute as Phil. After meeting on the first day of class, Phil and Phylicia became inseparable. Over the next two years, Phil served as Phylicia's tutor and eventually her mentor. Upon her graduation, Phylicia married Phil. The dynamic duo worked tirelessly to establish their longtime dream, the successful clothing line known as FELIX: Classic Apparel for Men and Women.

They have two children, Felix, 40, and Trish, 38. Felix, the current CFO of FELIX, has been married to his wife, Ashley, for seven years. Felix and Ashley have two sons, Felix Jr., 10, and Tanner, 8. Trish is the savvy marketing manager for FELIX.

For the last 35 years, FELIX has established a reputation for its modern, classic casual and business apparel for both men and women. Its headquarters is in Atlanta, Georgia with two additional offices in New York City (NYC) and Los Angeles (LA). The company has 210 full-time employees and 75 part-time employees and interns.

FELIX ORGANIZATIONAL CHART

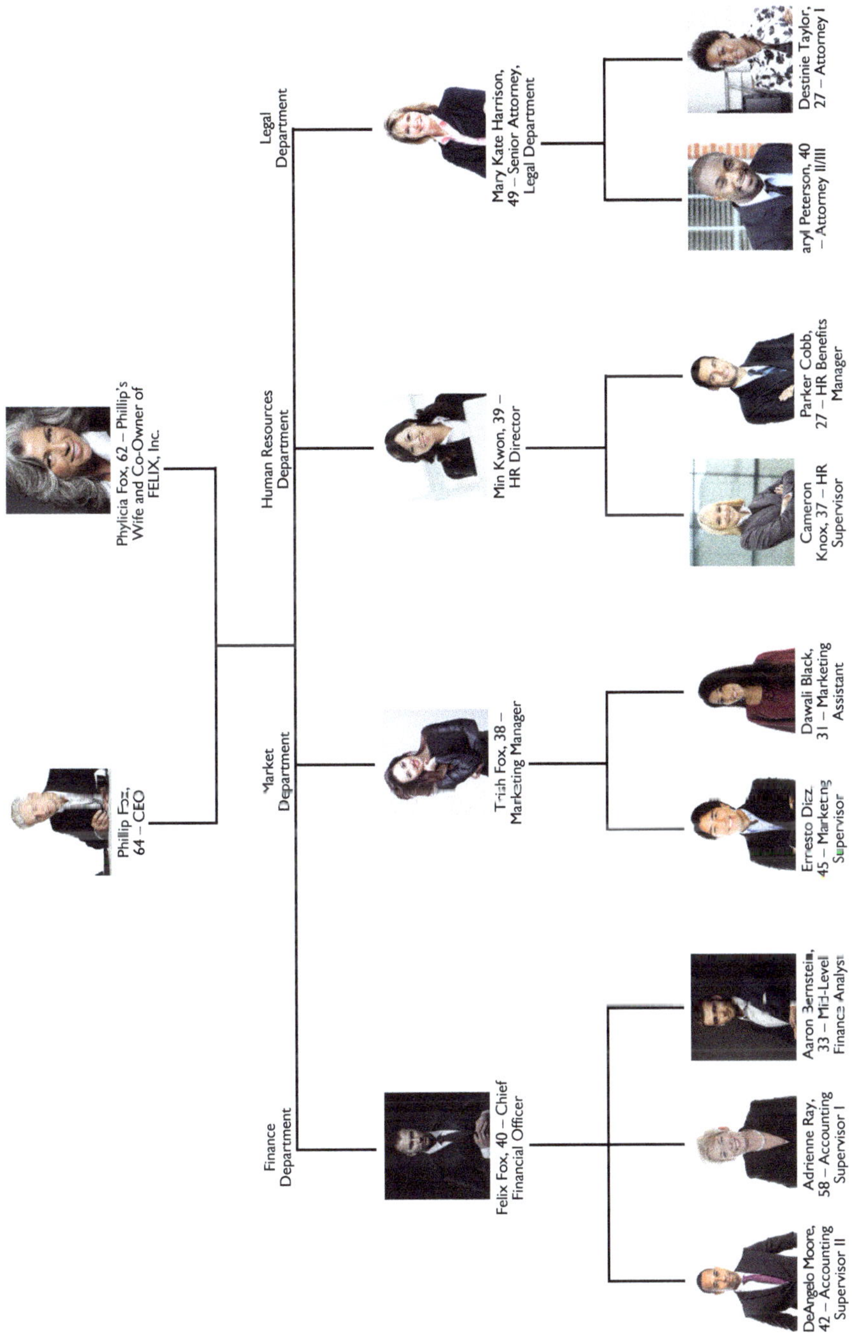

ABOUT THE AUTHORS

D.N. McDonald, Esq. is an assistant professor of Business Law and Management at Alabama State University and a former high school law instructor. McDonald has taught courses in employment law, negotiations, contracts, business law, business ethics, communications, torts, and family law.

Kim F. Smith, MBA is a management instructor at Alabama State University who formerly worked in human resources. Smith has taught courses in business orientation, business communications, human resource management, organizational behavior, direct marketing, and business law.

CASE STUDY I

AN ADDITION TO THE FELIX FAMILY

OBJECTIVES

Students will be able to:

A. identify legal and ethical issues that may arise during the interview and employment process;
B. critique interview and employment processes; and
C. formulate legal arguments and weigh the facts of the case study against present employment laws.

SUGGESTED CLASS TIME

3–4 class periods

TERMS TO KNOW

Define the following terms:

A. business ethics;
B. duty-based ethics;
C. outcome-based ethics;
D. social contract ethics; and
E. personalistic ethics.

PRELIMINARY ACTIVITY

Locate a job description of an entry-level analyst. Create a list of five relevant interview questions for this position. In addition, design a rubric that interviewers can use to score applicants.

WHO'S IN THIS STORY?

Aaron Bernstein, 33 FELIX Mid-Level Finance Analyst  © Shutterstock/eurobanks	Andreas Garcia, 22 FELIX Entry-Level Finance Analyst Applicant 1  © Shutterstock/se media
Adrienne Ray, 58 FELIX Accounting Supervisor 1  © Shutterstock/Zdenka Darula	Katherine Payne, 40 FELIX Entry-Level Finance Analyst Applicant 2  © Shutterstock/Luba V Nel
Tony Sampson, 25 FELIX Entry-Level Finance Analyst Applicant 3  © Shutterstock/InnervisionArt	

SETTING

Atlanta, FELIX Headquarters–Finance Interview Room

CASE SCENARIO

In January, FELIX releases announcements for three highly competitive job placements in its corporate headquarters. FELIX aims to hire three new personnel who are graduating seniors or recent graduates to work in the Finance, Marketing, and Human Resources (HR) Departments. Each department will place one new hire within its respective area. All hiring decisions must be made by the end of April. As of March 30, Finance is the only department that has not conducted interviews and selected a new employee.

Felix Fox, the Chief Financial Officer (CFO) of FELIX, previously directed DeAngelo Moore to ensure that the best applicant is selected for the entry-level finance analyst position. DeAngelo has reviewed the applications provided to him by Adrienne Ray. Adrienne and Aaron Bernstein are set to conduct the interviews for the three best applicants on April 10. Based on a review of the applicants and the interviewers' recommendations, DeAngelo will make the final hiring decision. He informs Adrienne that a new hire must be chosen from the three applicants because of time constraints.

All applicants were assessed on the following criteria and were directed to respond to three questions as a part of the application process:

The applicants provided the following information in their applications:

Hiring Criteria

The selected applicant must be team-oriented, self-motivated, and self-directed. In addition, the selected applicant must possess excellent communication skills.

Interview Questions

1. *What is one of the most challenging situations that you have encountered?*
2. *How did you handle the situation?*
3. *What did you learn from this experience?*

Finance Interview Room, 9:30 a.m.

Applicant 1: Andreas Garcia, 22 – He attends the prestigious Atlanta Park University on a full academic scholarship. He is majoring in accounting and has a 3.86 grade point average (GPA). He desires to take the Certified Public Accountant (CPA) Exam soon after graduation.

Interview of Applicant 1

Adrienne: Welcome to FELIX corporate headquarters, Mr. Garcia.

Andreas: Thank you for having me, Ms. Ray and Mr. Bernstein.

Aaron: Please have a seat.

Andreas: Thank you, sir.

During the interview, Andreas reveals his primary lifetime challenge: when he was nine years old, he had to leave his parents and younger siblings in Mexico to live with extended family in Georgia. He shares that he became a U.S. citizen seven years ago and believes that his family would benefit greatly from living in America. Eventually, he desires to move the remainder of his family to live with him in the United States. Despite the rigors of being a full-time student, Andreas manages to work 30 hours per week as a paid intern at a local CPA firm. He informs Adrienne and Aaron that he has learned the importance of paying attention to detail and utilizing effective verbal and written communication skills, which have been the keys to his success as an intern.

Aaron: Do you have any further questions for us, Mr. Garcia?

Andreas: No, sir. I appreciate your time, and thank you for interviewing me for this position.

Adrienne: I have one final question. If a translator was needed, would you feel comfortable speaking to your people on the corporate customer service line?

Andreas (*with a strained expression*): If it was a part of the job description, then yes.

Applicant 2: Katherine Payne, 40—She is a fifth-year graduating senior at Riverdale College. She receives some tuition assistance from a grant for non-traditional female college students. She is majoring in finance. Her GPA is 3.10.

Interview of Applicant 2

Adrienne: Hi, Katie. It's been way too long. You look great!

Katherine: Hey, Adrienne. Thanks, and how are you? This place has changed so much since the last time I picked you up for lunch. Wow . . . how long ago was that? At least a year ago, right?

Aaron: Oh, I wasn't aware that you two knew each other. Hello, Ms. Payne. I'm Aaron Bernstein.

Adrienne: Oh, sorry, Aaron. This is Katie . . . I mean, Katherine Payne.

Katherine: My apologies, Mr. Bernstein. Nice to meet you.

During the interview, Katherine mentions that she works as a part-time secretary at a local non-profit organization for 20 hours per week. After her divorce, she decided to return to college 18 years after graduating from high school. She reveals that her biggest challenge has been attending college at a later stage in life while raising her two teenage daughters. She expresses that her work as a secretary has given her a greater appreciation for all positions, from entry-level to executive. Through her experiences, she has truly realized that companies would not function properly without efficient people at all levels.

Aaron: It was nice to meet you, Katherine. I left the business cards in my office. Excuse me while I get one for you.

Aaron exits to retrieve his business cards, while Katherine and Adrienne walk toward the interview waiting area. Meanwhile, Andreas returns to the interview waiting area to retrieve a company business card. Katherine and Adrienne are now chatting in the waiting area. He overhears Adrienne speaking casually to Katherine, who he then discovers is another applicant. He witnesses Adrienne hug Katherine and tell her to say hello to her parents. Andreas leaves without being seen by Adrienne or Katherine.

Applicant 3: Tony Sampson, 25—He is a graduate of Florida College. As a mathematics major, he graduated with a 3.21 GPA and was President of the Mu Alpha Theta Chapter. He has been teaching trigonometry, pre-calculus, and calculus at a high school in Miami, Florida for two years.

Interview of Applicant 3

Aaron: Mr. Sampson, what has been your focus since graduating from college?

Tony: Well, besides developing professionally as a teacher, I have been preparing to take the CPA Exam. I am scheduled to take it in three months. I want to ultimately open my own CPA firm. I've already started looking at office spaces.

Adrienne: How do your plans fit the entry-level finance analyst position with FELIX?

Tony: I'm not sure exactly. The position was simply of interest to me. I am exploring my options at this time.

Tony also explains that his main hardship has been the death of his grandfather who was his role model. Tony could not answer any questions related to FELIX.

Interview notes taken by Adrienne and Aaron contained the following comments.

Adrienne's Notes

Andreas Garcia: serious personality, solid academic foundation, unlikely to fit within FELIX corporate environment, seems unwilling to work in customer service and other areas in the company, heavy speaking accent

Katherine Payne: great personality, balances work, academic, and personal responsibilities well, team player, great company knowledge

Tony Sampson: average interview, did not appear to be really interested in entry-level analyst position, likeable personality, overall good fit for FELIX culture despite lack of company knowledge

Applicant Choice: K. Payne

Aaron's Notes

Andreas Garcia: personable, likely to meet challenges of job, solid experience that relates to the available entry-level position, strong communication skills

Katherine Payne: has very good credentials but seems too friendly with Adrienne

Tony Sampson: has nice personality but seems more interested in pursuing CPA interests, appears to be a fast learner even though he lacked company knowledge

Applicant Choice: 1. Andreas Garcia; 2. Katherine Payne

A week later . . .

DeAngelo decides to offer Katherine the position after Adrienne convinces him that she is the overall best fit for the company. Katherine accepts; however, after FELIX conducts a background check, HR discovers that eight years ago she was convicted of possession of a controlled substance. DeAngelo contacts Katherine to ask her questions about the conviction. Because she possessed a small quantity of the drug and it was her first offense, Katherine received probation with mandatory substance abuse counseling. Katherine explains that she previously had some difficulty dealing with her divorce and made the bad decision to use marijuana to relieve stress. Nevertheless, she has overcome that part of her life and will not make the same choices again.

FELIX is a drug-free workplace and has a zero-tolerance policy against hiring individuals for certain criminal convictions. Its policy does not take into consideration the length of time that has transpired since a conviction. Because of the FELIX criminal conviction policy, DeAngelo revokes the job offer to Katherine and then, after speaking with Adrienne, selects Tony as the new employee.

DISCUSSION QUESTIONS

1. Consider the credentials of each applicant, the hiring process, and the selection of the final applicant. Who do you believe was the best applicant, and why?
2. Were the questions that Adrienne and Aaron asked Andreas appropriate for an entry-level finance analyst position? Explain your answer.
3. Assess the fairness of this hiring process. Based on your assessment, who could be potentially responsible for any challenges in the interview and hiring processes? Explain in detail the potential liability of and consequences for FELIX, DeAngelo, Adrienne, and Aaron.
4. Does Andreas have any legal claim(s) against FELIX? If so, what legal options does he have to resolve the claim(s)?
5. Does Katherine have any legal claim(s) against FELIX? Explain your answer.
6. What are the ethical considerations for companies like FELIX that enforce strict background check policies regarding drug convictions?
7. Should previous drug convictions completely exclude applicants from securing certain types of employment? If so, what are the legal issues that would arise from such employment policies?

SELF-ASSESSMENT

Explain the concept of business ethics. Research and explore your personal ethical perspectives from the following philosophies. Determine the philosophy that best suits you. As a class, engage in dialogue on the significance of ethical hiring practices.

a. Duty-Based Ethics, (e.g., Religious ethical standards, Kantian ethics, and the Principle of Rights)
b. Outcome-Based Ethics, (e.g., Utilitarianism)
c. Social Contract Ethics
d. Personalistic Ethics

APPLICATION ACTIVITIES

1. Choose either Equal Employment Opportunity Commission (EEOC) background check policies or the do's and don'ts of conducting interviews as a topic.
   a. Research the topic and prepare an outline.
   b. Write a research paper on the topic with a focus on diversity and cultural awareness.
   c. Present your findings on the selected topic, highlighting the importance of cultural sensitivity.
2. In pairs or in small groups, compose company background check and drug use policies. Each student group should share the policies with the class. Compare your group's policies with those of actual companies.
3. Complete a career ladder on an entry-level finance analyst position.
4. Rank the importance of the employment skills mentioned in the case scenario for the entry-level finance analyst. How do your rankings compare to those set forth on such sites as Careerbuider.com and Monster.com or in business magazines like *Forbes* and *Business Week*?

CASE STUDY 2

HIRING HODGEPODGE

OBJECTIVES

Students will be able to:

A. state the requirements of an age discrimination case;
B. explain the defenses to an age discrimination claim;
C. analyze the use of company background checks; and
D. compose a business memorandum.

SUGGESTED CLASS TIME

2–3 class periods

TERMS TO KNOW

Define the following terms:

A. age discrimination;
B. background check;
C. legal claim; and
D. non-disclosure clause.

PRELIMINARY ACTIVITY

Review the *Age Discrimination in Employment Act of 1967*. Briefly outline the elements needed for a plaintiff to prove a successful case of age discrimination. Discuss the elements as a class.

WHO'S IN THIS STORY?

Note to the Reader: This is a non-dialogue case scenario. These characters are mentioned in the story.

DeAngelo Moore, 42
FELIX Accounting
Supervisor II

© Shutterstock/Hugo Felix

Min Kwon, 38
FELIX HR
Director

© Shutterstock/Dragon Images

Adrienne Ray, 58
FELIX Accounting
Supervisor I

© Shutterstock/Zdenka Darula

Andreas Garcia, 22
Entry-Level Finance
Analyst
Applicant 1

© Shutterstock/se media

Katherine Payne, 40
Entry-Level Finance
Analyst
Applicant 2

© Shutterstock/Luba V Nel

Parker Cobb, 27
FELIX HR
Benefits Manager

© Shutterstock/vgstudio

Mary Kate Harrison, 49
FELIX Senior
Attorney

© Shutterstock/kurhan

Cooper Jones, 36
Attorney for
Katherine Payne

© Shutterstock/OFOLIA

SETTING

Atlanta, FELIX Headquarters—DeAngelo's Office and the HR Department; The Law Offices of Cooper Jones; and Katherine Payne's Home

CASE SCENARIO

On April 20, DeAngelo receives a letter from Tony, who was Applicant 3 for the entry-level finance analyst position. In the letter, Tony declined the FELIX job offer because he decided to remain a teacher while he takes the CPA Exam and develops a business plan for his own CPA firm. With the new hire deadline looming, DeAngelo contacts Andreas as he is the only one remaining in the applicant pool. DeAngelo calls Andreas and extends the offer to him. Andreas accepts. The next day, Andreas has an 8:30 a.m. appointment with Parker Cobb, a FELIX HR Benefits Manager, to complete new hire paperwork, including information for a background check.

Meanwhile . . .

Unknown to FELIX employees, Katherine meets with a civil attorney, Cooper Jones, to discuss her allegations of age discrimination and FELIX's overly broad background check and drug use policy. The attorney informs her that she should consider filing a complaint with the EEOC first. Katherine is apprehensive because the process could potentially take much longer based on the EEOC's case volume. Cooper agrees to conduct some preliminary research during his first opportunity on April 21.

Later in the day, Katherine arrives at home and receives a telephone call from Adrienne. They have known each other for a long time, and their parents are members of the same country club. Because of pressure from her parents, Adrienne wants to make sure that Katherine is not upset about the job situation. Adrienne's parents have vehemently expressed how embarrassed they are at the whole predicament, especially since the situation has placed a strain on their social interaction. Adrienne tells Katherine that Andreas was her last choice for the job but admits that he has been selected since Tony declined the job offer. Adrienne is unaware that Katherine is recording the entire conversation. Katherine calls Cooper and plays the recording to him. He promises to call DeAngelo at FELIX in the morning.

The next day . . .

While meeting with Parker, Andreas informs him that he is concerned about a statement that Adrienne made during his interview. According to Andreas, she said verbatim, "If a translator was needed, would you feel comfortable speaking to your people on the corporate customer service line?" He explains how offensive the statement was and asks Parker if it is customary to ask such questions during an interview. Parker contacts DeAngelo; they meet with Andreas in the HR department. DeAngelo states that he will speak to Adrienne regarding her interview question.

At 10 a.m., DeAngelo is in his office and is transferred a call. Cooper introduces himself and schedules an appointment with him for that afternoon. In the meeting, Cooper plays the tape recording of the conversation between Katherine and Adrienne. DeAngelo states that he has no comment and will call Cooper back in a few days. Highly upset, DeAngelo demands a meeting in his office with Adrienne, Mary Kate Harrison, Min Kwon, and Cameron Knox to discuss what can be done to avoid a major lawsuit. After developing a strategy, DeAngelo contacts Cooper. During the conversation, but before Mary Kate and Min can object, DeAngelo offers to temporarily hire Katherine as a full-time finance intern for six months with a possibility of permanent hire based on performance evaluations. To avoid litigation, this special internship package consists of full employee benefits. Cooper agrees to present the offer to Katherine. He later informs her of the offer and strongly suggests that she accept it. He does not believe that she has a plausible age discrimination case. Katherine accepts the offer and will start the internship on June 1. After the stressful meeting in DeAngelo's office, Min realizes that Cameron, her HR Supervisor, never attended the meeting.

DISCUSSION QUESTIONS

1. Did Adrienne make the right decision in calling Katherine and speaking to her? What ethical issues are raised by this telephone conversation?
2. What should happen to Adrienne at FELIX as a result of this conversation? Explain.
3. Was Cooper correct in informing Katherine that she did not have a plausible age discrimination case against FELIX? Explain.
4. What defenses could FELIX present regarding Katherine's claim of age discrimination?
5. Does Katherine have a legal claim regarding an overly broad background check? By agreeing to accept DeAngelo's job offer, has Katherine relinquished any rights to pursue claims of age discrimination and background policy issues? Explain.
6. Did DeAngelo make the best decision by offering a job to Katherine? What other options could FELIX have explored and presented?
7. Should Mary Kate approach DeAngelo regarding his impromptu offer to Katherine? Defend your position.
8. Was it appropriate for Andreas to inform Parker about Adrienne's statement? Why or why not?
9. If you were Katherine, would you have accepted the six-month internship? Explain.
10. What is the law for recording conversations in your respective state?

SELF-ASSESSMENT

In leadership roles, one will be responsible for delegating and making vital decisions in the workplace. As a pre- or post-activity, complete the "Your Preferred Decision-Making Style" Exercise located in the Appendix.

APPLICATION ACTIVITIES

1. Adrienne has presented two management issues, specifically her interview question to Andreas and her telephone conversation with Katherine. Compose an internal office memo from DeAngelo to Adrienne regarding her conduct. Include any appropriate disciplinary actions in your communication.
2. Write and present a skit between DeAngelo and Adrienne as he addresses the two management issues mentioned in Application Activity #1
3. Prepare a sample settlement agreement between Katherine and FELIX concerning her temporary employment. Determine whether a non-disclosure clause should be included.
4. Each student in the class selected an ethical philosophy that best suited their individual perspectives in the Self-Assessment in Case Study 1. Apply your selected ethical philosophy to Adrienne's two management issues. Determine what should happen to Adrienne and how it will impact the stakeholders involved.
5. In one to two paragraphs, state how Parker could have responded to Andreas' concerns regarding Adrienne's statements. In your answer, consider the timeliness of Andreas' statement. Should he have waited until another incident occurred, or was he correct in bringing it to Parker's attention now?

CASE STUDY 3
INCOMPETENT LEADERSHIP—THE BREEDING GROUND FOR EMPLOYEE SABOTAGE

OBJECTIVES

Students will be able to:

A. identify problem areas that may cause employees to become disengaged in their work;
B. describe the negative impact that can be associated with nepotism;
C. demonstrate problem-solving skills in a hands-on team activity; and
D. recognize effective leadership styles.

SUGGESTED CLASS TIME

2–3 class periods

TERMS TO KNOW

Define the following terms:

A. leadership style;
B. participative leadership;
C. transformational leadership;
D. charismatic leadership;
E. service-oriented leadership;
F. situational leadership; and
G. nepotism.

PRELIMINARY ACTIVITY

Review the following five effective leadership styles: participative, transformational, charismatic, service-oriented, and situational. Research common signs of poor leadership and compare them.

WHO'S IN THIS STORY?

Felix Fox, 40
FELIX CFO

© Shutterstock/doodko

DeAngelo Moore, 42
FELIX Accounting
Supervisor II

© Shutterstock/Hugo Felix

Adrienne Ray, 58
FELIX Accounting
Supervisor I

© Shutterstock/Zdenka Darula

Katherine Payne, 40
FELIX Finance
Intern
(Temporary Employee)

© Shutterstock/Luba V Nel

SETTING

Atlanta, FELIX Headquarters—Finance Department

CASE SCENARIO

Although Felix has a Master of Business Administration (MBA) from Atlanta Park University, he has never worked for anyone other than his father. Many of the FELIX employees consider him to be a neophyte boss, who has the pleasure of benefiting from nepotism. Even though he seems knowledgeable about the retail industry, Felix is mainly focused on self-preservation and appearances. For instance, Felix rarely handles challenging situations in the office and depends heavily on his team, but he rarely gives them credit for their work. Under his leadership, there is a lack of trust among the team, and employees are slowly becoming disengaged and passively hostile. To make matters worse, Felix usually does not admit to his own mistakes and quickly blames others when situations do not go as planned.

On Monday morning . . .

Adrienne is still upset with Katherine about last week's incident. She feels hurt and double-crossed after learning that Katherine covertly taped their conversation. To prove to Felix that she can put personal differences aside, Adrienne plans to behave professionally toward Katherine, even if she has to force herself to bury the simmering negative feelings toward her.

As Felix arrives at the office, he sees Adrienne introducing everyone to Katherine, the new temporary finance intern that DeAngelo hired to avoid a potential lawsuit. He is not pleased to have Katherine at FELIX and does not like the fact that his team is being forced to hire her.

He blames Adrienne for her inability to keep her personal and professional lives separate. She had no business discussing private office hiring decisions with Katherine. Now, FELIX is obligated to appease Katherine for the next six months! What will he do with her should she perform well on the job? He has no intentions of keeping her. Surely, she cannot be trusted if she is capable of taping Adrienne, who is supposedly her friend. Moving forward, Felix decides to observe her carefully.

Out of his peripheral vision, Felix notices Adrienne and Katherine walking toward him. He hates having the tough conversations, which is why he values teamwork and dependability. He only feels the need to micromanage when he believes that problems will occur.

Adrienne: Good morning, Felix. I want to introduce you to Katherine Payne, our new finance intern.

Felix: Good morning, Adrienne. Katherine, it's nice to meet you. Welcome to FELIX.

Katherine: Thank you, Mr. Fox. I'm happy to be here.

Felix: Great. Please call me Felix. Adrienne, once you've helped Katherine get settled, I'd like to speak with you about the status of the funding for the upcoming fashion internship project. As a matter of fact, when DeAngelo arrives, let's have an impromptu meeting. Katherine, you may attend the meeting as well.

Adrienne: Sure.

As Adrienne and Katherine walk away, Felix decides that he will give Katherine a proper welcome. He will make sure that she has plenty of work to keep her occupied on her first day.

Later that morning . . .

Looking stressed, DeAngelo walks into the office in a hurry. He is overwhelmed and under enormous pressure, yet again. Today, he has to assist Felix with finding the capital to fund several projects, a task that Felix should already know how to do.

Felix: DeAngelo, good morning!

DeAngelo: Hello, Felix. Sorry, I'm a little late. I had a flat tire this morning and had to call AAA. How are you doing? Do you need me to do something?

Felix: Your tire is fixed now though, right?

DeAngelo: Yes, it is.

Felix: Okay. Well, now that you're here, we need to have a meeting in about ten minutes. I need to find out where we are with the fashion internship project. It will be here before you know it. Get Adrienne and Katherine. Meet me in the conference room.

DeAngelo: Right, but . . .

Felix: Have them there in ten. Thanks!

Frustrated, DeAngelo turns and leaves without saying another word. Felix believes he is motivating the team by calling these mandatory impromptu meetings, but in reality, they take the focus away from more pressing projects. Several team members have complained that Felix does not respect their time and fails to appreciate what they do for the company. Although Felix is aware of this, he does not seem to care. He feels that he is the boss and everyone in the company ought to respect that fact.

DeAngelo enters Adrienne's office and observes her training Katherine on how to use the accounting program and answer the phones. He notices that Adrienne is being overly nice to Katherine. Her exuberant compliments are exaggerated and just a hint below the point of appearing fake.

Adrienne: Hey, DeAngelo. Felix wanted me to tell you that we have a meeting today.

DeAngelo: Yes, I just saw him. He's ready for us now.

Adrienne: Now? I'm training Katherine. *(She nods her head, and then rolls her eyes at Katherine.)*

DeAngelo *(looking suspiciously at Katherine)*: I don't think that matters right now, but doesn't the secretary or Aaron normally conduct this training? Never mind, we need to go so that we can finish working on our other projects.

Adrienne: Yes, I will be glad when I can get back to my real job. All of this switching gears from one project to the other and assuming training duties is wearing me down. Goodness, I'm tired already! I'm not sure what's going on with me, but I can't seem to keep up. It's like my days are endless.

DeAngelo: I understand! I'm feeling the same way. I was hoping to make a few calls this morning and tie up some loose ends, but they will just have to wait.

Adrienne: If we don't get this project, you know who's going to be blamed, right?

Katherine observes Adrienne and DeAngelo. She makes a mental note to document their behavior as soon as she is alone. After all, she knows that the company plans to dismiss her after six months.

In the meeting . . .

Adrienne looks at DeAngelo, shakes her head, and sighs heavily. She is frustrated because Felix has yet to make the necessary calls to investors and clients. He failed, yet again, to solidify the funding for the marketing campaigns and internship partnerships with local colleges and universities.

DeAngelo has his own frustrations and under normal circumstances, he would be able to provide Adrienne with words of encouragement. However today, he too is challenged with keeping his emotions intact. He is angry with her for placing the company in a precarious situation.

Katherine observes Adrienne and DeAngelo's body language. They both look tense and are exchanging looks while sighing heavily. Trying to appear as if she is a team player, Katherine interjects.

Katherine: Can I help you guys with anything? If necessary, I can make several calls to clients today.

Felix: Yes, you can do that, Katherine. Adrienne, be present and listen to Katherine's conversations to make sure that she represents FELIX accurately. Also, be sure to find out if our university partners are ready for the competition in the spring. DeAngelo, there are some contracts in my office. Take a look at them to make sure everything is in order. We do not want to promise to fund anything that won't yield a profit. Check with the marketing department to see what they need with regard to the new urban clothing line. Review their budget while you are at it. Mistakes, at this juncture, aren't an option. I'm not so sure this spring line is worth all of the money that the marketing department says it needs to launch it. We'll meet again in three days to see where you guys are with this.

DeAngelo: Felix, I know that this is important to you, but what about our other projects that have deadlines before the university internship and the spring fashion show project? We need to have time to review those contracts and meet with the clients should we foresee changes.

Felix: Don't worry about that. I'm sure you all will be done by then. You don't need that much time. Keep me informed of your progress. Oh, start crunching the numbers for the robust women's apparel project. Someone told me the other day that the plus size market is booming! We're done here!

Katherine and Adrienne exit the conference room.

Katherine *(leans toward Adrienne and discretely asks)*: So, what is Felix going to do? Does he always just delegate?

Adrienne: Why do you need to know? I mean, it's not as if you'll still be here by then anyway.

Surprised and hurt by Adrienne's comment, Katherine walks away angrily.

DeAngelo: Adrienne, when you get a minute, can you please stop by my office? I need to talk to you about something.

Adrienne: Ah . . . sure.

DISCUSSION QUESTIONS

1. In your opinion, what is incompetent leadership? In the case scenario, is Felix disrespectful and/or incompetent? Explain.
2. Under what circumstances do you believe that nepotism is appropriate?
3. How can Felix build a strong team? Is it evident that certain team members do not respect one another? If so, what can Felix do about this? Or is he a part of the problem? Explain.
4. Compare Felix's leadership style to those described in the Preliminary Activity. Is he an effective leader? Why or why not?
5. If Katherine decides that she wants to remain at FELIX, how can she regain her team's trust?
6. Are DeAngelo and Adrienne handling their issues with work overload professionally? Should they ignore it or talk with Felix? Explain.
7. How does a manager know when his/her team is disengaged? Is Felix's team showing signs of disengagement? How can he reverse these behaviors?

SELF-ASSESSMENT ACTIVITY

Goals

The goals of this exercise are

- to energize participants through an experience that relates to their work realities
- to allow participants to practice effective teamwork behaviors while accomplishing a task with an ambiguous goal
- to observe how participants react to change.

Materials

The materials needed for this exercise are

- newspapers (a 6-12-inch stack for each team)
- one roll of masking tape for each team
- one roll of string or twine for each team
- one pair of scissors for each team

Alternatively, this exercise can be done using firm tofu, food coloring, tooth-pics, plastic knives, and a few sheets of newspaper to protect the work areas. The food coloring is introduced when the "aesthetically appealing" criterion is added.

Time

- 45 minutes for set-up and exercise
- 30-60 minutes for debriefing

Instructions for Facilitators

1. Form groups of 10 or fewer participants (groups of five to seven people work best).
2. Each group should select and observer. Give observers instruction sheets.

3. Explain that the task is to build a free-standing tower, using only the material provided: newspapers, tape, string, and scissors.
4. Point out that the groups are in competition with each other. The criteria for the wining tower are height and structural soundness.
5. The groups have 25 minutes to complete their towers. After providing instructions, check for questions and begin timing.
6. Ten minutes into the exercise, add the criterion that the towers must also be aesthetically appealing. Let the groups know that the prize winner will be judged by a group voting process, and that each group gets one vote.
7. At 25 minutes, stop the activity. Direct the groups to clean up their areas. Give them five minutes to look at other towers and 10 to meet again as teams and decide for which tower to cast their votes.
8. Tally the votes, announce a winner, and award a prize.

Debrifing

Discuss the experience in teams. Instruct the observer to begin by sharing his or her comments, and then open up the discussion to the entire team. Each team should identify at least three things learned or three observation to share with the larger group. Take approximately 30 minutes for this part of the debriefing.

Bring the teams together for approximately 15 minutes to share what they have learned and observed with the larger group.

Key Points

In debriefing and discussion, be sure to discuss the following points. They may emerge spontaneously or the facilitator may raise them.

- What did the teams do well?
- What could the teams have done better?
- Did each team have a common vision at the start of implementation? At any time?
- Were everyone's ideas and inputs considered?
- Did the teams respond effectively to the change in criteria?
- How did the team handle time pressure?
- Were the team's tasks, resources, and roles clear to each team member?

Instructions for Observers

Instructions for observers can be found in Structured Experience 12-6. Located in the Appendix

Desired Outcome: Teams can use their experiences in the game to overcome work problems and relational issues.

APPLICATION ACTIVITIES

1. Write three to four paragraphs supporting or dispelling the benefits of nepotism in your future business or workplace. Read the article "Nepotism" by Ron Prokosch located in Appendix D.
2. Develop a script from either Adrienne or DeAngelo's perspective addressing the work overload issue with Felix. Include key factors that an employee would want to bring to an employer's attention. Be prepared to present the script in class.

CASE STUDY 4

PRESENTEEISM—WEARY, WORRIED, AND WORN OUT

OBJECTIVES

Students will be able to:

A. understand how presenteeism impacts employee performance and office productivity;
B. recognize the manager's role in creating a healthy work environment; and
C. identify personal stressors and discover methods to limit their effects.

SUGGESTED CLASS TIME

2–3 class periods

TERMS TO KNOW

Define the following terms:

A. sick leave;
B. emotional intelligence;
C. absenteeism; and
D. presenteeism.

PRELIMINARY ACTIVITY

Read the article titled "7 Ways to Measure Employee Performance" located in Appendix G. Locate another article regarding measuring employee performance. Identify any discrepancies and updates concerning how employees are evaluated.

WHO'S IN THIS STORY?

Ernesto Diaz, 45
FELIX Marketing
Supervisor

© Shutterstock/Andresr

Dawali Black, 31
FELIX Marketing
Assistant

© Shutterstock/Rob Marmion

Parker Cobb, 27
FELIX HR
Benefits
Manager

© Shutterstock/vgstudio

SETTING

Atlanta, FELIX Headquarters

CASE SCENARIO

Marketing assistant Dawali Black has been working eighty billable hours for seven-days-a-week over the past three months. She is responsible for creating Debonair, a cutting-edge media campaign geared toward jetsetting executives. Dawali is under immense pressure from her boss, Ernesto, to finish the campaign three weeks before the target date.

Ernesto is so adamant about developing a successful media campaign ahead of schedule that he does not care how long Dawali has to remain after work to complete the task. His primary goal is the deadline, not her feelings. Dawali explains to Ernesto that she is working hard but needs to conduct more focus groups to ensure that FELIX is sending appropriate public relations (PR) messages.

The project is in its early stages, and Dawali is waiting for a follow-up call from the designers. The clients are putting the final touches on a portfolio of professional wear, which Dawali plans to share with focus groups. As she justifies possible delays on the project to Ernesto, he appears irritated and reiterates his position on completing the project early.

Last year, major competitors were able to reveal their new men's clothing line two months before FELIX's. As a result, FELIX's shareholders incurred significant profit loss. Trish, the CEO's daughter and Marketing Manager, threatened to fire employees. This year, Trish desires a line that consists of a variety of trendy suit styles that could easily transform into casual wear. Debonair has to be perfect! Ernesto cannot afford any mishaps on this project. Dawali has no choice but to deliver a spectacular product line or find employment elsewhere.

Dawali: Yes, I understand. I will provide you with an update on my progress in a few days. But Ernesto, tomorrow is a holiday, and I have family coming to visit from out of town.

Ernesto ignores Dawali's futile attempt to remind him that the office is closed for the next few days.

Ernesto (*sighing heavily*): Dawali, you are not the only one working hard around here to complete projects. Do whatever it takes, but by Monday morning, I want to review the communication materials and be provided a demonstration of the PR piece. The clock is ticking!

He quickly turns away from her and with long, purposeful strides, goes into his office. Ernesto then calls his wife, retrieves his coat, and walks past her without speaking. He is leaving the building. Dawali is unaware of what or if anything is causing Ernesto to behave in this manner. He has never spoken so harshly to her. He usually encourages and helps her, especially when they have tight deadlines. Lately, his demeanor has changed and he seems easily irritated and brash.

Dawali wonders if she has done something wrong or if what Ernesto said is true, and she needs to become more productive. She has to show Ernesto that she cannot only get the job done but that she can handle the pressure. No matter what it takes, she will have the materials he requested on Monday.

Feeling the onset of a migraine, Dawali, for first time in five years, fears that she could lose her job. Instead of going home at the end of the day to rest and recharge, she continues to work for hours. By the time she leaves the office, the temperature has dropped to below freezing.

The next day . . .

When Dawali arrives at the office at 6 a.m., no one is there to greet her. She figures that she will get some work done during the holiday before her family arrives at 6 p.m. The night before, she stayed up cleaning the house and preparing dinner for her guests. She notices that the stress and lack of sleep are taking a toll on her. Today, she is feeling light-headed, feverish, and sick to her stomach. Dawali hopes that she has not caught the flu. She plans to call Parker later to see exactly how much sick leave she has left. Clearly, she does not want to disappoint Ernesto and upset Trish. She needs her job, so she takes more over-the-counter medicines and forces herself to work nonstop for 12 hours.

On Monday morning . . .

As soon as Ernesto arrives at work, he goes into Dawali's office.

Ernesto: Good morning, Dawali.

Dawali (*coughing and sneezing*): Good morning, Ernesto. How was your holiday?

Ernesto: It was okay. Isabel's family came to visit us from Mexico. The kids were glad to see their abuela. My mother-in-law will stay with us for a while. Isabel is . . . well, she needs her mom's support right now.

Dawali: Oh, is everything okay?

Ernesto: It's a private matter. How about we focus on work? By the way, is the project completed?

Dawali (*sneezing and blowing her nose*): Yes, I worked on it all weekend. I have already placed it on your desk. I can discuss it with you once you've looked at it.

Ernesto: Are you sick? You don't look well.

Dawali: Oh no, I'm fine. I have some medicine in my purse. I think it's just a cold. I'm going to get some green tea in a minute. My throat is a little scratchy and sore, but I'll be okay.

Ernesto: Oh, no! Well, if you are sick and something is wrong with this campaign, who is going to fix it before Wednesday's deadline?

Dawali: I will, I guess. If I have to be here, then I will be here.

Ernesto: Good. I will go over the materials now.

Dawali feels awful, but she cannot share that with Ernesto. She is beginning to show signs of a severe fever and can barely hold up her head. To make matters worse, the effects of the medicine are making her drowsy.

At mid-morning . . .

Parker walks by Dawali's office and notices that she has her head resting on the desk. She is shaking and breathing heavily and her coat is draped over her shoulders.

Parker: Hello, sleepy head.

Dawali can barely focus but recognizes Parker's voice. Standing in the doorway, he looks at her with an expression of concern.

Dawali: Hi, Parker. I'm sorry. I must have dozed off.

Parker: It's not even 10:30 in the morning. What time did you get here?

Dawali: Around 6 a.m. I guess I'm physically winding down, sorry.

Parker notices that Dawali is sweating and shivering. When she talks to him, her teeth are chattering, but she does not seem to notice. She is coughing and holding her head.

Dawali: Have you seen Ernesto? I want to make sure that I do not have to make any changes to the project I submitted to him this morning.

Parker: No, I'm sorry. I haven't seen him yet. But, I'm much more concerned about you. Are you feeling sick?

Dawali: What did you say?

Parker pauses and contemplates whether he wants to enter her office. He does not want to become ill.

Parker: Dawali, honey, if you are feeling sick, you should go home. The flu is going around, and we can't afford to have everyone in the office sick. You do know that the flu is contagious, right?

Dawali: Parker, I can't go home. Ernesto needs me to fix any issues with the *Debonair* project as soon as possible. I need to work. I don't get paid to sit at home. We all know how men view women in this office. If we don't perform, we are overlooked or fired. No, I need to be here.

DISCUSSION QUESTIONS

1. What is sick leave, and how is it generally accumulated?
2. Is Ernesto being unreasonable with his demands concerning the project deadline? Explain.
3. Based on the case scenario, is Ernesto experiencing personal issues that may be impacting his emotional intelligence? As a manager, what steps could you use to minimize the negative effects that your personal life may have on your work environment?
4. In the case scenario, Dawali is concerned about losing her job. If she has received above-average performance evaluations in the past, then why is she concerned about losing her job now? Explain.
5. How should Parker respond to Dawali being sick at work? If you were the HR Benefits Manager, what would you do? How would you handle her last comment regarding possible inequity between men and women in the office?
6. Should Ernesto be reprimanded by FELIX management for his treatment of Dawali? Use specific examples from the case scenario to support your answer.
7. Do you believe that Ernesto's treatment of Dawali stems from his personal family issues? Support your answer.

SELF-ASSESSMENT

Assess your stress level by completing the Stress Questionnaire located in Appendix F.

APPLICATION ACTIVITIES

Complete the exercises in groups of four to five students:

1. In Appendix E, read the article titled "Underlying Factors Contributing to Presenteeism and Absenteeism" by Tammy Prater and Kim Smith. Has anyone in your group ever experienced presenteeism? If so, write a paragraph describing the experience.
2. Investigate the cost of presenteeism in the workplace. How does it impact the workplace?
3. Re-read the case scenario, and identify other workplace issues. Recommend suggestions on how to address them.
4. Find out the steps in creating an effective marketing plan. Develop your own marketing plan for a real or fictitious business, and share it with the class.
5. How should you respond when your team member treats you poorly? Write a response from Dawali's perspective to Ernesto. In your response, take into consideration that Dawali desires to remain employed at FELIX.

CASE STUDY 5

FRIENDS, WHERE'S THE MONEY?

OBJECTIVES

Students will be able to:

A. define pay equity;
B. explain how an employer justifies differences in pay;
C. describe the legal elements for unequal pay in the workplace; and
D. examine how social media use may impact employment.

SUGGESTED CLASS TIME

2 class periods

TERMS OF KNOW

Define the following terms:

A. pay equity;
B. comparable worth;
C. unequal pay;
D. gender discrimination;
E. work-life balance; and
F. retroactive pay.

PRELIMINARY ACTIVITY

Locate and review the *Equal Pay Act of 1963*. Identify and list the elements needed to prove unequal pay in the workplace. In a paragraph, respond to the following prompt: Do men and women presently have equal and fair treatment in the workplace? Supply examples to support your position.

WHO'S IN THIS STORY?

Ernesto Diaz, 45
FELIX Marketing Supervisor

© Shutterstock/Andresr

Isabel Diaz, 45
Ernesto's Wife

Min Kwon, 38
FELIX HR Director

© Shutterstock/Dragon Images

Sam Kwon, 40
Min's Husband

SETTING

Atlanta, FELIX Headquarters; The Diaz Home; and The Kwon Home

CASE SCENARIO

At the Diaz Home, 6:07 a.m.

Isabel: Ernie, we need to talk.

Ernesto: About what, Izzy? I'm going to be late for work if I don't leave now. I'm really stressed out over these deadlines. I need to talk to Dawali. She's been working extremely hard, and I have been abrupt with her lately. We've all been working too much. Didn't we talk last night?

Isabel: You mean the one-minute conversation that we had right before you fell asleep? Ernie, look at me!

Ernie (*looking at Isabel*): Lo siento, Izzy. Sí, mi amor? Yo estoy escuchando ahora.

Isabel: Antonio got into another fight at school yesterday. I have a conference with one of his teachers and the assistant principal at 10 this morning. I wanted to know if you could attend.

Ernesto: This morning?! No, you know I can't. I need to talk to Antonio again. I don't know what's gotten into him. Why is he acting up at school all of a sudden?

Isabel: This hasn't been sudden, honey. You've been so busy with work that I didn't want to bother you. I just told you about the last two fights. You work so hard to provide for us. With the endless marketing deadlines, meetings, and work issues, I just didn't want to stress you even more. Ernie, you've worked at least 70–80 hours a week for the last three months. You've been dealing with your wonderful boss, Trish. You better hope that I don't see her anytime soon.

Ernesto (*sighing heavily*): Izzy . . . we've discussed this already.

Isabel: No, Ernie. You're always at work. You do a great job. Despite all of your efforts, Trish didn't want to give you a raise. The last salary increase that you had was four years ago. With all of your hard work, you still had to speak to Trish about giving you a raise. Then, you had to go to her boss before you were even heard! And to think that the only other FELIX supervisor to get a raise was DeAngelo. What about Min and Mary Kate? They work just as hard as the men.

Ernesto: Iz, let's focus on Antonio. Then, I've got to get to work.

Three days later, Min is in her office at FELIX headquarters . . .

After pacing around her office, Min decides to call her husband, Sam.

Sam: Hello.

Min: Sam, do you have a few minutes to talk?

Sam: Of course. Is something wrong? You sound upset.

Min: I'm the HR Director, so how did I not know that DeAngelo and Ernesto received salary increases. How can FELIX justify DeAngelo and Ernesto receiving raises when Mary Kate and I have been working there longer than they have? Besides, we work just as many hours as they do.

Sam: Min, please calm down. There has to be some logical explanation for this.

Min: Whatever, Sam. Year after year, I have been told to be patient. Well, I've been patient, and I still have not received a raise in six years. Ernesto has gotten two raises at FELIX, and he has less time in the company than I. DeAngelo has only been with FELIX for five years, and this is his second raise, too. Mary Kate has worked for FELIX for 17 years, and her last raise was before I came to FELIX.

Sam: Min, I'm on your side. I just want you to consider all other factors besides seniority in determining who gets a raise. What about productivity? Experience? Education? Those matter as well.

Min: Are you saying that I'm not educated? That Mary Kate is not educated? That we're not productive? You know that's not true!

Sam: Min, please. What's the real issue here? Is there something else going on?

Min: You've got to read Ernesto's wife's social media post.

Sam: What does her post have to do with anything? You can show it to me once we get home, but you need to focus. Try to calm down, Min. We'll handle this together.

At the Kwon Home later that day . . .

As Sam walks through the door, Min rushes him over to the computer.

Min: Sam, there it is. Read Isabel's post.

Izzy Diaz
June 5 at 1:29 p.m.

This morning was challenging, but there is always something to be thankful for. My husband finally got a raise after all of his hard work. I want to encourage all of you who are struggling to keep moving forward. It will happen for you in time. Because I am a woman, I want to send extra encouragement to my working female friends. Even though I don't work outside of the home anymore, I still remember how hard it was. I listen to my husband's stories all of the time. It is still hard for women in the workplace. When we are assertive, we are told we are attitudinal or too demanding. We also continue to struggle with getting the same pay as men while working the same amount of hours with similar experience and education. It is time for companies to stop discriminating. I long for the day that my husband will share stories of equality for all instead of what I hear now.

23 likes 8 comments

DISCUSSION QUESTIONS

1. How could FELIX justify pay increases for Ernesto and DeAngelo when they were hired after Min? List the justifications in order from the strongest to weakest.
2. Apply the facts of the case scenario to the elements of the *Equal Pay Act of 1963*. What would Min have to prove in order to have a successful case? What would be the likely outcome of Min's lawsuit against FELIX?
3. Could Isabel's social media post lead to disciplinary action against her husband, Ernesto? Locate a legal case to support your position.
4. Is it unethical for Ernesto to discuss employment situations with his wife? Is it illegal? What types of boundaries should be established when discussing job-related situations with a friend, family member, or significant other?
5. Is Ernesto dealing with an issue of work-life balance? If so, what can he do to create more of a balance? Is it possible to avoid such an imbalance, or is it an inevitable part of having a family and pursuing a career? Explain.
6. Research the *Lilly Ledbetter Fair Pay Act*. Based on this Act, if Min proves her case, is she eligible for retroactive pay? Why or why not?

SELF-ASSESSMENT

Review your personal social media accounts. Objectively consider whether there are any pictures, posts, and information that an employer would find questionable. Based on those considerations, make a list of what items should be removed or modified. How can these impact your personal brand? How will these changes benefit you in the future?

APPLICATION ACTIVITIES

1. Assume that Min shares Isabel's social media post with FELIX executives. Explain how FELIX should respond to Isabel's post from a corporate perspective. Include the disciplinary action, if any, that may occur.
2. In small groups, research the potential pitfalls associated with social media and employment grievances and termination cases. Present this information to the class.
3. Invite your supervisor to class to discuss the hiring, disciplinary, and/or termination processes associated with social media for potential and current employees.

CASE STUDY 6

FRIENDS, COLLEAGUES, OR BOTH?*

OBJECTIVES

Students will be able to:

A. list how federal law advocates for women concerning violent acts;
B. identify appropriate workplace boundaries;
C. define insider trading;
D. predict how workplace boundaries protect employees and companies; and
E. apply Rule 10 b-5 of the *Securities Exchange Act of 1934*.

SUGGESTED CLASS TIME

2–3 class periods

TERMS TO KNOW

Define the following terms:

A. insider trading;
B. confidentiality;
C. securities;
D. trading blackout; and
E. domestic violence.

PRELIMINARY ACTIVITY

In 2013, Congress updated the *Violence Against Women Act* (VAWA), the federal law that aims to combat domestic and sexual violence against women. Review VAWA, and write three or more important protections that it provides.

WHO'S IN THIS STORY?

Min Kwon, 38 FELIX HR Director 	Cameron Knox, 37 FELIX HR Supervisor 
Parker Cobb, 27 FELIX HR Benefits Manager 	Brandon Knox, 37 Cameron's Husband 

© Shutterstock/Dragon Images

© Shutterstock/Maksim Shmeljov

© Shutterstock/vgstudio

© Shutterstock/wavebreakmedia

SETTING

Atlanta, FELIX Headquarters—HR Department

CASE SCENARIO

Parker: Cameron, I'm only asking because I care about you. Please know that I'm not trying to pry or be too intrusive. You're my supervisor, but you're also my friend. Besides, you've taught me everything I know. You were even there for me when I told my parents that I'm gay. You also encouraged me to not hide it from Min or anyone else at FELIX. You've been a huge support to me, Cam. I just want to know what's going on so that I can help. This is the third meeting that you've missed in a month. Min returned from the meeting yesterday asking where you were. I don't know how much longer I'll be able to cover for you, especially when I don't even know what's going on.

Cameron: I didn't mean to put you in an awkward position. I'm fine, really. I simply needed some personal space yesterday.

Parker: I understand that, but you just left the office in the middle of a work day without letting anyone know. Was there an emergency? Is Brandon okay? Your daughter, April? Is everything good at home?

Cameron: Why wouldn't everything be okay? What have you heard? Have you seen something?! Why don't you just . . .

When someone knocks at Cameron's office door, she stops the conversation by placing her index finger to her lips to silence Parker. After composing herself, she turns toward the door.

Cameron: Come in.

Min: There the two of you are. Cameron, I need to speak to you before our afternoon meeting. Meet me in my office in five minutes.

Cameron: Yes, Min.

As Parker rises to leave, he gives Cameron a friendly hug of support. He notices that she winces.

Parker: Are you hurt? Wait! Has he hit you again?! Is that what's going on?

Cameron: Leave it alone, Parker!

Parker: Cam, you promised that you would leave if he hit you again! Not only is he controlling all of your money, but he is also abusing you and interfering with your work. You've got to put an end to this. I know a great divorce attorney. Please just call him!

Cameron: I don't want a divorce, Parker! We're working it out. He promised that this was the last time. I have to do a better job at home. I've been working far too much and neglecting my husband and daughter. Anyway, I have to go. Min is waiting on me.

In Min's office . . .

Min: Cameron, this is the third meeting that you've missed this month. I've been lenient thus far because you've always been an exceptional employee. Nevertheless, I fear that you're developing a pattern of neglect for job responsibilities. I really needed your expertise at the meeting with DeAngelo and Mary Kate regarding Katherine Payne's potential lawsuit against FELIX. Even though that issue has been resolved, the training that you recently received in the New York office would have strengthened our negotiating position. The only explanation that you've given me is that you had some questions for Aaron in the Finance Department but that still does not excuse missing even one meeting. At this point, I must . . .

Min continues to speak but a distracted Cameron does not hear what she says. A few minutes later, Cameron leaves Min's office and returns to her own. Her cell phone rings.

Brandon: Cam, do you have the stock information?

Cameron (*whispering*): Brandon, I told you not to call me about this at work. I got it, but it would be best if we waited until I get home. If anyone finds out, do you know what could happen to me? To us? What about April?! Since your brother is a broker, it will be too easy to trace this back to us!

Brandon: Shut up, and listen! We're already close to filing bankruptcy. You owe April and me. All those hours that you spend at work, we should be able to profit off of old man Phil Fox. He surely has been profiting off of your hard work. And if you don't want me to take April from you, then you better supply me with any useful information about the upcoming FELIX contract for the release of the new urban clothing line.

During Cameron's telephone conversation with Brandon . . .

Parker knocks on Min's door.

Parker: Min, do you have a minute? I want to speak to you about Cameron. I'm concerned about her.

Elsewhere in the FELIX Corporate Office . . .

An email is sent to all FELIX employees reminding them of confidentiality on the urban clothing contract and imposing a trading blackout of the acquisition of FELIX stock for a number of days.

DISCUSSION QUESTIONS

1. Evaluate the relationship between Cameron and Parker. In your answer, consider whether it is appropriate given their supervisor–employee relationship.
2. What ethical issues could arise due to the closeness of Cameron and Parker's relationship? How could they try to prevent these ethical issues from occurring? Explain how their interaction could potentially lead to workplace problems in the future.
3. Assess Cameron's balance of work and home life issues. What are her primary challenges? How can she resolve them?
4. Is Cameron a victim of domestic violence (DV)? If so, what are her options to overcome this situation? Does Parker have reasonable cause to be concerned for Cameron's safety and well-being? Is he legally obligated to contact someone on her behalf? On April's behalf? How could his intervention impact their workplace relationship?
5. Define security and insider trading. Read Rule 10-b5 of the *Securities Exchange Act of 1934*. After applying the elements of insider trading to the facts in the case scenario, determine whether Cameron has violated the law. Has anyone else violated it? If so, what potential consequences do Cameron and others face?
6. Why are insider trading and other fraudulent activities against the law? In the case scenario, who are the stakeholders who could be potentially harmed by the actions of Cameron and Brandon?

SELF-ASSESSMENT

Based on the issues in the case scenario, assess how the lack of confidentiality impacts individuals, groups, business environments, and communities. As a journal entry, write about an incident in which someone violated confidentiality in a personal or work-related situation. State two examples in which it may be best to violate confidentiality. What was the impact of the confidentiality violation?

APPLICATION ACTIVITIES

1. In the case scenario, Min stated, "At this point, I must . . ." as she was speaking to Cameron regarding her missed meetings. Imagine that you are a fellow HR Director from whom Min is seeking advice. Provide a response to Min regarding what to do with Cameron in this situation. Assess the appropriateness of how Min started her meeting with Cameron as it relates to what you may have learned in a business communication course.
2. At the close of the case scenario, Parker enters Min's office and states that he is concerned about Cameron. With a partner or in small groups, compose the message that Parker would deliver to Min. Each group must share its message. Evaluate the quality of its content from a manager's perspective.
3. Invite the campus Title IX Compliance Officer, a DV guest speaker from a community organization, or a local sexual assault prosecutor to class to discuss VAWA and violent crimes against women.

4. Select one of the following topics: the ethics of confidentiality in the workplace or appropriate relationship boundaries in the workplace.
   a. Research the topic and prepare an annotated bibliography in the form of the Modern Language Association (MLA), American Psychological Association (APA), or Chicago Manual of Style (CMS).
   b. Write a research paper on the topic with a focus on how to maintain confidentiality and handle platonic friendships in the workplace.

CASE STUDY 7

NO ONE'S BULLIED AT WORK, RIGHT?

OBJECTIVES

Students will be able to:

A. define workplace bullying, abusive work conduct, and abusive work environment;
B. describe how absenteeism relates to the work environment and worker productivity;
C. design an anti-workplace bullying campaign; and
D. compile research and present findings on international workplace bullying laws.

SUGGESTED CLASS TIME

3–4 class periods

TERMS TO KNOW

Define the following terms:

A. workplace bullying;
B. abusive work conduct;
C. abusive work environment;
D. absenteeism;
E. worker productivity; and
F. retaliation.

PRELIMINARY ACTIVITY

Read "Workplace Bullying and Ethical Leadership" by law professor David Yamada, author of the Healthy Workplace Bill, in the *Journal of Values-Based Leadership*. Identify and learn the definitions for workplace bullying, abusive work conduct, and abusive work environment.

WHO'S IN THIS STORY?

DeAngelo Moore, 42
FELIX Accounting
Supervisor II

© Shutterstock/Hugo Felix

Adrienne Ray, 58
FELIX Accounting
Supervisor I

© Shutterstock/Zdenka Darula

Aaron Bernstein, 33
FELIX Mid-Level
Finance Analyst

© Shutterstock/eurobanks

Katherine Payne, 40
FELIX Finance Intern
(Temporary Employee)

© Shutterstock/Luba V Nel

Andreas Garcia, 22
FELIX Entry-Level
Finance Analyst

© Shutterstock/se media

SETTING

Atlanta, FELIX Headquarters—Finance and HR Departments

CASE SCENARIO

Adrienne: Aaron, I appreciate all of your hard work. I know that you did a great job managing the office while I was gone last week for ethics training.

Aaron: Well, you know that I'm a team player, but I don't understand why you had to attend the ethics training again. No one that I know of has had to repeat it in the same year. You know, I heard that the incident with Katherine is the reason why you had to do it again. Is that true? If she's a troublemaker, I surely don't want her starting any problems for me.

Adrienne: Where did you hear that information?! Isn't anything confidential anymore? Well, since you already heard . . . but this conversation stays in this room, understand?

Aaron: Of course.

In a low voice, Adrienne tells Aaron how Katherine recorded their telephone conversation, her background check issue, and her previous threats to sue FELIX.

Aaron: Well, that's just ridiculous. Are we hiring criminals now? If she's a drug addict, then that's her problem. Why should we have to suffer for it? I welcome the help from Andreas, but Katherine really seems like trouble. I'll make sure that she doesn't bother me though.

Adrienne: Yeah, Aaron. You and me both. I'm just glad that my parents have stopped pestering me about her. Okay, let's get back to work. We have a lot to do.

The next day . . .

After a morning of introductions, trainings, and meetings, Adrienne, Aaron, Andreas, and Katherine are debriefing prior to taking a lunch break.

Adrienne (*while looking at Katherine*): Andreas, I can tell that you're going to be a great *permanent* addition to our department.

Aaron quietly chuckles while cleaning off the conference table.

Andreas: Thank you, Adrienne. I look forward to learning as much as I can and working as a team player with everyone here. Katherine and I worked well together today, too.

Katherine: Thanks, Andreas. Adrienne, I'm excited about what I'll learn in the next six months.

Adrienne: Really? Well, isn't that great for you, Katherine. Andreas, you can leave for lunch now.

Andreas exits the room.

Adrienne: Katherine, just because you're a temporary employee at FELIX doesn't mean that you can leave Andreas to do all of the work. We are team players here. If you don't know how to work on a team, then you're in the wrong place. Honestly, I expected more from you today. Lucky for us, you are a criminal and didn't get the full-time job; otherwise, we'd be stuck with your *subpar* performance for God knows how long. Oops, did I just say that? I apologize, Katherine.

Aaron (*chuckling*): Oh, I'm sorry. Yes, we both do. Remember, Adrienne, that we must be careful. She might be recording us. We don't want her running to tell her big-time lawyer anything.

Adrienne: I'm not stupid, Katherine. I know that you're watching everyone at FELIX, but please know that we're watching you, too. You're not the only one that knows how to document.

As Aaron and Adrienne continue to laugh and talk about her, Katherine's face turns red with embarrassment. With tears in her eyes, she leaves the conference room.

Over the next few weeks, Katherine faces various incidents at FELIX. She submits her three top-priority projects on time; however, Adrienne informs DeAngelo that she did not submit them until after the deadline. The entire finance department is scheduled to attend a local workshop that is only a few miles from FELIX. Since it is raining heavily outside, Katherine asks Adrienne if she can ride with her because she left her car at a local repair shop for maintenance and took a cab to work. Adrienne says yes. At the designated time to leave, Katherine cannot find Adrienne. She finally calls a cab but is 30 minutes late for the workshop. She walks into the workshop and disrupts the presentation.

Katherine: Excuse me. I'm so sorry for interrupting.

Embarrassed, Katherine hurriedly takes a seat next to DeAngelo. He leans toward Katherine and whispers to her.

DeAngelo (*in a firm voice*): Tardiness to workshops is unacceptable. Don't let this happen again.

Extremely frustrated, Katherine stares at Adrienne angrily. Adrienne smiles knowingly at her. Highly upset, Katherine feels her heartbeat increase and begins to sweat profusely. She rises to go to the restroom. After calming down and noticing a pause in the presentation, Katherine returns to the workshop and takes a seat.

After working for two months at FELIX, Katherine has a heavier workload with shorter deadlines than Andreas or anyone else in the department. When Katherine has questions, she must ask Adrienne for clarification. Adrienne often ridicules her by stating that even her undergraduate interns do not ask such elementary questions and by commenting that the drugs Katherine used must have impaired her brain. Katherine tries to address her concerns with DeAngelo, but he tells her about the importance of teamwork and that she must overcome personality differences if she plans to succeed at FELIX.

Following DeAngelo's instructions, Katherine attempts to talk to Adrienne about her workload and how she perceives she is being treated.

Adrienne: How can I help you, Katherine? DeAngelo tells me that you have some sort of problem with your workload.

Katherine: Well, Adrienne, my concern is about the amount of work that I'm being given in comparison to Andreas and other people.

Adrienne: I don't understand. How do you know how much work Andreas and other people have?

Katherine: It's obvious that I have more work to do. I arrive earlier and leave later than most full-time employees.

Adrienne: I don't think that it's fair to compare your workload to others based on when you arrive and leave work. How is your time management? Is it effective? Did you start working with a strong enough foundation, or do you lack the necessary skill set to do your job?

Katherine (*sighing heavily*)**:** You know what I mean, Adrienne.

Adrienne: Actually, I don't. If you are unprepared to meet the demands of the job, this is not anyone's fault but your own. You wanted the job so much that you were ready to sue for it. Now it's yours, so do it!

As Katherine exits Adrienne's office, she begins to sweat and her hands shake uncontrollably. With her heart racing, she walks to the restroom. Upon entering, she becomes dizzy and grabs the counter to keep herself from falling. She then begins to cry.

Meanwhile in the HR department . . .

The day after Parker spoke to Min about his concerns regarding Cameron, Min calls Cameron into her office. Cameron realizes that Parker has spoken to Min. She is upset but does not let Parker know how she feels. A few days later, Parker reminds Cameron about a federal government deadline. Cameron promises to stay after work and review his information before it is submitted. Nevertheless, she leaves work without letting him know and does not answer his telephone calls. Parker stays at work until 11:30 p.m. to ensure that the submission is correct and complete.

He has to arrive at work by 7 a.m. to finalize preparations for a meeting with other FELIX departments. After the meeting, Parker gets feedback on his annual performance review that is conducted by Cameron. He is extremely concerned about her comments stating that he is unorganized and too talkative at work. She recommends that he engages in less socializing and focuses on becoming more organized, completing tasks, and managing his time.

DISCUSSION QUESTIONS

1. Revisit Adrienne's conversation with Aaron regarding her second ethics training and her statements about Katherine. What ethical issues are raised based on this conversation?
2. Based on the definition of workplace bullying, evaluate the actions of Adrienne, Aaron, DeAngelo, and Cameron. Compare how DeAngelo, Adrienne, and Aaron treated Katherine versus how Cameron interacted with Parker. Do their actions amount to workplace bullying? How are they the same and how do they differ? If not, what types of actions would need to occur against Katherine and Parker to qualify as workplace bullying?
3. Cite examples of abusive work conduct that are present in the case scenario. Has an abusive work environment been created? In your answer, include incidents of any retaliatory behavior that has occurred.
4. How should Katherine and Parker respond to their colleagues' behavior? As a temporary employee, does Katherine have the same rights as Parker? Explain.
5. Identify the stakeholders at FELIX. What are the potential consequences of workplace bullying on these stakeholders?
6. Compare absenteeism to bullying in the workplace. Identify the physical symptoms that Katherine experienced in the case scenario. Research how often employees are absent from work as a result of an abusive work environment. Did Katherine experience stress-related symptoms in response to the treatment she received? If so, how could this impact worker productivity?
7. How should FELIX management respond to any acts of workplace bullying? Explain.

SELF-ASSESSMENT

Research updates on U.S. workplace bullying laws. Are you in support of the Healthy Workplace Bill in its entirety? Why or why not? If not, how would you amend the bill?

APPLICATION ACTIVITIES

1. In Appendix H, read the article titled "Workplace Bullying: A Review of Its Impact on Businesses, Employees, and the Law" by D.N. McDonald, Edward D. Brown, and Kim F. Smith. In small groups, provide one example of a workplace bullying incident that you have witnessed, heard of, or experienced. How did the person that was bullied respond? How were these situations handled and/or resolved by management? Share the group's example with the class.
2. In small groups, research the components of at least three anti-bullying campaigns. Pursuant to the general components in the researched campaigns, create a FELIX Workplace Bullying Policy.
3. Research and gather facts from online resources, such as the Workplace Bullying Institute website, about workplace bullying. Construct pro and con arguments about workplace bullying. Have a class debate on the topic.
4. Select one of the following countries. Research its workplace bullying laws, and prepare a presentation for the class.

   a. Sweden
   b. Canada
   c. Australia
   d. France
   e. United States
   f. England

CASE STUDY 8
THE ILL-PREPARED AND NOT-SO-FOCUSED EMPLOYEE

OBJECTIVES

Students will be able to:

A. recognize the significance of a thorough employee interview and selection process; and
B. evaluate the impact that secretarial positions have on an organization.

SUGGESTED CLASS TIME

2–3 class periods

TERMS TO KNOW

Define the following terms:

A. termination and
B. disciplinary action.

PRELIMINARY ACTIVITY

Locate a job description and note the duties of a(n) secretary/administrative assistant. Make a list of the top five most important responsibilities for this position. In addition, create ten interview questions for a potential candidate.

WHO'S IN THIS STORY?

Min Kwon, 38
FELIX HR Director

© Shutterstock/Dragon Images

Cameron Knox, 37
FELIX HR Supervisor

© Shutterstock/Maksim Shmeljov

Stephanie Lane, 24
FELIX HR Secretary
(New Hire)

© Shutterstock/Vadim Ivanov

SETTING

Atlanta, FELIX Headquarters—HR Department, Meeting Room

CASE SCENARIO

Coni DeGraves has been the FELIX HR secretary since the company was founded. Because of unexpected medical issues, she is suddenly retiring and will be greatly missed by the entire FELIX family. She is a highly competent employee and an efficient multi-tasker. Due to Coni's vital role within the department, Min and Cameron must hire immediately. FELIX advertises the position for two weeks. Out of twenty-seven applicants who are carefully screened, only four applicants are called for an interview. The first applicant is dismissed because of profane music on her voicemail. In spite of the music, Cameron leaves a message, but the candidate never returns her phone call. The second applicant is five minutes late to his interview. The third applicant answers his cell phone during the interview and apologizes profusely for the interruption. Despite explaining that the call concerns an ill family member, Min and Cameron consider his actions unprofessional. Desperate, they are conducting an interview with the final person, Stephanie Lane, in the department's meeting room.

Min: So, Stephanie, can you tell us why you would be the best applicant for the secretarial position? Why should we select you for the job?

Stephanie: Well, if you look at dat . . . um résumé, I got alotta secretary experience. I worked at a small advertisement firm as a part-time secretary while I got my college degree in PR. I am good at customer service and have very good telephone skills. I'd love to work for FELIX while I get my master degree in public administration. I start taking my classes next semester.

At her response, Min and Cameron quickly exchange a look of concern.

Cameron: Can you give us an example of how you've successfully handled a difficult situation?

Stephanie: What do you mean? You mean when something bad happened on the job?

Cameron: Yes, that's what I mean.

Stephanie: Okay. I kept da calendar for da firm's office manager, Mrs. Polk. Due to no fault of my own, da office manager had a scheduling conflict one day. While Mrs. Polk was talking to an important client down da hall, somebody else's client came to my desk and said dat dey had arrived for a meeting wid Mrs. Polk and Mr. Ingram, one of da head guys at da firm. I double-checked da calendar and found dat da person relieving me had placed dis client at da right time but on da wrong day. I asked da client to have a seat and if dey wanted bottled water or coffee. After dat, I went to Mr. Ingram's office to speak to his secretary. She was able to help me and da client. Da situation turned out okay. I learned a good lesson dat day about being helpful and asking for help when needed.

Min (*eyeing Cameron again*): Thank you, Stephanie.

Cameron: Min and I reviewed your cover letter. It appears that you write well. This is important with the secretarial position. We need to fill it with someone who has strong verbal and written communication skills. We've informed you of the available job benefits. Oh, one last thing. Whomever is selected for the position will be subject to a supervisory review every three months.

Stephanie: I understand and appreciate dat compliment. I will do my best to meet your needs if chosen for dis job.

Cameron: Min, do you have any more questions?

Min: No. I've asked all of mine.

Cameron: Stephanie, thank you for coming. We will notify you by the end of the week with our decision.

Stephanie: Dank you for the interview. It was nice to meet you.

Stephanie exits the HR meeting room. Min and Cameron begin to discuss her interview while they review Stephanie's cover letter again.

A Portion of Stephanie's Cover Letter

Stephanie Lane
I Grindera Road
Druid Hills, Georgia 30322

Attn: Cameron Knox
FELIX Headquarters
0 Peachtree Street NW
Atlanta, Georgia 30303

Dear Ms. Knox:

I am writing in response to the Administrative Assistant opening at the FELIX Headquarters in Atlanta, Georgia. I am confident that my knowledge base, secretarial experience, communication skills, and commitment to service make me a superb candidate for this position.

While working at an advertising firm, I learned that administrative assistants are the initial representatives for companies. I witnessed firsthand the positive and negative impact that competent and incompetent customer service can have on the reputation of a company as well as its owners and employees. By meeting the challenges of daily stressors and long-term projects, I honed secretarial skills that have enabled me to solidify my ability to work as a team player or individually to problem solve to creatively meet the demands of an ever-changing work environment.

. . .

Min: What do you think about her, Cameron?

Cameron: I think that she's our best applicant. I mean, look at her cover letter. We need a strong writer. But, did you notice her speech? Will it be a problem? She's going to answer our phones and interact with our clients.

Min: Yes, I noticed it. She's not as polished as Coni, but her writing is strong.

Cameron: Yes, maybe there is a reason for the issues with her speech, but with our time crunch, we need to hire someone right now. Besides, from what we can see, her writing is comparable to Coni's.

Min: Yes, you're right. Call her tomorrow to offer her the position. We don't have time to waste.

The next day, Cameron calls Stephanie to offer her the job. Stephanie accepts and completes her new hire paperwork. She begins training with Coni on the following Monday; Coni trains her for two weeks. Coni prepares a binder of standard FELIX business letters for Stephanie to refer to when necessary. A retirement party is held for Coni at the end of the two weeks.

Stephanie is now performing general tasks, such as sending faxes, answering telephones, and transferring calls. During Stephanie's third week on the job, Cameron notices that she arrives late one day and is often texting at her desk. A few employees also mention to Cameron about Stephanie having loud phone conversations in the hall while she passes by their offices. They find it disruptive, especially when they are meeting with clients.

One afternoon, Min asks Stephanie to prepare a memo to clarify a company policy for another department. Min informs Stephanie that she will have to compose the content of the letter based on her verbal instructions. Min does not provide her with a deadline.

Since she was not given a deadline, Stephanie decides to wait until the next morning to begin crafting the letter. Instead, she looks for outfit ideas online and makes posts on social media. One of her posts is a selfie at her office desk with the caption "GEORGIA CUTIE." When Stephanie arrives 20 minutes late the next morning, she notices a note from Min detailing four tasks: 1. forward yesterday's memo to her immediately; 2. review employee promotion files; 3. return three clients' telephone calls; and 4. write an additional memo for Min. Stephanie completes the first memo and forwards it to Min two hours later.

A Portion of Stephanie's Memo

To: DeAngelo More From Men Kwong

Re HR Confidintial Info

Dear D'Angelo,

You contacted this office two weeks ago asking about the company policy. The company policy say that two minimally must sign off on any and all financial reviews in the finance department. You are right when you say that one person can't sign off. Please keep following this policy to protect FELIX and Finance department. Keep up the very good work.

She writes the second memo, makes the telephone calls, and reviews the files by 3 p.m.

That afternoon, Cameron receives a call asking why confidential employee information was left for the wrong person on someone's voicemail. In a brief meeting to discuss Stephanie's progress, Min and Cameron converse about the liability that FELIX may face because of Stephanie's breach of confidentiality. They also compare her cover letter to her first memo. Min and Cameron find a number of typos and grammatical errors in it. They are also baffled by the differences in her writing style.

Cameron meets with Stephanie to discuss all of their concerns. Stephanie apologizes and says she is overwhelmed. She states that she will correct her behavior and pay closer attention when completing assignments.

Three weeks later, Stephanie is still texting, having loud conversations, and using social media at work. Although she was instructed to follow Coni's letter format, her written communication has also not improved.

Min and Cameron meet for a second time to discuss Stephanie's lack of progress. They must decide what to do.

DISCUSSION QUESTIONS

1. Consider the role of a(n) secretary/administrative assistant. What is the importance of this position? How does it add value to an organization? What qualities and skills should a person in this position possess?
2. In the case scenario, identify the problems that Min and Cameron are having with Stephanie?
3. From a managerial perspective, what options do Min and Cameron have to address Stephanie's poor performance?
4. Did Min and Cameron act within a reasonable time to address problems with Stephanie? How could they have been more proactive in addressing their concerns? Explain.
5. Identify reasons why Min and Cameron might want to avoid terminating Stephanie. Provide an explanation for each of the reasons identified. If termination is not a corrective option, then highlight the best two alternatives for improving Stephanie's performance.
6. Review the content of Stephanie's interview. Discuss the relationship between a person's verbal communication and written communication.
7. In the case scenario, Min and Cameron noticed Stephanie's difficulty in pronouncing words beginning and ending in "th." In a secretarial position, effective communication skills are vital. Should Min and Cameron have asked her questions during the interview about her speech issues? If so, could any legal ramifications stem from that type of questioning? What could be some legitimate reasons for Stephanie's speech impediment? Explain your answer.
8. What reasonable explanation(s) exist for the differences in the quality of Stephanie's cover letter and memos? How can Min and Cameron avoid hiring someone with these disparities in the future?
9. In their haste, what mistakes did Min and Cameron make in their interview process? What impact could this have on the HR department and FELIX?
10. What legal and ethical issues could arise from Stephanie's breach of confidentiality? Rate them from the most serious to the least serious. Support your answer.

SELF-ASSESSMENT

Objectively assess your verbal and written communication skills as an employee. What are your strengths? In what areas do you need further improvement? Develop a plan to improve in these areas.

APPLICATION ACTIVITIES

1. In small groups, select students to play the roles of Stephanie and Min and/or Cameron. Write and perform a skit demonstrating the second official conversation that Min and/or Cameron must have with Stephanie. Determine what decisions must be made regarding Stephanie's future at FELIX.
2. As a manager, what would be the cost factor in firing Stephanie compared to providing her training to improve her communication skills? In your respective disciplines, interview an HR representative at an organization for which you desire to work. Discuss the main points of the case scenario with the representative. Ask what mistakes Min and Cameron made in the interview and how the case should be resolved. Share your experience with the class.
3. Review and revise Stephanie's first memo to Min.

CASE STUDY 9
PERCEPTIONS OF BEAUTY

OBJECTIVES

Students will be able to:

A. recognize the significance of cultural awareness and diversity in the workplace;
B. understand the benefits of an employee health and wellness program;
C. consider the impact of individual biases and cultural perceptions on employees and work culture; and
D. determine how comments about colleagues affect workplace relationships and environments.

SUGGESTED CLASS TIME

2–3 class periods

TERMS TO KNOW

Define the following terms:

A. diversity;
B. cultural awareness;
C. health and wellness program; and
D. professional image.

PRELIMINARY ACTIVITY

Locate a journal article concerning the global impact of obesity. Visit the *Gallup*, and read about U.S. obesity rates to understand the three criteria of obesity. Compare the statistics to those in another country.

WHO'S IN THIS STORY?

Adrienne Ray, 58
FELIX Accounting
Supervisor I

© Shutterstock/Zdenka Darula

Aaron Bernstein, 33
FELIX Mid-Level
Finance Analyst

© Shutterstock/eurobanks

Dawali Black, 31
FELIX Marketing
Assistant

© Shutterstock/Rob Marmion

Destinie Taylor, 27
FELIX Attorney I

© Shutterstock/REDAV

SETTING

Atlanta, FELIX Headquarters and Employee Lounge

CASE SCENARIO

Aaron arrives at work wearing a Kenneth Cole New York extreme black slim fit suit with black Prada Spazzolato buckle loafers that are polished to the point of perfection. He is a handsome man, and his fashionable style and refined taste earn him plenty of compliments from both the men and the women in the office.

Aaron is a self-proclaimed health nut who fits perfectly in a business where good looks appeal not only to customers, but also to clients. Everyone in the office knows that he loves to exercise. At the close of most work days, Aaron changes out of his stylish business attire into a form-fitting Nike pro basketball shirt with matching shorts. At least four days a week, he heads to the local YMCA where he plays on a competitive adult basketball team.

Although Aaron does a great job as a mid-level finance analyst, he requires some finesse in the area of interpersonal skills. His enthusiasm for health and wellness often rubs his co-workers, who are less than naturally svelte, the wrong way. Some even consider him to be downright insensitive and rude on many levels. On this particular Friday morning, Aaron may go a bit too far.

Aaron: Good morning, Destinie! How are you?

Destinie: I'm great, Aaron. How are you?

Aaron: Oh, just dandy. Wow, you look beautiful today. Are you meeting with a trainer or something?

Destinie: No, not at all. I don't even own a gym membership. I've just been trying to eat better these days and get more rest. I heard that doing this alone can help you keep the unwanted pounds off and avoid certain health issues.

Aaron: Yes, that's true. But nothing beats a consistent exercise routine. You should join the YMCA. I can put you in touch with a serious trainer. I mean, you look great, but once you hit 25, if you're not careful, things just automatically start to spread.

Destinie gives Aaron a quick look of shock for his off comments. Aaron sees the quick change in Destinie's demeanor and clears his throat, as he runs his fingers through his hair.

Aaron: I mean the weight just starts to shift after that age, right? At least that's how my wife explains it to me. She works pretty hard at staying in shape, but it's a challenge.

Destinie: Yes, I'm sure. Well, Aaron, I have a lot of work to do this morning. So, if you don't mind . . .

Aaron: Oh! Yes, of course. Hey, wait! Did you change your hair?

Destinie pretends like she does not hear him. She refuses to explain how she can go from a short natural kinky afro to a long silky look in a matter of hours. She does not have the energy or the patience to be politically correct, as Aaron had already irritated her with the trainer comment.

Although Destinie is in her late twenties, Aaron's comment about women "spreading" in her age group only reminds her of the negative self-images women may have concerning looks, size, and age. She believes that the double standard between men and women is unfair. Men could have a head full of gray hair and still be considered debonair. When women begin to age, they may be regarded as over-the-hill and unattractive.

Destinie is not what some people would consider naturally thin. At a size 10, she has womanly curves. When compared to most of the women in the fashion industry, she is not considered model material. She decides that she will mentally file Aaron's comments and focus on her pile of work.

As Aaron proceeds toward his office, he sees Dawali Black coming out of the restroom wearing a form-fitting black knee-length dress with butterfly sleeves. She is adjusting a colorful Navajo custom-made beaded belt with matching bracelets, necklace, and earrings. She has long bangs that swoop to the side and two loosely braided ponytails that are wrapped with leather strings and black rubber bands at the end.

As he watches Dawali, Aaron notices that she is wearing very little make-up and surprisingly looks stunning for someone in her early thirties. Aaron silently questions why she has to ruin the outfit with that Indian garb. Everyone in the office is well aware that Dawali is American Indian. Why does she have to remind them of it all the time?

Dawali looks up and sees Aaron watching her. She smiles, says hello, and waves but unnecessarily continues adjusting her belt to avoid interacting with him. She quickly walks past Aaron, makes a bee-line toward her office, and closes the door. Dawali never feels comfortable around Aaron. He rarely says anything that is considered overtly disrespectful, but she senses that he does not like her very much.

A few weeks ago, Dawali heard Aaron talking to Adrienne about a documentary concerning Indians being banished from their lands and experiencing an extinction of their culture. He tells Adrienne that maybe the reason Dawali wears Indian accessories and has a dream catcher hanging in her office is to restore some connection to her lost heritage. Dawali never mentioned the conversation to Adrienne because she agreed with Aaron and said that all this diversity and gender talk are just a waste of time.

From his perspective, Aaron notices that Dawali is merely cordial to him and not as friendly as she is with other co-workers. He wonders why since he has always been nice to her. Ultimately, in his mind she is insignificant to him. She does not impact his work life and he is only required to collaborate closely with her when she asks for additional funds to support a marketing project.

During lunch time in the employee lounge . . .

Adrienne: Hi, Destinie. How are you? I haven't seen you or Dawali all day. You guys must be busy.

Destinie: Oh, hey, Adrienne. Yeah, it's been a day. I have an issue with one of our clients, and I've been on the phone all morning trying to iron out some contract discrepancies.

Dawali: Hello, Adrienne. Yes, I've been busy too. I'm working on a new marketing campaign. It has been a challenge trying to meet deadlines when the client keeps changing his mind about what items he wants us to debut.

Adrienne: Wow, you all have had a lot to do today!

Destinie and Dawali (*at the same time)*: Yeah.

Aaron enters the employee lounge to get some coffee. He stops to watch the news report about a new terrorist group and listens to how the United States has identified its spokesman. The terrorist leader sent an audio message claiming the group has expanded to western Africa to recruit and gain allegiance from another dangerous militant organization.

Aaron: Man, this terrorist situation is a real threat.

The women look at him and then stare at the television to see what he is watching.

Destinie: Yes, that's really scary, especially since they are recruiting here too.

After several commercials, the news returns but switches to the latest report on health issues that plague America. The medical reporter, an assistant professor of neurosurgery at a prestigious university and news medical spokesman, begins talking about how diet sodas are just as bad for you as regular sodas.

Adrienne: Oh great, so now I can't consume diet drinks! I've been trying to lose weight forever, but at my age it's just harder to get off. I hate drinking plain water all of the time. It becomes annoying. I'm even thinking about joining the health and wellness program here at work.

Destinie: I didn't know that you were on a diet, Adrienne. Yes, I understand about the difficulty of losing weight at a certain age. I mean, just today, I was told that you can almost give up on maintaining your figure in your late twenties if you aren't careful.

Aaron's eyes shift quickly to Destinie then back to the TV. He does not want to have a weight loss debate with Destinie. After all, she is an attorney, and she knows how to argue a point. He has seen her in action and dares not provoke her. On the other hand, Adrienne is not as defiant as Destinie. She blushes and shifts uncomfortably near Dawali and takes another quick survey of what she is eating for lunch.

Adrienne: Well, I've been trying to diet. I just haven't been consistent like I should.

Dawali, trying to block out what she heard Adrienne say a few weeks ago, offers her words of encouragement.

Dawali: Well, my sister is a nurse. She said the easiest way to diet is to substitute one bad eating habit gradually with a good one. Eventually, you will replace all of your bad eating habits.

Aaron cannot contain himself. He has to help these women because they are confused about what it takes to incorporate and maintain a healthy diet and lifestyle. He takes a sip of his black coffee and decides to offer them some unsolicited advice.

Aaron: Well, Adrienne, age has nothing to do with it. It's about establishing and adapting to a healthier lifestyle.

Adrienne: What? Excuse me!

Aaron: I mean, no offense, but if you really want to get healthy, you have to get serious about it. Did you know that obesity counts for about 10% of the deaths that occur in America! High blood pressure, cholesterol issues, and heart problems all are associated with an unhealthy lifestyle. Physicians have the nerve to say that obesity is a disease. It's not a disease, it's a choice.

Did you all know that we are the fattest country in the world?

C'mon, Adrienne, look at your lunch today! You have salty chips, a huge 12-inch meatball sub on white bread with extra meat and cheese. That alone is over 1,900 calories, and that's just the sandwich! If you add the chips and 24-ounce diet soda, then you're eating enough calories for three meals in one sitting.

Geez, how can you function with that sitting in your stomach all day? I'd feel sluggish and ready to take a nap. No wonder you can barely move around. All of that heavy breathing would stop too if you selected healthier foods and exercised. I'm not trying to be rude, but I noticed your clothes were a little snug today too.

Listen, if you need a trainer to help you get started, I can find you one who's reasonable. I think we all should be cognizant of our professional image. I mean we work in the retail industry. It's all about looks here. Yeah, I know the perfect trainer for you. I'm going to refer you to Sam. She's a great trainer for women your size. No offense, but I'm just trying to help you out since you said that you want to shed a few pounds.

Dawali and Destinie are in shock and cannot believe what they just heard. Aaron has apparently lost his mind talking about weight in a room full of women, one of which happens to be his boss!

Adrienne is embarrassed by his comments and becomes instantly angry. Who is he to scold her about her eating habits? She has the right to eat whatever she wants. Her clients could care less that she is overweight; they care more about her competence. She composes herself and tries to rebound quickly.

In the past, she has heard Aaron's off comments about how the women in the office should portray a professional image not only in their wardrobe selection, but also in their physical appearance. At this moment, she feels that he is superficial. His comments are hurtful since she assumed that they are friends. She and Aaron have worked together for years.

Aaron knows that Adrienne was not always this overweight. She underwent surgery for a medical condition and could not exercise regularly, so her weight gradually increased. She also stopped smoking per her physician's orders and that made her crave sweets in place of cigarettes. Before she knew it, she had gained several pounds. It makes her self-conscious and bitter. Her self-esteem suffers and so do her personal relationships. He also notices that her energy level is low, and she misses more days of work. He is tired of having to do his work and hers on the days that she is absent.

Destinie *(lightly touching Adrienne's arm)*: Adrienne, are you okay?

Adrienne clears her throat. She manages to fight back tears and turns to lock eyes with Aaron, who is still sipping on his coffee.

Adrienne: Yes, thank you, Destinie. Aaron, I realize that you think everyone should exercise, eat as healthy as you do, and adhere to your standards of beauty, but not everyone does. Some of us struggle with weight, living a healthy lifestyle, and looking fashionably flawless. We mere mortals do the best we can.

Adrienne gathers her lunch and leaves the employee lounge. Dawali and Destinie continue to look at Aaron in disbelief. He watches Adrienne as she exits the room and turns to face Destinie and Dawali.

Aaron: I don't know why you all are looking at me like that. I just told her the truth. Besides, you all do not have to worry about controlling your weight. You all are gorgeous and nicely built. By the way, Destinie, I have wanted to tell you something since this morning. Your hair looks so much better like this.

DISCUSSION QUESTIONS

1. Is a person's weight a legitimate concern in the workplace? Do weight and appearance really matter in certain industries? Under what circumstances would it be legal for employers to discriminate based on physical appearance? Do you consider this practice ethical? Explain your answer.
2. Do you agree with Aaron's views on his colleague's professional image? Why or why not?
3. Should Adrienne be concerned about the image her weight has on clients in face-to-face situations? Explain.
4. Employees suffering from obesity can put a strain on company insurance costs, result in lost productivity, and affect the corporate image. With this in mind, how can a company legally force employees to shed pounds?
5. Should Aaron be disciplined for his insensitivity toward women in the workplace? Was he uncivil? As his supervisor, how would you speak to him about his behavior?
6. Describe how Aaron's statements could impact his relationship with Adrienne.
7. If you were Destinie, how would you respond to Aaron about his hair comment? Should Destinie let Aaron know that what he said offended her? Write a brief paragraph detailing what you would say.
8. If you were the HR Director and Destinie, Adrienne, or Dawali came to you to complain about Aaron, what steps should you take to avoid possible litigation and disruption in the office? Explain.
9. Should Dawali approach Adrienne and Aaron about the comment she heard a few weeks ago or forget about it? How could her unresolved feelings toward Adrienne and Aaron impact work relationships? Explain your answer.
10. What type of non-verbal signals is Dawali sending Aaron? If so, what advice would you give either Dawali or Aaron on how to rectify the situation?

SELF-ASSESSMENT

Keep a journal for the next three days. Record all of the comments that you hear regarding a person's weight. Be prepared to share your findings with the class.

APPLICATION ACTIVITIES

1. Locate and watch *Overweight in the Workplace* (HBO: The Weight of the Nation) and/or another video on obesity on the Internet.
2. Write your reflections on the video. How did you feel about it? If FELIX were your company, what would you do to combat obesity in the workplace and/or minimize the stigma employees suffering from obesity face?

CASE STUDY 10

I'M NOT INTERESTED ANYMORE

OBJECTIVES

Students will be able to:

A. identify and give examples of hostile work environment and quid pro quo sexual harassment;
B. outline the challenges that employees and companies face with workplace dating; and
C. devise an employee fraternization policy.

SUGGESTED CLASS TIME

2–3 class periods

TERMS TO KNOW

Define the following terms:

A. hostile work environment sexual harassment;
B. quid pro quo sexual harassment; and
C. fraternization.

PRELIMINARY ACTIVITY

Read the definitions of hostile work environment and quid pro quo sexual harassment under *Title VII of the Civil Rights Act of 1964 (Title VII).* Cite at least three examples of each type of sexual harassment.

WHO'S IN THIS STORY?

Mary Kate Harrison, 49
FELIX Senior Attorney

© Shutterstock/kurhan

Daryl Peterson, 40
FELIX Attorney II

© Shutterstock/Charlotte Purdy

Destinie Taylor, 27
FELIX Attorney I

© Shutterstock/REDAV

Female Worker 1, 29
FELIX

Female Worker 2, 34
FELIX

SETTING

Atlanta, FELIX Headquarters—Legal Department and *Nikhauli's Restaurant*

CASE SCENARIO

Daryl and Destinie have been secretly dating for three months. Daryl is surprised at how much he has come to care for Destinie in such a short time. Tonight, they are having a late dinner at posh downtown Nikhauli's Restaurant.

Destinie: Dinner was great as usual.

Daryl: Yes, it was. I hate that we have to go home now.

Destinie: Well, we'll see each other again in about nine hours at the office.

Daryl: Destinie, you know that's not the same.

Destinie: Daarryylll, stop it.

Daryl: Baby, are you still nervous about people finding out about us? I told you not to worry about it. We can make this work.

Destinie: Yes, I'm still concerned! I could lose my job. You know I've been at FELIX for less than a year.

Daryl: Destinie, we're both consenting adults. You've done a stellar job since your arrival in the legal department. You've become a valuable member of the team. What are you worried about? I told you that FELIX does not have a formal policy against employees dating each other. It's not like I'm your supervisor or anything. We work together, that's all.

Destinie: I know, I know. But, you're up for a promotion soon. If you get it, then you will be supervising me. What do we do then? Just give me some time to think about it. I've come too far to make a mistake now that could jeopardize my career.

Daryl: So that's what we are? A mistake?

After an awkward pause, Daryl asks Destinie if she is ready to go. Seeing her nod, he stands and pulls out her chair. Silently, Daryl and Destinie leave the restaurant. Daryl hails a cab for her. They awkwardly hug each other good night.

The next day at the close of business—Legal Department Meeting Room . . .

Mary Kate: Great briefing about FELIX background check policies, Daryl. Destinie, Daryl tells me that you conducted the research on this project. Great job to both of you! That will be all. I'll see you guys tomorrow.

Mary Kate exits. Daryl turns to Destinie and grabs her hand. Pulling her hand free, Destinie faces Daryl.

Destinie: Daryl, I can't see you anymore. I value my career too much.

Daryl: Baby, don't do this. We have something good going here. We can make it work.

Destinie: I'm sorry, Daryl, but this has to end.

Over the next several weeks, Daryl struggles with his feelings for Destinie, who appears unaffected by their breakup. Finally accepting that their relationship is over, Daryl focuses on moving forward with both his personal life and career.

Mary Kate: Congratulations on your promotion, Daryl! Try to enjoy the feeling this weekend because your new supervisory duties start next week.

Daryl: Thanks, Mary Kate.

Mary Kate: Hey. Why so solemn? I thought you'd be more excited about the promotion.

Daryl: Oh, I am. I am. Just focusing on work is all. Thanks, again.

As Daryl walks to his office, Destinie exits hers.

Destinie (*whispering*): Hey, babe. Congratulations. Is it okay if I follow you to your office? I have some files that I need to review with you.

Daryl (*looking surprised*): Thanks, Destinie. Can we review the files on Monday? I'm leaving in ten minutes.

Destinie: We need to do it today. Mary Kate wants an update on Monday.

Daryl: Okay. Well, let's go to the meeting room.

After reviewing the files, Destinie and Daryl exit FELIX 40 minutes later.

Destinie: Can I treat you to an after-hours cocktail to say congratulations?

Daryl: I don't know if that's such a good idea, Destinie. I've done my best to keep my distance and respect your wishes about not continuing with our relationship. But frankly, you're sending me mixed signals. What's up with all the personal text messages when we're on company time? I'm not trying to be rude, but it's got to stop. This is what you said you wanted, but suddenly over the last week, you have been contacting me under the ruse of work. What's up with that?

Destinie: So that's why you've turned down my last invitation to dinner? Are you not answering my calls for the same reason? I miss you, Daryl. Can't a girl change her mind?

Daryl: No, our work situation has changed. I just think it's best to maintain status quo. Have a great weekend.

Over the next month . . .

Daryl continues to maintain a professional distance from Destinie despite her continued requests to spend time together or go to dinner. He is extremely uncomfortable with her persistence. On one afternoon in particular, Daryl and a male co-worker are talking in the garage after work when they hear giggling behind them. Daryl turns to find Destinie walking with two other female workers. He says hello and turns away.

Female Worker 1: Hey, Tiger. I mean, Daryl. Would you like to hang out this evening? I hear you're loads of fun.

Female Worker 2: Hey, handsome. Rrrrrrr, I like the name Tiger. It fits you. Just like the suit that you're wearing . . . nice and tight.

Shocked, Daryl does not respond but looks at Destinie. She rolls her eyes and continues to walk past him. His co-worker, who is surprised by the ladies' catcalling, looks at Daryl but says nothing. As they walk away, the female workers continue to speak loudly about Daryl.

DISCUSSION QUESTIONS

1. Discuss the pros and cons of dating a fellow employee within the same company but who works in a different department, versus dating a fellow employee who works in the same department. Determine whether there is a difference in these two situations.
2. Prior to Daryl's promotion, was it inappropriate or unethical for Daryl and Destinie to date since they are both FELIX employees? What about after his promotion? Explain.
3. Is Destinie sexually harassing Daryl? Are the two female co-workers sexually harassing him? If so, what type(s) of sexual harassment? State the elements for the relevant type(s) of sexual harassment and apply the facts of the case scenario to support your position.
4. Assess the actions of Destinie and the two female employees toward Daryl and the male co-worker. Are these women violating any of their rights?
5. Consider your answer to Question 4. With regard to time and place, are the women's actions appropriate? If these women made the same statements on the weekend while they coincidentally encountered Daryl and the male co-worker in the mall, would they be violating their rights?
6. What is the impact of the women's actions on Daryl and the male co-worker in the FELIX work environment? Will the women be impacted as well? Explain your answer.
7. Based on *Title VII*, should Daryl speak to Destinie and the female workers privately regarding the garage incident? Explain. What are the advantages and disadvantages of initiating a private conversation with them?
8. In addition to having a private conversation with Destinie, what other options could Daryl use to deal with this workplace issue? Assess the quality of each option.
9. Does Daryl's new supervisory position create additional sexual harassment concerns should Destinie's behavior continue? Explain.
10. In order to protect himself against any future actions by Destinie, how should Daryl proceed? What should he do first, second, and so forth?
11. Should FELIX implement an employee fraternization policy? Explain.

SELF-ASSESSMENT

Reflect on the issue of employees dating within the same company. Write a journal entry discussing your personal opinion on whether employees should be permitted to date and why.

APPLICATION ACTIVITIES

1. In small groups, research company employee fraternization policies. Based on your research, create a FELIX Employee Fraternization Policy.
2. In small groups, create your own scenarios for quid pro quo and hostile work environment sexual harassment. Compose sample answers, and perform a skit for both scenarios. Ask the class for input on how management should resolve these situations.
3. Read two recent federal and/or state cases on sexual harassment. From the plaintiff's perspective, what are the difficulties in proving a case of sexual harassment? What defenses are available for defendants and/or employers in these cases?
4. Research current statistics on workplace dating. How are companies dealing with this trend?

CASE STUDY 11

HOLIDAY HEADLINES*

OBJECTIVES

Students will be able to:

A. identify appropriate business etiquette;
B. recognize potential corporate liability at social events; and
C. organize a networking event.

SUGGESTED CLASS TIME

3–4 class periods

TERMS TO KNOW

Define the following terms:

A. business etiquette;
B. employer liability; and
C. social host liability.

PRELIMINARY ACTIVITY

Research state laws pertaining to holiday parties and employer liability. Then, locate articles that offer guidelines that companies should follow to ensure a safe and litigation-free holiday season.

WHO'S IN THIS STORY?

Min Kwon, 38
FELIX HR Director

Sam Kwon, 40
Min's Husband

Cameron Knox, 37
FELIX HR
Supervisor

Brandon Knox, 37
Cameron's Husband

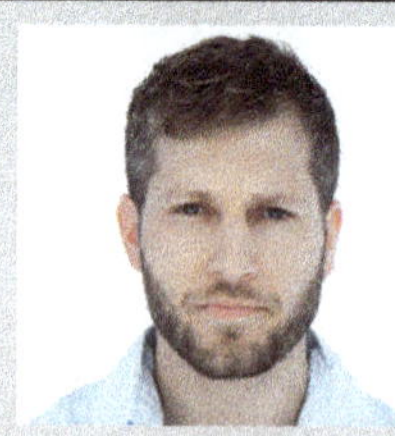

Parker Cobb, 27
FELIX HR
Benefits Manager

Mary Kate Harrison, 49
FELIX Senior Attorney

Aaron Bernstein, 33
FELIX Mid-Level Finance
Analyst

Dawali Black, 31
FELIX Marketing
Assistant

Patricia (Trish) Fox, 38
FELIX Marketing
Manager

Daryl Peterson, 40
FELIX Attorney III

Felix Fox, 40
FELIX CFO

SETTING

Downtown Atlanta, FELIX holiday party location

CASE SCENARIO

At the end of every year, FELIX holds its holiday soiree at the most exquisite hotel in Atlanta. The party is a sophisticated and extravagant affair with some of Atlanta's most elite, including local politicians as well as the company's community stakeholders, employees, clients, and models, in attendance. FELIX's holiday event has been listed in the Atlanta Monthly Exposé as one of the city's Top 20 annual holiday fundraising events.

Felix: Good evening, everyone. On behalf of FELIX, we would like to thank you all for coming to our end-of-the-year party and fundraising event. We are proud of the eight new clothing lines, which may move us into international territory. We should all be excited about that. Also, we welcome Paulo Fabrizio de Reis from Rio de Janeiro, Brazil as one of our newest designers. Paulo, where are you? Wave your hand. *(Felix points in Paulo's direction.)* Oh, there he is. Paulo has some wonderful ideas for our women's collection. All I can say about it is stay tuned!

As you know my dad, Mr. Phillip Fox, believes in giving back to the community. He has donated thousands of dollars each year to worthy causes in the Atlanta area. Because of your staunch support, we were able to donate $2.5 million to the shelter for the homeless project, $3.5 million to HIV/STD prevention services for at-risk youth, and $4 million in scholarships and internships to underprivileged high school and college students who want to pursue careers in the fashion industry. Please give yourselves a round of applause. You are making a positive difference in so many lives. We look forward to continuing our partnership with you in the new year.

This evening, we have plenty of food, beverages, entertainment, and goodie bags. We also are offering taxi services should you require them. Please enjoy yourselves! Our event is now underway. You may proceed to Ballroom A. The ushers will direct you to your respective tables.

As Min and Sam walk to the ballroom, they see Mary Kate.

Min: Good evening, Mary Kate.

Mary Kate: Hi, Min. Hello, Sam. You both look great.

Min: Thanks. So do you.

Sam: Good evening, Ms. Harrison. It's nice to see you again.

Mary Kate: Nice to see you as well, and please call me Mary Kate. Okay, where do we sit? We should have name tags, right?

Min *(looking at her husband)*: We should ask the ushers, honey. Oh, never mind. There we are. *Min notices the name tags on the table.*

Mary Kate: Min, did you place all of the executives at the same table?

Min: No, I told Stephanie to place people from different offices together. This is the only time we have an opportunity to meet some of our clients and colleagues from the other offices. Why? Did that not happen at our table?

Mary Kate: Well, I just noticed that all of us are from the same office and are in leadership positions.

Min: Oh no, that's a mistake. Unfortunately, I can't change it now. I will address it with Stephanie. I gave her a seating chart weeks ago. I'll have Cameron pay closer attention to the seating charts the next time.

Mary Kate: I didn't mean to suggest that you move anyone. I hope you did not think that was what I meant. It was just an observation.

They both hear familiar laughs and turn toward the direction of the sound. Mary Kate and Min notice Dawali and Daryl laughing as they enter the ballroom. Dawali has her arm intertwined with Daryl's. Mary Kate and Min exchange looks. FELIX just implemented a new policy that prohibits fraternization in the office. Daryl sees them both, smiles, and walks in their direction.

Daryl: Good evening, ladies and gent.

Min, Mary Kate, and Sam (*simultaneously*): Good evening.

Dawali: Hello. How are you guys doing? We were told to come to table ten. Wow, you all look lovely!

Min: Thank you, so do you.

Mary Kate: Thanks, Dawali.

Daryl pulls out a chair for Dawali and waits for her to be seated. He gently grazes her shoulders and slides his hand down her arm then sits beside her. Dawali smiles at him and turns to speak to her co-workers.

Dawali: Hey guys, I've seen so many celebrities here tonight. My niece would go crazy if I told her JJ and the group Machiavelli were here! I'll take a picture of them later and send it to her phone. Even though it takes an entire year to organize this event, I love the holiday party! Thanks for helping me this year with the seating arrangements and other tasks, Min. Wait, where is Parker? Is he not coming?

Min: You're welcome, Dawali. As for Parker, he should have been here by now. Maybe he's running late.

Hearing the last part of the conversation, Cameron walks up to the table.

Cameron: I'm sure he'll be here. Parker loves having a good time.

Dawali: Hi, Cameron. Wow, you look spectacular!

Cameron: Thanks. So do you and everyone else at the table. This is my husband, Brandon.

Brandon scans the room, looking out for the nearest bar.

Brandon: Sit down, honey. I met them at the last holiday party, remember? Good seeing you all again.

Everyone nods and looks around the room.

Daryl: I don't get out often, so where's the bar? Dawali, would you like something to drink?

Dawali: Not right now, but thanks for asking, Daryl.

Brandon: It's over there. It's the first thing I spotted when we got here. I'll go with you, Daryl. Cameron, do you want anything?

Cameron: No, thank you. Are you drinking tonight?

Brandon: Cam, don't start. Daryl, it's this way, man.

Daryl looks at Cameron but decides to follow Brandon to the bar without saying anything.

Min: Well, they're beginning to serve dinner. Good, I'm starving.

Dawali: I'm starving, too. I haven't eaten all day because I wanted to fit into this dress!

All of the women laugh and nod in agreement. A few minutes later, Parker arrives with his friend, and they sit at the table.

Parker: Good evening, everyone. This is my friend Hollace. Hollace, this is my boss, Min and her husband, Sam. Dawali works in Marketing, and over here is Cameron. Where is your hubby tonight, Cam?

Cameron: He's at the bar with Daryl.

Parker: Okay. Did Daryl bring a date?

Dawali: Nope. He and I arrived at the same time.

Parker: Oh, I see.

Dawali blushes and tries to hide a smile.

Dawali: Wait, no. We're just friends. I mean, co-workers.

Brandon and Daryl return to the table with drinks in hand. Brandon has two drinks while Daryl has one. Cameron looks at Brandon's drinks and decides to remain quiet. She refuses to discuss his drinking habit in public and knows better than to embarrass him in front of her co-workers. Instead, she discretely gains Parker's attention and motions him to talk in private.

Cameron *(whispering to Brandon)***:** Honey, I'm going to the ladies room. I'll be right back.

Brandon waves her off and gulps down one of his tall drinks. Parker waits a few minutes before he too makes an excuse to leave the table.

Parker: Cam, are you okay? You seem a little tense.

Cameron: Not really. Have you noticed that he's already started drinking, as if he didn't have four drinks before we left home.

Parker: Oh, no. Is he drinking that much tonight? But then again, Cam, he's a man. He can handle it. How is everything else coming along with you guys? I noticed the long-sleeve gown. It's beautiful and you look amazing, but you aren't going to be able to hide those bruises forever.

Cameron: Parker! I don't want to discuss that right now. What I want to know is are you going to behave tonight? You remember the talk we had after the last holiday party?

Parker *(laughing at the memory)*: You know how I like to have fun. Hollace will be my designated driver.

Cameron: Be careful, Parker. I know we work in the fashion industry and this is Atlanta, but we also work with some very conservative clients and employees. Just make sure that you can handle the backlash, if there is any. Remember that last week Felix contacted Min about incorporating a mandatory business etiquette seminar. We didn't have enough time to hold it before this gathering, but we'll have it next year.

Parker: I know, you're right. Thanks, Cam. You better go to the restroom. Brandon is looking this way.

Cameron: Whatever, Parker. Go back to the table, and try to behave.

Before Parker returns to the table, he stops by the bar and orders four Long Island Iced Teas. Two for him and two for Hollace. He is going to enjoy the festivities. It has been a long year, and he is in a celebratory mood. Parker sees Trish mingling with guests on her way to the bar.

Parker (*addressing the bartender*): Can you put that on a tray? There is no way I can carry all of those drinks by myself.

Trish: Hey, Parker! How are you liking the party so far?

Parker *(turning to face Trish)*: Oh hi, Trish! The party's fabulous. The marketing department did an excellent job with the fundraising campaign. I heard we gave away millions of dollars this year.

Trish: Yes, the campaign was a success. Next year, we will need to raise a lot more money. We hope to start an afterschool fashion program for elementary students in four counties. We are looking at properties and locations now. We need to recruit the next generation of designers way before the high school and college levels. It is all about changing minds through effective marketing strategies.

Parker: Wow, you've really thought this through.

Trish: Yes, well, that's why I'm in marketing. Have fun tonight because come Monday, we're back at work!

Parker: I know, right! Save me a dance. I know you like to do the Macarena!

Trish: Whoa, do they still do that?

Parker: Tonight they will because I am going to request it. You need to join me on the dance floor when the song comes on!

They both laugh and return to their tables. As Parker sits down, the band plays a slow song.

Daryl: Finally a song I can dance to. Dawali, would you like to dance?

Parker: Oh, I was going to ask her, but you go ahead, Daryl. You've been staring at her all night long, anyway.

Dawali: Oh my gosh, Parker! It's just a dance. I dance with you all the time.

Everyone at the table looks at Parker.

Parker (*shrugging his shoulders*): What?

Parker sips on his Long Island Iced Tea.

Dawali: Sure, Daryl, I would love to dance. Please, don't step on my feet. These shoes are killing me.

Daryl: I won't. I promise. As for the shoes, take them off.

After a long night of dancing and several mixed drinks, Parker is ready to leave the party until he hears one of his favorite old school dance songs. Motioning to Hollace to join him on the dance floor, Parker dances wildly with a drink still in his hand. Singing loudly, he bumps into a corporate sponsor and his wife. Noticeably intoxicated, Parker continues his antics by grabbing Hollace, running his fingers through his hair, and laying his head on his shoulder. Parker seems to forget that they have an audience and are at a corporate event.

Aaron: Felix, what is going on here?

Felix: What are you talking about, Aaron? Everyone is having a great time!

Aaron: That's the problem. Look at the dance floor! Wait, is that Parker?

Felix: No, that's not Parker. Wait! Yes, it is! Oh no, what will our guests think?

Aaron: Well, maybe you need to tell him to quit. Don't you think that this is inappropriate?

Felix: Yeah, you're right. I will have Min talk to him on Monday. I expected a little more class from him.

Felix is not pleased with Parker's behavior, and neither is Aaron. Min spots Parker and Hollace on the dance floor.

Min: What! Did you see that?

Sam and Brandon (*simultaneously*): Yes!

Min: Parker should know better.

Cameron: Oh my! Too much for a corporate event. I talked to him about this earlier tonight.

Mary Kate *(clearing her throat)***:** Yes. Well, I think I've seen enough for one night. I'm going home, but someone needs to make sure that Parker uses the taxi service tonight.

Cameron: Well, Parker told me that Hollace is his designated driver.

Min: If I were you, Mary Kate, I'd document this situation.

Mary Kate: You do the same. Nice seeing you all again. Enjoy the rest of your evening.

After the song, Parker and Hollace return to the table. In slurred speech, Parker bids everyone a good night. Daryl decides this is an appropriate time to leave the party as well. He grabs Dawali's hand, and they tell everyone good night. Cameron notices that Parker is pulling out his car keys. She tries to convince him to take a cab, but he refuses. Parker and Hollace leave the soiree loudly singing the DJ's current selection. Thirty minutes later, they are involved in a car accident. The police arrest Parker for driving under the influence while Hollace is transported to the hospital with severe injuries.

DISCUSSION QUESTIONS

1. What is the importance of business etiquette at work-related events? Even outside of normal business hours, should employees adhere to business etiquette at after-hours functions? Explain your answer.
2. State examples of how business etiquette was not adhered to in the case scenario. How could these behaviors be corrected? Whose responsibility was it to correct each behavior?
3. Should FELIX have implemented a mandatory HR business etiquette seminar prior to hosting the holiday event? Why or why not? How can an employer establish boundaries regarding holiday party behavior?
4. What is social host liability? Who is at risk in this case scenario?
5. What is the impact on FELIX for Parker's behavior at the holiday event? Should Parker be asked to leave FELIX based on his actions and visible inebriation? Explain.
6. Could FELIX be liable for Parker's accident and Hollace's injuries? Why or why not?
7. As an HR professional, was Parker violating policies his office may have put into place? If so, how should he be reprimanded?
8. Is Cameron negligent for allowing Parker to drive after she observed him drinking at the holiday party? Support your answer.

SELF-ASSESSMENT

Create a list of do's and don'ts to remember when attending a corporate function. Based on the devised list, how can you create a positive impression as a representative of your company?

APPLICATION ACTIVITIES

1. Assume that you are at a networking event.
   a. Create a five-minute elevator speech to use at a corporate function and/or
   b. Organize a networking event among your peers. Consider inviting corporate sponsors to your event.
2. Min suspects that Dawali and Daryl may be in a relationship. If you were Min, how would you handle this delicate situation considering FELIX's new fraternization policy?
3. Develop a letter of reprimand to Parker concerning his behavior at the holiday soiree. Decide whether the letter should become a part of his permanent employee record.
4. Research companies that have been sued for tort liability concerning office parties and alcohol-related accidents. To begin, Google the legal case about Dr. Jared Purton and Marriott International, Inc.
5. Devise and present a professional etiquette seminar.

CASE STUDY 12
COMPETING IN STYLE

OBJECTIVES

Students will be able to:

A. understand why it is important that companies establish and develop a sustainable succession plan to attract premium talent;
B. recognize the importance of adhering to pre-selected competition guidelines; and
C. establish a recruitment process for a company or student business organization.

SUGGESTED CLASS TIME

3–4 class periods

TERMS TO KNOW

Define the following terms:

A. succession plan;
B. soft skills; and
C. technical/hard skills.

PRELIMINARY ACTIVITY

Research how companies recruit and retain high-quality employees. Share your findings with the class.

WHO'S IN THIS STORY?

Felix Fox, 40 FELIX CFO  © Shutterstock/doodko	Trish Fox, 38 FELIX Marketing Manager  © Shutterstock/DC Studio
Ernesto Diaz, 45 FELIX Marketing Supervisor  © Shutterstock/Andresr	DeAngelo Moore, 42 FELIX Accounting Supervisor II  © Shutterstock/Hugo Felix
Dawali Black, 31 FELIX Marketing Assistant  © Shutterstock/Rob Marmion	Destinie Taylor, 27 FELIX Attorney I  © Shutterstock/REDAV
Cameron Knox, 37 FELIX HR Supervisor  © Shutterstock/Maksim Shmeljov	Gabriel Deveaux, 60 Dean, School of Fashion 
Jon Claude de Marco, 46 Professor of Fashion Marketing and Management 	Phil Fox, 64 FELIX CEO  © Shutterstock/Ruslan Guzov

SETTING

Atlanta—DeKima University, Academy of Fashion

CASE SCENARIO

During the spring, FELIX has its annual FASHIONISTA competition at DeKima University's Academy of Fashion (DAF) in downtown Atlanta. The faculty recommends junior and senior students majoring in fashion with a minimum of a 3.5 GPA to compete for a year-long paid internship with FELIX. Students may be offered full-time employment at the end of the internship program. The purpose of the competition is for FELIX to develop a pipeline of highly skilled employees who understand the full spectrum of fashion. This year's competition starts now.

Gabriel: Good morning, DAFFERS! We are excited to feature the top four candidates who will participate in this year's FASHIONISTA competition. As you know, the winner will receive a paid internship in the amount of $60,000 for one year at Atlanta's very own elite fashion company, FELIX. The candidate will also have an opportunity to debut his or her couture line during Fashion Week in Paris, France. Today's winner will showcase several original pieces in F^3 (FELIX's *Future Flair*) Magazine and have select items sold at FELIX's Atlanta and New York City stores.

Jon Claude: Each candidate is incredibly talented and is prepared to compete in an extremely competitive global fashion environment. The students represent the best DAF has to offer. We wish them all the best. The panel of judges is comprised of the most respected professionals in the fashion industry. Each judge evaluates apparel accessory combinations, color schemes, shoe choices, makeup and hair, stitching, fabrics, and designer themes. Candidates will also have a panel interview in which they must respond to a series of questions. Only the team members from FELIX will make the final selection. FELIX representatives, along with world-renowned designers, artists, models, marketers, trendsetters, and fashion critics, are here to take part in today's occasion. Candidates, please come forward to draw a number out of the red stiletto heel so that we can determine the line-up.

As the candidates draw numbers, Felix approaches the microphone and begins to speak.

Felix: Good morning. My name is Felix Fox, CFO of FELIX, and this is my sister and Marketing Manager, Trish.

Trish: Good morning, DAF! How are you doing?! Are you ready to see some fabulous fashion?

The crowd screams wildly.

Felix: Our father, Phil Fox, is the founder and CEO of FELIX. According to the latest issue of *Global Finances International* money market magazine, FELIX is the number one fashion company in the United States and ranks among the top ten for overseas sales!

Trish: You may not know this, but our dad is the product of unfortunate events. Like many of you, he did not come from money. Still, he dared to dream big, but life seemed to get in the way. Orphaned at the age of six when his parents died in a car accident, my father had to learn perseverance. As an only child and the product of parents who were also only children, Phil Fox had no living relatives to care for him.

Felix: He grew up in New York City's foster care system until the age of 18. Every day, someone told him that he would never amount to anything. Does that sound familiar? How many people have told you that a career in fashion will not feed you and that you should select a different major? The naysayers said the same thing to my dad. But that all changed when a local judge who, by the way, sentenced him to do time in a juvenile detention center, looked past the behaviors of a troubled teen and saw potential. Because of him, my father was able to change his life.

Trish: After graduating from a prestigious fashion institute, he went on to establish FELIX right here in Atlanta, Georgia. If he can do it, so can you!

Felix and Trish: Ladies and gentleman, please give a round of applause for our dad, the ultimate entrepreneur, Philip Fox.

The audience applauds.

Phil: Thank you, Felix and Trish, for telling that story. If there is anything that I would like for you to take away from my life story, it is that opportunities are all around you. It is up to you to take advantage of them when they present themselves. Opportunity does not care about your humble beginnings, ethnicity, or income level. It does not wait for the weary to decide whether or not they are ready. It comes, and then it leaves. Today, the opportunity is here for the right student.

Ladies and gentleman, I am not going to give a lengthy speech because that is not why you're here. You are here to see four students compete for a deal that will change their lives for the better. Each year, this platform allows students to feature their creative talents, and some go on to become famous designers around the world. A life in fashion put me on the right track, and it led me here. Because of the compassion and opportunities that I was given so long ago, I want to help someone else. Professor Jon Claude de Marco, do we have our line-up?

Jon Claude (*looking at Phil, then toward the DJ*): Yes, Phil, we do! We will proceed in the following order: Brooks, Henderson, Santiago-Moralez, and Lopez. Have the candidates provided our technicians with their music?

The DJ nods his head.

Jon Claude: We are ready to begin.

After hours of watching the competition, the FELIX panel has to decide on the final candidate. The panel is now having private conversations among themselves regarding the student designers.

Trish: They were all spectacular. But for what we need in marketing, I think Brooks is our guy.

He knows the business, and he put together an edgy collection that we have not seen at FELIX or anywhere else for that matter. We could use him. Plus, he is gorgeous!

Destinie: Looks do not count in this decision, Trish.

Trish: Yes, Miss Attorney. I was just making an observation. He's very talented. How is that?

Destinie: That's better. But my next question would be, "What constitutes "talent" in this case?" They are all talented.

Felix: I think his collection and delivery are too edgy. He has a hip-hop-type flair to him that may move FELIX away from its mission. Besides, some of his pieces don't fit the FELIX clientele. Some of our customers are too sophisticated for this line.

Dawali: The mission is to provide quality clothing to professional men and women. Why doesn't his line fall into that? I think even professionals would like to dress down now and then.

Trish: Thank you, Dawali. That's exactly my point! His line can include a more professional look.

Did you not see the last suit he featured? The smoky colors and tailored style of the suit mixed the American and the British style of dress. It was brilliant!

DeAngelo: I have to agree. The suits at the end were cutting edge. I would purchase them if I were a younger professional. However, I'm not sure if Brooks would fit in our work culture. I watched him interact with the other candidates, and he does not appear to get along with any of them. He also doesn't seem to do well under pressure. When his music went out, I thought he would lose it right there. He seems temperamental.

Destinie: I agree with that to some extent. For our purpose, I think a superior level of creativity should be a factor as well. I enjoyed Lopez's professional line more so than Brooks'. The models she chose reflected the shape and size of the average woman and her designs looked good on all of them. Her line would fit perfectly with the plus-size collection we plan to run in the fall.

Cameron: I liked Lopez as well. She is very articulate and could answer the questions HR put together for the competition. We specifically wanted to know what inspired their designs. Not only did she use bright colors and textures associated with her heritage, but she also incorporated her vision of the next generation of FELIX customers. I liked that!

Ernesto: Yes, I did too. It would also give us more diversity in the creative design department.

Lopez's designs were risky. She had bold colors and exotic prints that almost appeared to collide with her theme. Luckily for her, it was not distracting, and it worked in her favor.

DeAngelo: I enjoyed her designs, but from a man's perspective, would you want your wife to wear that?

Cameron: No, I wouldn't wear her clothes, but I know women who would.

Ernesto: She isn't trying to appeal to my wife who's over 40. She's attempting to appeal to someone like Dawali or Destinie.

Cameron: That may be true. She knows how to use the classics in her favor. She seems like a team player, too. Did you see how she helped Santiago-Moralez fix his model's dress when she accidentally ripped it? The other candidates didn't move.

Felix: Teamwork is vital in the marketing and creative design departments. We don't have time for the internal competition. We have enough of that from others. She would be an asset in the office. Plus, you have to admit, Lopez is smoking hot!

Destinie: I hope I didn't hear what you just said. I know Ashley would beg to differ.

Felix: What? My wife wouldn't mind. All I said was that she's pretty. That's not illegal!

Destinie: No, but judging her solely on that and not the pre-selected competition guidelines

could pose a problem for FELIX.

Cameron: Be careful, Felix. We are not judging these candidates on how they look. If we were, they would both win! We need someone with leadership skills and talent to one day move into the director position in the creative design department. We are looking for the best person who will provide FELIX with an advantage over its competitors.

Dawali: Okay, so have we decided on a winner?

DISCUSSION QUESTIONS

1. Based on the content of the panel discussions, inappropriate statements were made by FELIX representatives. Identify each speaker and the comments made. Why are the comments inappropriate? How could these comments impact FELIX in the future?
2. In most companies, the ability to work in teams is vital. Do you think that the panel judged Brooks and Lopez appropriately based on what companies look for in team members?
3. What is the difference between soft and technical/hard skills? How important are soft skills, such as attitude and demeanor, in teamwork? Are soft or technical/hard skills more important? Explain.
4. Should Destinie and Cameron document what Felix and Trish said about the candidates? Why or why not? If they decided to document their comments, what are some repercussions the panel could face? How would such documentation impact team relationships?
5. As a judge in a competition or an interviewer in an interview, how important is it for you to adhere to pre-selected guidelines and criteria? How can failing to adhere to this process impact the integrity of the company and the competition as well as the credibility of the panel?
6. Are physical characteristics one of the determining factors in selecting representatives of a company? Can a lawsuit be the consequence of making a decision based solely on physical appearance? Locate and write a brief summary of a legal case in which a company was sued for discriminatory hiring practices based on physical appearance.
7. Research articles on how to make a great first impression. Compile a list of attributes that employers look for in potential employees. Based on the information compiled, how can you make a great first impression at your next interview?
8. How long does it take for someone to make a first impression? What was DeAngelo's first impression of Brooks? How did he conclude that he was not a good fit for the FELIX work culture?
9. What is a succession plan, and why is it important? Is FELIX's FASHIONISTA competition a sustainable succession plan? Is it an appropriate way to identify quality talent for the company? What other activities can FELIX engage in to internally and externally groom quality talent? Do you believe creating an internship of this magnitude will be able to attract premier talent, or should FELIX do other events? Explain.
10. Based on the conversations in the case scenario, is Felix ready to assume his father's responsibilities as CEO? Support your answer.

SELF-ASSESSMENT

Create a survey that will solicit feedback on your strengths and weaknesses as a student and potential employee. Consider your career goals when creating the survey. Interview instructors, family members, and friends to gain personal insight. Based on feedback received, devise a plan on how to maintain and develop these areas to become more competitive.

APPLICATION ACTIVITIES

1. According to your respective major, how would you assist FELIX with developing a sustainable succession plan?
2. In small groups, identify a business or student organization for which you aspire to work or volunteer. Pinpoint its strengths, weaknesses, opportunities, and threats (SWOT Analysis) of the business or student organization. Design a succession document or recruiting plan.

CASE STUDY 13

EMPLOYEE OFF-DUTY CONDUCT*

OBJECTIVES

Students will be able to:

A. comprehend the employment at-will doctrine;
B. recognize employee statutory right to privacy;
C. determine when employee off-duty conduct warrants discipline; and
D. compose a public relations (PR) response to address negative press.

SUGGESTED CLASS TIME

4–5 class periods

TERMS TO KNOW

Define the following terms:

A. employment at-will doctrine;
B. seniority;
C. worker productivity; and
D. bias.

PRELIMINARY ACTIVITY

Students should review stipulations in the employment at-will doctrine for their respective states. Write the stipulations for group sharing and class discussion.

WHO'S IN THIS STORY?

DeAngelo Moore, 42
FELIX Accounting
Supervisor II

© Shutterstock/Hugo Felix

Adrienne Ray, 58
FELIX Accounting
Supervisor I

© Shutterstock/Zdenka Darula

Rebecca Ray, 32
Adrienne Ray's
Daughter

Waiter, 28
Nikhauli's
Restaurant

SETTING

Atlanta, FELIX Headquarters and Nikhauli's Restaurant

CASE SCENARIO

Lately, work has become extremely stressful for Adrienne. Her attitude toward co-workers is strained. Although several weeks have passed since Aaron made comments concerning her steady weight gain, she is still angry with him. She feels humiliated and cannot bring herself to confront him just yet. To add to her level of frustration, she works closely with Katherine. When FELIX hired Katherine to avoid a lawsuit, their relationship changed, and Adrienne no longer considers Katherine a friend. Feeling disengaged in her work and isolated from her team, Adrienne decides to call her daughter Rebecca for a little support.

Rebecca: Hey, Mom!

Adrienne: Hi, honey, how are you?

Rebecca: I'm fine. Is everything okay with you? You sound a little tired.

Adrienne: No, I'm just . . . I don't know. I need a break from here. Do you want to go to Nikhauli's for dinner tonight?

Rebecca: Oh, yes! We haven't gone there in a long time.

Adrienne: Yes, it's the only restaurant where I haven't run into a co-worker. This city is too small!

Rebecca: Yes, it is. Let's meet around 6 p.m. and order green apple margaritas!

Adrienne: Do I have to be the designated driver tonight, Becca?

Rebecca (*laughing*): No, Mom, but I may have to be one for you. You sound down. I'll see you at 6 p.m. then, okay?

Adrienne: Okay. I'll call you when I'm on my way.

Rebecca: Great. Love you. Bye.

Adrienne hangs up the phone and spots DeAngelo at the copy machine. She rolls her eyes and slowly gets up from her seat.

Adrienne: DeAngelo, I have a note on my desk to see you concerning the Alonso account.

DeAngelo: Yes. Good morning, Adrienne. Let me finish up here, and I will meet you in your office.

Adrienne: Sure, but is there something you need me to do?

DeAngelo: Ah, yes. I will talk with you about it.

Adrienne looks at him suspiciously and returns to her office. What is DeAngelo's problem now? Ever since his promotion, he has been micromanaging her accounts. Always second-guessing her, he needs to relax. It's not like she is new to the finance and retail businesses. She has more experience than he and has worked at FELIX longer. If anything, he should be asking her for advice, instead of trying to tell her what to do.

DeAngelo *(pausing at the entrance of Adrienne's office)*: Hey, Adrienne, I spoke with Mr. Alonso, and he had some concerns with the way his account is being handled.

Adrienne: What do you mean "being handled"?

DeAngelo: Well, he said that you were not working with him on his account and wanted to have someone else overlook it.

Adrienne: Wait a minute! Is that what he told you? DeAngelo, Mr. Alonso wanted me to omit certain financial figures and provide him with discounts that I am not authorized to give. He is trying to borrow money from the bank, but he already has a large sum of money tied up with us to debut his new couture dress line. It makes his boutique look financially unhealthy. I told him that he had to honor the contract he had with us, and if he wanted to amend it, he would have to go through our legal department. He didn't want to do that.

DeAngelo: Well, Adrienne, I do understand. However, there were some other comments he made concerning your professionalism.

Adrienne: My professionalism?

DeAngelo: Yes, he said that you were rude to him the other day, and he felt as though you were unwilling to work with him. He said that he explained to you that he was trying to grow his company and had to take out another loan. He just asked that you allow him to defer some payments, and he would make them up later since he's a long-standing customer.

Adrienne: No, that's not true. He asked me to lie about how much he owed. To me, that's a significant breach of accounting ethics. I did not want to put FELIX at risk should we undergo an internal or external audit. I'm sure you wouldn't want that either, DeAngelo.

DeAngelo: Yes, you're right. But, I also cannot afford to lose Mr. Alonso's account and personal contacts either. I hope you understand that this isn't personal. I'm going to have to assign his account to someone else. We can't afford to lose a client over personality differences.

At this point, Adrienne is visibly upset and breathes deeply to keep from lashing out at DeAngelo. He is her boss, but he is not defending her like he should. She believes that he is using her situation to show Felix that he can make difficult decisions.

Adrienne: I can't believe this! I have done the right thing here, so why do I feel as though I'm the one being punished?

DeAngelo: Adrienne, you are not being punished here. We have to satisfy our client even if that means finding another financial supervisor to handle his account. We will do what is best for FELIX.

Adrienne: Fine. I'm not going to argue over this. But when another financial advisor won't yield to his demands, then what are you going to do?

DeAngelo (*ignoring her last comment*): I am going to call Mr. Alonso and tell him that I'll be handling his account until we can find a replacement contact person.

Adrienne: Wait! So, are you going to give him what he wants? That will make me look incompetent to a client. That's not right!

DeAngelo (*proceeding toward the door*): I am going to do what's best for our client.

DeAngelo leaves Adrienne's office and quietly closes the door. Adrienne is livid and is tempted to call Mr. Alonso to tell him that he was wrong about her. She is very professional and even more competent than DeAngelo. However, she knows that if she calls the client, she is opening herself up to more criticism. She decides to hibernate in her office for the rest of the day. Later, Adrienne calls Rebecca and tells her that she is on her way.

At Nikhauli's Restaurant . . .

Arriving at the restaurant, Adrienne sees Rebecca who is waiting for her in the foyer.

Adrienne *(hugging her daughter)*: Hey, Becca, let's get a booth in the back. I need two green apple margaritas to start. I'm so upset right now. Once he seats us, I will tell you all about it.

Waiter: Ray, party of two?

Rebecca: Yes. Can we have a booth in the back?

Waiter: Yes, ma'am. Follow me.

The waiter directs the ladies to a booth in the back of the restaurant.

Waiter: Is this booth all right?

Adrienne: Yes, this is great. Thank you.

Waiter: Lucy will be your server. I can take your drink orders. What would you like?

Rebecca: I'll start off with water with lemon.

Adrienne: Bring me two green apple margaritas. No, scratch that. I need a brandy . . . two of them!

Rebecca: Wow, Mom, you must've had a bad day. What happened?

Adrienne: Well, to start, DeAngelo took an account away from me because a client complained that I wasn't willing to work with him. The man wanted me to lie and say that he didn't owe us a certain amount of money so that he could qualify for another business loan. The bank isn't stupid. What a jerk!

Rebecca: Oh wow, Mom. I'm sorry. Are you okay?

Becca and Adrienne are so focused on their conversation that they do not notice the waiter standing there until he clears his throat to get their attention.

Waiter: Here are your drinks. Is there anything else I can get for you?

Adrienne looks at him and rolls her eyes. She is angry at DeAngelo and Mr. Alonso but displaces those feelings onto the waiter.

Adrienne: Yes, you can just get Lucy, the blonde over there, so that we can order our food. How about that?

The waiter is surprised by Adrienne's sudden change in attitude. He exits to find the waitress to take their order, but she is busy with other customers. He returns to Adrienne and Becca's table to inform them of the delay.

Waiter: Ma'am, I apologize, but Lucy is occupied with a large party, so she asked that I take your order instead. I am going to be your server tonight. Would that be okay?

Rebecca: Yes, sure. I already know what I'm going to have. Bring me the steak, steamed broccoli, and whipped potatoes. Can you bring us more bread? Mom, have you decided what you want?

Adrienne has gone through her drinks like water. Rebecca is concerned that she is drinking too much too fast and on an empty stomach. Her mother is unpredictable when she drinks. She has no social filter.

Rebecca: Mom! What do you want to eat? You need to order something soon.

Adrienne: Oh, bring me a Caesar salad with the dressing on the side. No chicken, just the salad. Oh, and two more drinks.

The waiter eyes Rebecca and notices that she is not drinking.

Waiter: Miss, would you like to order a cocktail as well?

Rebecca: No, thank you. I have a feeling I'm going to be the designated driver tonight.

Waiter: Mmm, I'm sure. I'll go get your drinks, ma'am.

Adrienne: What does that mean? What did he just say?

Rebecca: Nothing, Mom. Calm down. Eat some bread. You need to put something in your stomach. By the way, why are you eating a salad?

Adrienne's voice is getting louder. She is irritated and wants to vent.

Adrienne: Because I work with some stupid Jews and black people! Aaron the Jew told me to lose weight. I tried to hint to him that I had health issues that made losing weight difficult, but noooo, his steroid behind wouldn't listen. I hate that guy! As a matter of fact, I hate most of the people at my job. DeAngelo, the Affirmative Action black man, is an incompetent fool who was promoted over me.

Rebecca (*looking around the restaurant and leaning in closer to her mom*): Oh my goodness, Mom! Lower your voice!

Adrienne: Why? I don't know anyone here. Do you?

Rebecca: That's not the point! You don't know if someone knows the people you are talking about. You just never know.

Adrienne: I don't care!

The waiter returns with two more brandies for Adrienne.

Waiter: Ma'am, I'm sorry. I don't mean to be rude, but some of the other patrons are complaining about the loud noise. Can you please tone it down a little?

Rebecca: I'm sorry. Yes, of course.

The waiter leaves and speaks to the patrons at the next table.

Adrienne: You want me to keep it down? Humph! I have worked at FELIX longer than he has!

Rebecca: Who, Mom?

Adrienne: Have you been listening to me? I'm talking about DeAngelo! FELIX pretends like it respects and welcomes diversity, but it's a sham! It doesn't! DeAngelo, with his stupid NAACP card-toting tail, was promoted over me.

Rebecca: Mom, please!

Rebecca is visibly uncomfortable. Her mom is beyond tipsy, and she is gulping down the two additional drinks the waiter brought her.

Adrienne: What?! It's true. Felix only promoted him so that the company could look like it is color blind. But no one ever questions whether it is gender-blind too! It's just that people notice skin tone more often. Did you know that Dawali thought that DeAngelo was cute? Yeah, the little skinny Indian princess used to watch him all the time! I would see her. Although she was smitten, she pretended like she didn't care for him. Can you imagine them together? HA! I don't think so. That would be the darkest baby ever with slick hair. Oh, I forgot, silly me. DeAngelo is infertile. It's impossible for them to have a kid. He and his wife, who looks like a macchiato version of Heidi Klum, had to adopt. I hope he loses the account with Alonso. If DeAngelo gives Alonso what he wants, I'm going to blow the whistle on him!

Rebecca: Oh, thank God, our food is here. You need to eat! Please no more drinks, Mom. Have some water.

Adrienne: I don't want any water!

Rebecca speaks quietly to the waiter.

Rebecca: Please no more drinks for her. She's not a heavy drinker, and I think she's had enough.

Adrienne: Becca, don't speak for me, and stop looking at me like that. All right, I'll stop. No more drinks. I'll just finish this one.

Rebecca: Thank goodness! Go ahead, Mom, and finish the story. You need to get this out of your system. You need to vent so that tomorrow, you can go back to work and just do your job. Your co-workers are under the impression that you like them, right? Don't lead on that you don't! You need your job. You don't want people to get wind of this little tirade. They'll brand you as a racist.

Adrienne: Yeah, I know, right.

When Rebecca starts to cut into her steak, she notices the couple across from them is staring disapprovingly at her mom. They're whispering, so she can't hear what they are saying. The woman looks as if she's texting, but Rebecca isn't so sure. She hopes no one heard the comments that her mom said. If it ever got back to FELIX, her mom would have to deal with more than losing a client.

DISCUSSION QUESTIONS

1. Do you think that DeAngelo handled the Alonso account properly? Did he have a legitimate reason to take the account away from Adrienne? Explain.
2. What is the appropriate protocol for a supervisor to handle client–employee personality conflicts? Explain your answer.
3. Should seniority outweigh worker productivity as the determining factor for promotion decisions? Support your answer.
4. Based on the statements concerning gender bias in the case scenario, would Adrienne's comments be considered rude and her response to Mr. Alonso considered inappropriate for both males and females alike? Explain.
5. When can employers discipline employees for non-work-related behaviors, actions, and/or activities?
6. If you were the restaurant manager, how would you deal with Adrienne? Is it ever appropriate to ask a patron to leave? Explain.
7. If you were the waiter, how would you respond to Adrienne? Would you continue to serve her under the circumstances in the case scenario? Do you think the waiter had a responsibility to address Adrienne's comments?
8. Do you think there is a problem with Adrienne's comments? Should she be able to say whatever she wants in private and away from work responsibilities without it potentially impacting her job? Why or why not?
9. How could Adrienne's comments negatively impact her daughter's employment? At the restaurant, did Rebecca have a responsibility to intercede during Adrienne's rant? If so, how?
10. Do Adrienne's underlying feelings for her co-workers warrant FELIX developing a workplace diversity program? To foster an environment of respect and tolerance, would it be beneficial for companies to discover culturally insensitive attitudes of their workers? How can companies like FELIX nurture cultural sensitivity and tolerance in the workplace? If they do not, how could it impact their companies?

SELF-ASSESSMENT

1. Create a survey of five questions that surround issues in the case scenario. Have at least ten people complete your survey, and present your results to the class.
2. For one week, note any comments you hear, positive or negative, that relate to race, ethnicity, gender, and age. Note how you felt when you heard these comments.

APPLICATION ACTIVITIES

1. In teams, research five major Fortune 500 companies that have fired employees for inappropriate, non-work-related behavior. Present the information in a PowerPoint presentation.
2. Based on your findings from the Preliminary Activity, use the information to support whether Adrienne should be disciplined.
3. In groups of four, develop a skit that addresses an issue concerning cultural, racial, and/or gender bias. Devise questions for the audience. Discuss how a manager should respond to the challenges presented.

CASE STUDY 14
A PR NIGHTMARE

OBJECTIVES

Students will be able to:

A. define agency, general agent, special agent, and crisis communication plan;
B. describe agency authority and evaluate how agency relationships work;
C. understand and explain the purpose of a public relations (PR) firm;
D. assess the challenges faced by companies due to employee actions; and
E. create a PR commercial.

SUGGESTED CLASS TIME

3–4 class periods

TERMS TO KNOW

Define the following terms:

A. agency;
B. agency authority;
C. principal;
D. agent;
E. general agent;
F. special agent; and
G. crisis communication plan.

PRELIMINARY ACTIVITY

Research companies, sports teams, and/or educational institutions whose executives, employees, students, or other representatives engaged in derogatory comments concerning race, gender, religion, national origin, color, disability, sexual orientation, and/or age. How did the organizations react to these situations? What kind(s) of PR responses did they use to counter such negative exposure?

WHO'S IN THIS STORY?

Phil Fox, 64
FELIX CEO

Phylicia Fox, 62
Phil's Wife and
Co-Owner of FELIX

Trish Fox, 38
FELIX Marketing
Manager

Ernesto Diaz, 45
FELIX Marketing
Supervisor

Blake Golden, 51
FELIX PR Agent

SETTING

Atlanta, FELIX Headquarters—Board Room, 5:27 a.m.

CASE SCENARIO

Two hours ago, Phil summoned Phylicia, Felix, Trish, DeAngelo, Ernesto, Mary Kate, Min, and Blake Golden, the PR agent, to an emergency meeting for 5:30 a.m. Everyone except for Blake has arrived.

Phil (*visibly upset*): Thank you all for meeting me so early this morning. Needless to say, I am beyond livid. Last night, I received a call from Frazer, Moore, and Jenkins, our PR firm. They somehow discovered the recording of Adrienne's rant in Nikhauli's Restaurant before we did. Apparently, a couple that was seated next to Adrienne and her daughter Rebecca recorded Adrienne's drunken tirade. It has gone viral. My goodness, it is all over social media. The news is having a field day! What Adrienne has done threatens to ruin what I've worked so hard to build . . . what we all believe in. I . . . I . . .

Sighing deeply, Phil leans forward onto the table.

Phylicia: Honey, try to calm down. Remember what Dr. Morgan said.

Phil: Phylicia! Now is not the time, dear.

Trish: What?! Dad, are you okay?!

Phil: I'm fine! I'm fine! I'm sorry. I didn't mean to yell. The extent of this is weighing on me. We must discuss what to do with Adrienne. This is the first time that FELIX has ever encountered such negative press of this magnitude. I feel we should've had some procedures in place. Blake Golden should be arriving at any moment.

Trish: Is Blake a special agent or a general agent, Dad?

Phil: I'm not sure but likely a general agent. Why?

Trish: Well, I'm wondering whether we have him for this situation only or for all PR matters. Anyway, we should've released a statement hours ago. Our shareholders are rightly concerned about the impact that Adrienne's intolerant comments could have on the company. We could lose millions, not to mention the damage it could have on our corporate reputation.

Phil: When Blake arrives, Ernesto and you will be working with him to develop a crisis communication message to our shareholders and the community. Min, Mary Kate, and DeAngelo, I need you all to speak to the employees in your respective departments. Identify people who can assist in returning calls to our LA and New York affiliates. It's going to be a long day, everyone. Let's get to work.

Before everyone leaves, Blake walks into the board room and shakes hands with Phil.

Blake: Phil, hi. It's good to see you again, although I wish it were under better circumstances. Good morning, everyone. I barely made it through the news reporters outside of the building.

Everyone begins to talk loudly.

Phil: Quiet, please. Blake, continue.

Blake: Yes, sir. First, we need to send a company representative to give a short statement to the media. We could briefly state that FELIX's only comment at this time is that we'll have an official press release today at noon to respond to Adrienne Ray's comments. We should also mention that her comments do not represent us and are not supported by the company.

Phil: Can you do this now? I have your PR firm on retainer so you have full access to work on our behalf in bringing this debacle under control. My daughter Trish and Ernesto work in marketing. They are here to assist you.

Blake: Thank you, Phil. I will simply inform the reporters that we plan to make a statement at noon. Then, we'll look at your crisis communication plans. We only have a few hours to prepare.

After his brief statement to reporters, Blake meets Trish and Ernesto in the board room . . .

Blake: Where are your crisis communication plans?

Trish: I don't believe that we have any. Ernesto?

Ernesto: You're right. There aren't any.

Blake: What?! A company of your size must have one in place. Well, we'll have to create one for the future. For now, we need to get this done before noon. This is what we must do in the short-term. We have to create a crisis communication message that includes the following components. One, acknowledge the situation by demonstrating concern. Two, describe any counteractive measures that FELIX has taken. Three, offer directives and further information. Four, provide a rationale or reasoning for why this happened. And five, express regret and seek the community's forgiveness. We also need to devise a PR slogan and strategy that demonstrates how FELIX supports diversity. I want you to use the word "hate" in the slogan to reveal how much the company is against discrimination. I need you to both gather your teams and decide which group will complete the tasks. Phil needs the PR message no later than 11 a.m. so that he can prepare to deliver it. I also need someone to tell me what decision has been made regarding Adrienne's employment status.

Two hours later . . .

Trish: Blake, we have completed our tasks. We would like you to review them.

DISCUSSION QUESTIONS

1. Does FELIX need a PR firm to deal with the impact of Adrienne's comments? What could the company potentially lose if this situation is not handled properly? Explain your answer.
2. Did Phil make the right decision in choosing not to respond immediately to news reporters and calls regarding Adrienne's comments? Explain your answer.
3. What legal consequences could FELIX face due to Adrienne's actions?
4. Regarding the principal and agent's relationship, what type of agency authority has Phil given Blake? What is Blake able to do with this authority? What kinds of duties are required of both Phil as the principal and Blake as the agent?
5. What is the difference between a general agent and a special agent? How does one determine whether a PR agent is general or special?
6. Was it appropriate for Phil to direct Min, Mary Kate, and DeAngelo to speak with employees in their departments and to return calls to the LA and New York affiliates? Were his instructions provided at the appropriate time, or should he have waited to receive instructions from Blake? What could happen if the content of Phil's instructions conflicts with the crisis communications? Explain your answers.
7. What types of procedures should have been in place at FELIX to address this incident? What are the challenges companies face when they are forced to create crisis communication messages within a limited time frame?
8. Should FELIX continue to employ Adrienne or terminate her? In your opinion, is it the responsibility of the company to try to rehabilitate an employee through diversity training? Under what circumstances could this apply? Explain.
9. Should FELIX promote the belief that Adrienne's comments were wrong to protect the company's reputation only? Should FELIX leadership believe that her comments were wrong? Does the actual belief system of FELIX leadership impact the culture of the workplace? If so, how?

SELF-ASSESSMENT

If a co-worker made comments about you similar to what Adrienne stated in the case scenario, what would be your response? In a journal entry, write down how it would impact your feelings and how your behavior might change toward her. If you felt the need to confront her, what would you say?

APPLICATION ACTIVITIES

1. In small groups, create a crisis communication message following the format that Blake provided Trish and Ernesto: 1. acknowledge the situation/demonstrate concern; 2. state counteractive measures; 3. offer directives and further information; 4. provide a rationale or reasoning; and 5. express regret and seek forgiveness. Share your messages with the class. In addition to the message, determine the type of venue(s) in which it should be disseminated.
2. In small groups, devise a PR slogan and strategy following Blake's instructions of using the word "hate" to reveal how much the company is against discrimination. Develop a creative presentation that showcases the slogan and strategy to the class.
3. Using the slogan and strategy that you created in Application Activity #2, develop a PR commercial for FELIX.

CASE STUDY 15

CRIMES AND CLAUSES*

OBJECTIVES

Students will be able to:

A. define contract, breach, morality clause, and white collar crimes;
B. explain short swing profits in insider trading;
C. ascertain how a breach of contract occurs; and
D. distinguish between negotiation, mediation, and arbitration.

SUGGESTED CLASS TIME

2–3 class periods

TERMS TO KNOW

Define the following terms:

A. contract;
B. breach of contract;
C. morality clause;
D. white collar crimes;
E. distributive bargaining;
F. integrative negotiation;
G. insider trading;
H. short swing profits;
I. crimes of moral turpitude;
J. criminal fraud;
K. mail fraud;
L. wire fraud;

M. *Sarbanes-Oxley Act of 2002*;
N. mediation;
O. arbitration;
P. presenteeism; and
Q. social responsibility.

PRELIMINARY ACTIVITY

Individually, find example(s) of an athlete, celebrity, and/or employee who has lost an endorsement or job because of violating a morality clause. As a class, determine: a. the common mistakes made by these individuals and b. the preventative measures that could have been established to avoid the loss of endorsements and/or employment.

WHO'S IN THIS STORY?

Cameron Knox, 37
FELIX HR Supervisor

© Shutterstock/Maksim Shmeljov

Brandon Knox, 37
Cameron's Husband

© Shutterstock/wavebreakmedia

Min Kwon, 38
FELIX HR Director

© Shutterstock/Dragon Images

Parker Cobb, 27
FELIX HR Benefits Manager

© Shutterstock/vgstudio

Stephanie Lane, 24
FELIX HR Secretary

© Shutterstock/Vadim Ivanov

SETTING

Atlanta, FELIX Headquarters—HR Department and The Knox Home

CASE SCENARIO

The Knox Home, 5:30 a.m.

Cameron: Brandon, please! I'm begging you. You cannot purchase any more FELIX stock. Like I said before, your brother is a broker; your purchase of FELIX stock could easily be traced to us. FELIX employees received an email concerning the confidentiality on the new clothing contract. We are still under a trading blackout for acquiring FELIX stock.

Brandon: Well, keep quiet and stay alert. I am proceeding with my plans. And remember, you are just as guilty as I am. If I go down, you go down. We need this money to get out of debt.

Cameron's cell phone rings. Wondering who could be calling her, Cameron picks it up and sees Parker's name on the screen.

Cameron: Hello. Parker?

Parker: I apologize for calling so early this morning, but I just got off of the phone with Min. She is already at the office. Phil Fox wants everyone to report to work immediately. Min is currently in a meeting with Phil, his wife Phylicia, Felix, Trish, DeAngelo, Ernesto, Mary Kate, and Blake Golden, the PR guy. There is an issue that could potentially destroy the new clothing contract. Cameron, it is awful. Adrienne was recorded by a customer at Nikhauli's Restaurant saying some horrible things about the company. Because of Adrienne's statements, the supplier for the new clothing line is taking a stand because they've heard it too. The supplier is questioning FELIX's commitment to diversity and inclusivity in the workplace and in the community. So, they are threatening to not perform under the contract based on a morality clause.

Cameron: What?! What did Adrienne say?

Parker: Cam, you'll have to hear it for yourself. I don't wanna repeat what she said.

Cameron: Oh my gosh, Parker! This sounds terrible. So what about the morality clause? I thought those were usually in place for athletes and celebrities?

Parker: Well, Felix Fox is a celebrity, especially in the fashion industry. I've heard of some companies including them in employee contracts. As a part of the contract agreement, Felix was going to provide his name and face to further promote our supplier Sandleria Materials, who is extremely socially conscious and responsible. Mary Kate sent HR a copy of the contract in case we needed it for anything today. I'll read it to you from my email. The clause states in part, "*If FELIX or any FELIX representative, while under obligation to perform under contract with Supplier, engages in or is involved in a crime of moral turpitude, public scandal, or similar incident, that will likely offend the community at large, then Supplier may terminate the contractual agreement.*" If you recall, it took our legal department weeks to finalize the contract negotiations because Mary Kate did not want to agree to include the morality clause. Phil and Felix directed her to do so.

Cameron: So, is the supplier liable for breach of contract then?

While Cameron is talking to Parker, Brandon is pacing and tells her to end the call.

Cameron: Hold on, Brandon. Just a second.

Parker: Cam?

Cameron: I apologize, Parker. Brandon was telling me something. Now, I was asking you whether the supplier is liable for breach of contract.

Parker: Well, I'm not sure. That's a question for Mary Kate and her team. However, FELIX doesn't want to fight a legal battle, especially with the sensitive issue of the racial comments surrounding this situation. According to the contract, FELIX and the supplier must enter into negotiations regarding any contract issues prior to opting for litigation. Mary Kate, Daryl, and Destinie are preparing to negotiate our position on the morality clause. I don't know much about negotiations, but Mary Kate told me that she prefers a more integrative versus a distributive approach. If negotiations don't work, then they'll have to proceed to arbitration. Min says get to the office as soon as possible. We're looking at having another long day.

While Cameron is talking to Parker, Brandon tries to move the cell phone from her ear in order to get her attention.

Cameron: Brandon, stop it! Wait!

Brandon grabs Cameron's arm and tells her to end the call now.

Cameron (*wincing*): Okay . . . okay . . . Look, Parker. I've gotta go. I'll be in as soon as possible.

Cameron does not end the call before she turns to speak to Brandon.

Cameron: Brandon, listen to me! What you're doing is a bad idea. Since I gave you the stock information, you have sold and bought shares of stock three times. The first time you told your brother to buy 600 shares, the second time he purchased 500 shares, and the third time you sold 100. Where did you even get the money to purchase them? Parker just told me that the new contract is in jeopardy. We don't know what's gonna happen to the stock. We could lose everything!

Brandon: What?! Why didn't you tell me?! How did you not know this?!

Cameron: I just found out a minute ago when Parker called.

Brandon pushes Cameron to the floor.

Brandon: You are so stupid! What do you mean stop? I can't stop now! We can't stop! My brother and I already have people who think that they're investing in a real estate venture. We're taking their money and purchasing shares. You would be surprised how many elderly people will respond to emails and snail mail when they think it's for a good cause. They believe we're setting up a domestic violence shelter. Ha . . . the irony!

Cameron: Oh my goodness! Seriously? What's happened to you? Why are you being so mean? So awful? Why?!

Brandon (*tauntingly*): So awful? Why are you so stupid? Why do you say things to make me angry? Why do you make me do this to you?! I think you like it when I'm this way.

Cameron screams as Brandon slaps her. Their daughter April comes down the stairs from her bedroom, runs to her mom, and begins to cry. Unknown to Cameron, Parker is still on the line and has heard everything.

FELIX HR Department, 8:30 a.m.

Min exits her office and sees Parker in the hallway.

Min: Parker, did you speak to Cameron this morning? Where is she? I asked that everyone arrive as soon as possible.

Parker (*hesitantly*): Well, I spoke to her this morning. She may have had some issues with getting April to school.

Frustrated, Min turns away from Parker and walks to Stephanie's desk. Parker follows her.

Min: Stephanie.

Stephanie: Yes, Min?

Min: Has Cameron called this morning?

Stephanie: No, Min, she hasn't.

Min (*sighing*): As soon as she arrives, send her to my office. We have a lot of work to do. Parker, could you get two files from Cameron's office for me? They should be on her desk. They're the ones with blue sticky notes on the front of the folders. I need Stephanie to work on them while we meet with Phil today.

Parker turns and walks to Cameron's office. As he approaches, he hears faint sobbing coming from behind her office door. He knocks lightly and turns the knob. Standing in the doorway, he sees Cameron sitting in the dark and staring out of her window.

Parker: Cameron, I didn't know that you were here. Min is looking for you.

Cameron does not respond.

Parker: Cam? Are you okay?

Cameron: Just leave me alone. I need to be by myself right now.

Parker enters Cameron's office and closes the door.

Parker: Cam, you can talk to me. I'm your friend. This morning, I heard . . . you didn't hang up the phone and I heard everything that you said to Brandon. Look, I'm here for you, okay. But, I think that you're in over your head. You need to get some help.

Cameron: I said leave me alone. I'm not talking to you. You'll just run and tell Min anyway.

Parker pauses before speaking again.

Parker: Cam, I . . .

Cameron: I said go, Parker! Just leave me alone! Please!

Parker: Okay, I will . . . for now. But remember that no matter what, I am your friend. I'll leave you alone, but you should know that Min is looking for you.

Parker exits her office to allow her time to collect herself, but he plans to return in an hour. He knows that he must help Cameron before it is too late.

DISCUSSION QUESTIONS

1. Based on insider trading concepts, what are short swing profits? Is Brandon trying to make these profits? Explain.
2. Identify incidents of criminal fraud, mail fraud, and wire fraud in the case scenario.
3. What ethical and legal issues does Cameron face in the case scenario? Cite specific examples. In your answer, consider the potential consequences for Cameron if her role in providing confidential company information is discovered.
4. What is the *Sarbanes-Oxley Act of 2002*? What does Section 406 of this Act require? Would Cameron be classified under Section 406?
5. In this case scenario, is anyone liable for breach of contract? Who would be the non-breaching party? What damages would the non-breaching party likely seek, if any?
6. What arguments could the supplier assert to terminate the contract based on violation of the morality clause? What arguments could FELIX use to support its position that it has not violated the morality clause? Who do you think should win and why? What must FELIX consider prior to engaging in litigation with the supplier?
7. According to the contract signed by FELIX and its supplier, the parties must enter into negotiations first. What are the potential positive and negative outcomes of engaging in negotiations? What negotiation style, either distributive or integrative, would benefit FELIX more if the company desires to preserve its relationship with the supplier?
8. What are some plausible alternatives that FELIX and the supplier could use to settle the dispute? Explain.
9. In this case scenario, how does Cameron exemplify presenteeism in the workplace? Support your answer.

SELF-ASSESSMENT

Based on the research conducted in the Preliminary Activity, do you support morality clauses in whole or in part? Explain your position in a class journal entry.

APPLICATION ACTIVITIES

1. A friend of Cameron's is an HR supervisor at another company. Cameron confidentially informs him of Brandon's actions and her role in them. Present the advice that you would give her in an impromptu speech. Students should have three to five minutes to prepare a well-organized speech.
2. Based on individual student responses in the Preliminary Activity, hold a class debate concerning whether morality clauses should be included in employment contracts. Some questions to consider in the debate:
   a. Should morality clauses only include higher-level executives or include all employees?;
   b. Are morality clauses a means for companies to control employee conduct?; and
   c. Should an individual's personal life and morals dictate the kinds of endorsements and employment one holds? Why or why not?

3. In the case scenario, the supplier values social responsibility. If you were a business owner, which of the following four theories of social responsibility would you embrace and why?
   a. maximizing profits;
   b. stakeholder interest;
   c. moral minimum; and
   d. corporate citizenship.

CASE STUDY 16

THE BATTERED AND BRUISED INSIDER*

OBJECTIVES

Students should be able to:

A. illustrate how management should respond when the personal lives of employees impact the workplace environment;
B. write an internal business memorandum; and
C. conclude whether an individual is guilty of insider trading.

SUGGESTED CLASS TIME

2–3 class periods

TERMS TO KNOW

A. domestic violence;
B. insider trading;
C. Securities Exchange Commission (SEC); and
D. mitigating circumstances.

PRELIMINARY ACTIVITY

Conduct an online search to discover the danger signs of a domestic violence (DV) abuser and the warning signs that someone is being abused. As a class, share your findings, and discuss whether management should become involved when knowledge surfaces that an employee is a DV victim? If so, how?

WHO'S IN THIS STORY?

Cameron Knox, 37
FELIX HR
Supervisor

Cooper Jones, 36
Attorney

Parker Cobb, 27
FELIX HR
Benefits Manager

Stephanie Lane, 24
FELIX HR Secretary

SETTING

Atlanta, FELIX Headquarters—HR Department, and The Law Offices of Cooper Jones

CASE SCENARIO

After an hour, Parker decides to return to Cameron's office. He feels that it is time to confront Cameron regarding the telephone conversation that he overheard when she was talking to her husband Brandon. He is appalled that Cameron has been providing Brandon with FELIX stock information. Parker cannot believe that she is in this situation, and to make matters worse, Brandon is still abusing her. Parker is determined to persuade her to seek help today.

Parker: Stephanie, I am forwarding my calls to you while I'm on break. I will be in Cameron's office. Please do not disturb us unless it is an emergency. Thanks.

Stephanie: Parker, I'll try, but I'll probably have to interrupt because of dis Adrienne PR fiasco.

Parker: Just give me ten minutes.

Parker knocks on Cameron's door as he enters her office.

Parker: Cameron, how did your meeting with Min go? Whoa . . . why are you still sitting in the dark?!

As Parker turns on the lights in Cameron's office, she turns away from him.

Cameron: I didn't meet with her. She was called into another meeting with some other directors. I haven't left my office because I have a migraine. The lights make it worse. Please turn them off.

Parker: No, I won't. We need to talk. I've been calling you for the last 15 minutes, but you haven't been answering my calls. Look at me, Cameron!

Cameron (*facing away from Parker*): Now is not a good time, Parker.

Parker: I'm not accepting that. You can look at me, or I'll walk over to you. Choose what you prefer, but I'm not leaving until you talk to me.

Cameron finally turns to look at Parker.

Parker: Oh my goodness! Cameron! Your neck! It . . . it . . . it looks like you've been strangled! Did . . . Brandon . . . what in the world is happening with you? You must leave him. Today! If you don't, I'm going to tell Min. I'm going to tell someone! This has to stop now!

Cameron: I thought my makeup covered up the bruises. I wore a scarf into the building today so that no one would notice. I'll put it back on once I leave my office.

Parker: I don't care about the scarf! He's hitting you! He strangled you this morning! I know what else is going on, too. I know that you're committing insider trading with that . . . that . . . man you call a husband! You've been giving Brandon confidential information so that he can give it to his brother. Did you read the email that I told you about? This is serious. You could go to prison, Cameron! Have you thought about this? Have you thought about what would happen to April if both of you are sent to prison?

Cameron: Shhh! How did you find out about this? Have you told anyone?

Parker: I haven't said anything . . . yet. I overheard Brandon and you speaking over the phone. You didn't hang up the call after I informed you about the PR nightmare with Adrienne.

Cameron: What do you mean by yet?! Parker?!

Parker: You need to come clean before it's too late, Cam. It will be a difficult process, and I'm no lawyer, but there has to be a way to protect yourself and hopefully avoid prison time. I've been thinking. Brandon has been hitting you. I know that you would've never done this without him forcing you and without being afraid for your safety.

Cameron: He threatened to take April, you know. He threatened to kill me.

Parker: He's a coward, Cam. I will be a witness for you, but you've got to come forward. It's the only chance that you have. I'll go with you to speak to management, but first you need to get an attorney.

Cameron: I can speak to Mary Kate.

Parker: No. Mary Kate works for FELIX. Her responsibility is to the company first. We'll call Cooper Jones. He was Katherine Payne's attorney when she was pursuing a discrimination suit against the company. He has a great reputation.

There is a knock on Cameron's door. Parker opens the door and blocks Cameron from Stephanie's view.

Stephanie: I'm sorry to interrupt, Parker, but Min said dat she needs you . . . and she needs Cameron if she's available.

Parker: We'll be right there.

Closing the door, Parker turns to Cameron.

Parker: Okay. You've got one minute to get yourself together. Put that scarf on! But, Cam, we're getting you some help today. After we meet with Min, you're calling Cooper Jones. This situation stops now. You've got to get yourself together. Min needs you while she's helping to resolve this Adrienne matter. We also have to get ready for Stephanie's three-month job performance review. We may need to handle it if Min is called away again by Phil.

Later in the day . . .

Cooper: Well, Cameron, I'm glad that you've come forward. Your DV situation concerns me, and your insider trading participation is significant. First, regarding your safety, you should gather money and find shelter in order to protect yourself from further DV. This step is crucial. Second, we must inform FELIX management of these two issues and how the trauma from the abuse led you to provide Brandon with insider information. Third, mentally prepare yourself because there is a distinct possibility that you will face investigative and prosecutorial actions from FELIX and the SEC. I will handle the preliminary legal preparations. I know that all of this is overwhelming, but I'm here to help.

Cameron remains quiet.

Parker (*looking at Cooper*): Cameron and April can stay with me.

Cameron: I don't want to involve you any further, Parker.

Cooper: Cameron, it's your choice.

Cameron: Okay, but I need time to think.

Cooper: I understand, but once this begins, we won't be able to stop. I will start to prepare documents and to get ready to deal with FELIX and the SEC on your behalf. But, I don't need to move until you're ready.

DISCUSSION QUESTIONS

1. Did Parker overstep any professional boundaries by initiating this conversation with Cameron and urging her to seek an attorney? As an HR professional, does Parker have a responsibility to assist Cameron? Even though he is Cameron's friend, what is Parker's responsibility to FELIX? Explain your answer.
2. How have the employment roles and responsibilities of Cameron and Parker been affected by the occurrences in this case scenario?
3. Which member(s) of FELIX management should Cooper Jones inform first of Cameron's DV incidents and involvement in insider trading? Why?
4. Once FELIX is informed of this situation, will Cameron and Parker be able to retain their positions at FELIX? Describe the actions, if any, that FELIX could take should Cameron reveal that Brandon has threatened her life. Why or why not?
5. Should Cameron be prosecuted for insider trading? Should the SEC consider any mitigating circumstances in its prosecution of her? If so, what?

SELF-ASSESSMENT

What actions would you take to help friends or co-workers who are involved in abusive relationships? Would you assist them knowing that you could be at risk?

APPLICATION ACTIVITIES

1. Develop an internal memorandum with verbiage that addresses how FELIX will contain the highly confidential information disclosed by Cooper and Cameron in the event that a SEC visit occurs.
2. In small groups, conduct research, prepare a presentation, and present your findings on one of the following:
   a. how DV can negatively impact businesses and their employees; or
   b. the SEC process when insider trading is discovered and reported.
3. Research a company that has experienced insider trading issues. Consider the case scenario. Then, identify FELIX stakeholders, and discuss the impact that leaking the confidential information could have on these stakeholders.

CASE STUDY 17

RUFFLED FEATHERS—AN EMPLOYEE'S JOB PERFORMANCE REPRIMAND

OBJECTIVES

Students will be able to:

A. explain how an appropriate employee performance review is conducted;
B. examine and devise a company cellular phone policy; and
C. hypothesize the legal consequences of an unfair employee review process.

SUGGESTED CLASS TIME

2–3 class periods

TERMS TO KNOW

Define the following terms:

A. performance review;
B. policies and procedures;
C. probationary status; and
D. unfair treatment.

PRELIMINARY ACTIVITY

Google the top ten most common areas that employers consider for an employee performance review. As a class, discuss these areas, select the most important three, and explain your rationale for the selections. Review and familiarize yourself with the FELIX Employment Performance Review in Appendix K before reading this case scenario.

WHO'S IN THIS STORY?

Min Kwon, 38
FELIX HR Director

© Shutterstock/Dragon Images

Cameron Knox, 37
FELIX HR Supervisor

© Shutterstock/Maksim Shmeljov

Stephanie Lane, 24
FELIX HR Secretary

© Shutterstock/Vadim Ivanov

SETTING

Atlanta, FELIX HR Department

CASE SCENARIO

Min is not pleased with Stephanie's overall performance; nevertheless, she decides that her department cannot afford to be without a secretary. With the threat of losing the new clothing line still looming because of Adrienne's actions, FELIX is in emergency mode. Min realizes that now is not the time for a change in office personnel. Stephanie has been employed at FELIX for three months. Under Min's direction, Cameron and Parker continue to closely observe, correct, and train her when necessary. As mentioned in Stephanie's interview, it is time for her supervisory review. Min and Cameron will meet with her at 1:30 p.m. to discuss her evaluation.

In the HR Meeting Room, 1:37 p.m.

Min: Cameron, do you know where Stephanie is?

Cameron: She's probably returning a little late from lunch.

Min: That isn't a valid excuse. How can you be late to your own performance review?

Cameron: Now, Min . . .

There is a knock on the door of the meeting room.

Cameron: Come in.

Stephanie enters the meeting room with her purse and a to-go box from lunch.

Stephanie: Sorry I'm late, but I . . .

Min: Stephanie, please have a seat. We need to get started.

Cameron looks pointedly at Min, then motions for Stephanie to take a chair at the conference table.

Cameron: Well, where did you go for lunch, Stephanie?

Stephanie: Wesley's on Peachtree. I love dat restaurant. It has da best selection of appetizers and desserts.

Cameron: Mmmm, sounds yummy. I've heard of Wesley's. I'll have to check out the place.

Min: Well, ladies, I have to leave at 2:15 p.m., so let's get to the business at hand. Stephanie, you have been working at FELIX for three months. Before we offered you the position, we said that you would be required to have a quarterly performance review. This is your first. If you remain at FELIX, you will have three more this year. Typically, there are four performance reviews within the first year of employment while you are still in probationary status.

Stephanie: What do you mean by "if I remain"? Am I being fired?

Min: I didn't say that, Stephanie.

Stephanie: Okay. Because I really feel like I've improved a lot. You feel da same, right?

Cameron and Min shift uncomfortably in their chairs.

Cameron: Stephanie, before we focus on our observations, can you tell us how your transition has been at FELIX thus far?

Stephanie: In two words—slightly challenging.

Cameron: How so?

Stephanie: It's been hard to adjust to how fast stuff moves around here. I used to feel dat no place could be as fast as my old job at dat advertising firm, but it does not compare to FELIX. I have taken some time to reflect on your past comments and feel dat I have improved in all of da areas.

Min: Could you be more specific regarding your improvements?

Stephanie: Yes. You told me dat I was late for work five times in da first six weeks. I have not been late since you informed me. Cameron mentioned to me dat I was on social media during work hours. It came as a surprise to me because I was able to do dat at my last job. After she told me, I haven't gotten on social media ever since.

Cameron: We have noted that and applaud your efforts; however, we are still concerned about the excessive amount of texting and telephone conversations that you have. We are able to hear your entire conversations at times, especially when you have someone on speaker phone.

Stephanie: Well, I stopped having phone conversations in da hallway because you got complaints dat I was disturbing some employees and clients. So I started taking my calls in da office. If someone else comes in, I immediately stop and put dem on hold.

Min: The primary problem with this is that you are on company time. You are being paid to work and not to socialize. Based on your three-month performance, you are receiving a review categorized under the Improvement category.

Stephanie: Are you serious? Is it expected dat I should never use my cell phone or text? Can I ever use it, like in an emergency? Or when my doctor's office is calling? What am I supposed to do? Dis doesn't sound fair.

Min: Fair? Are you accusing us of unfair treatment? Really, Stephanie? Well, since you want to discuss fairness, was it fair of you to get someone else to write your cover letter for the job? Because based on the writing skills that you've been exhibiting since your arrival, you couldn't have possibly written your cover letter. Unfair is the fact that we have to waste time continuously editing your business letters.

Stephanie fidgets anxiously with her hands. Her face turns red as she works to maintain her composure.

Stephanie: I'm sorry, but you can't prove dat I didn't write my cover letter.

Min: You just confirmed the suspicions I've had all along.

Stephanie (*rising quickly from her chair*): Excuse me? What did you say?!

Cameron: Wait. Let's all calm down, please.

Stephanie (*looking from Min to Cameron*): Honestly?! I came in here for a review, not an assault! Min is being unfair! And you, Cameron . . . you've missed a few meetings yourself, so how can you say anything to me about my performance!

Cameron: You need to calm down. You're totally out of line, Stephanie.

Min: No one is assaulting you. No one has touched you or threatened you. You are taking our comments personally. Now, please have a seat.

Looking at her watch, Min realizes that she has to leave for her 2:15 p.m. appointment.

Min: Cameron, finish the review with Stephanie. I have to leave for my next appointment. I'll get an update from you upon my return. If you need some help, call Parker.

Without addressing Stephanie, Min exits the meeting room. Cameron looks at Stephanie who is still standing.

Cameron (*taking a deep breath*): Please have a seat, Stephanie. Let's not let our emotions take control of us.

Stephanie slowly sits down.

Stephanie: I'm sorry, Cameron. I'm fine now dat she's gone.

Cameron: That was highly inappropriate, Stephanie. I don't appreciate what you said. I've always tried to help you. You're not the only one overwhelmed around here.

Stephanie: I know. I apologize, okay? It won't happen again. I guess I'm really fired now, huh?

Cameron: Apology accepted. Let's move on. I'm unaware of any termination proceedings against you at this time. But, I have some suggestions on how you can improve your performance. Remember that you have three more reviews this year. You need to focus on these areas of improvement.

Stephanie: Yes, Cameron. I'm listening.

Cameron: First, company time is just that—company time. It is very important that you use your cell phone during break time only. Remember that loud office conversations are a no-no. Second, work on your time management. The office is extremely busy, and we all need to complete tasks as soon as possible. If someone gives you an assignment, then complete it then and submit it. Don't wait until the next day. Third, it's great that you haven't been late recently or on social media since it was mentioned to you. But honestly, Stephanie, this is all expected. These are not points of contention. They are simply what any employer would expect of you. You are not an intern; therefore, there is a certain level of professionalism that is warranted. Finally, you need to improve your business writing skills. You may consider enrolling in a writing or communications course. It is important that you address these issues before your next quarterly review.

Stephanie sits quietly after Cameron finishes sharing her points for improvement.

Cameron: Stephanie, do you have any questions or comments?

Stephanie: I really believed dat I was improving. Min didn't have to be so mean and unfair. She is a HR Director. She should know better.

Cameron: Stephanie, please focus on your improvements. Be careful of displacing your disappointment regarding your review onto Min. I'm here to help, so let me know if there's anything that I can do.

Stephanie: I will. Thanks, Cameron.

DISCUSSION QUESTIONS

1. What is the climate in the HR department during Min and Cameron's meeting with Stephanie? How does it change from the beginning to the end of the meeting? What suggestions would you offer Min and Cameron for improving how they conduct a performance review?
2. Evaluate Min and Cameron's supervisory skills by identifying both of their strengths and weaknesses. Was Min's demeanor toward Stephanie during the performance review appropriate? Were there underlying issues that Min could have resolved regarding Stephanie's performance prior to her review? Support your answer.
3. Did Cameron and Min provide Stephanie with a fair, honest assessment of her performance improvements? Explain your answer.
4. List the pros and cons of cell phone use in the workplace. Discuss your lists as a class. Are there any situations in which cell phone usage would be appropriate? Explain.
5. Develop a timeline for Stephanie to improve the areas discussed in her performance review. Consider the fact that the intent is to retain Stephanie and not terminate her.
6. Was Stephanie's response to Min's feedback regarding her insufficient writing skills appropriate? If you were Min, how would you note Stephanie's writing deficiency in her performance evaluation? Explain.
7. What are the possible legal consequences for a company if supervisors administer unfair performance evaluations?

SELF-ASSESSMENT

Consider your amount of texting and cellular phone use in class and/or at your workplace. Does it interfere with your level of focus as well as completion and understanding of tasks? How will your level of cellular phone use impact your grade in classes and/or at the workplace?

APPLICATION ACTIVITIES

1. Conduct an evaluation of Stephanie's three-month job performance by using the FELIX Employment Performance Review located in Appendix K. Discuss the similarities and differences between Min and Cameron's review and your own review of Stephanie's performance. What would you add or detract from Stephanie's performance review. Discuss your results with the class.
2. Research current company cell phone use policies. Create a cell phone policy that incorporates personal cellular phone use during office hours.
3. Visit three to five departments on your campus. Interview a secretary in each department to determine the most important aspects of the position. Based on your survey results, write a one-page report. Share your findings with the class.

CASE STUDY 18
EMPLOYEE CONDUCT, EMPLOYER LIABILITY

OBJECTIVES

Students will be able to:

A. summarize how employers may become liable for employee actions;
B. distinguish between frolic and detour in tort law;
C. determine what constitutes professional behavior; and
D. compile an employee performance evaluation.

SUGGESTED CLASS TIME

2–3 class periods

TERMS TO KNOW

Define the following terms:

A. tort;
B. respondeat superior;
C. vicarious liability;
D. frolic and detour;
E. indemnification;
F. performance evaluation;
G. lawsuit; and
H. injured party.

PRELIMINARY ACTIVITY

Research the concepts of respondeat superior and vicarious liability. Determine five ways that employees may cause an employer to be liable for their actions. Discuss your findings with the class.

WHO'S IN THIS STORY?

Adam Harris, 26 FELIX Delivery Driver 	Randy Andrews, 30 FELIX Delivery Driver 

SETTING

Atlanta, FELIX Headquarters—Loading Dock, and Delivery Vehicle—Interstate 20 (I-20)

CASE SCENARIO

Adam Harris has been employed with FELIX for two years and is one of the company's most dependable delivery drivers. He delivers FELIX merchandise to locations throughout Atlanta. Each morning, he arrives to work at 7:30 a.m., checks the delivery list, and signs for the deliveries and company vehicle. Normally, he leaves headquarters at 8:15 a.m. to start his route. Due to his stellar delivery and driving records, Adam trains the delivery drivers after they attend FELIX's driving seminar for new hires. Last week, Randy Andrews rode with Adam to observe how he engaged with delivery customers, operated the company vehicle, completed paperwork, and used the company gas card. Today, Adam will observe Randy and prepare him for his own assigned delivery route.

In part, the FELIX delivery policy reads:

Delivery drivers are not generally permitted to talk or text on personal cell phones. All delivery vehicles are equipped with wireless hands-free phones for drivers to receive incoming calls from FELIX and to call FELIX headquarters. In case of an emergency only, delivery drivers may use a personal cell phone after parking the delivery vehicle. All personal cell phone calls must be logged daily.

Randy: Hey, man. Thanks for letting me drive today.

Adam: No problem. I had nothing to do with it. You have to drive today as a part of your training.

Randy: All right. You ready to go? Where are we headed?

Adam: You tell me. If I were not here, how would you know where to go?

Randy: Oh, okay. Let me sign for the vehicle then.

Adam: Randy, what should you do before that? Follow the orders that you were given in the seminar.

Randy: I don't remember, bro.

Adam: Where are your notes from the seminar? Handouts? Anything that you can follow? If you don't know, I have to write this on your evaluation today.

Randy: Whatever, bro. I don't have a cheat sheet. What do I do?

Adam (*shaking his head*): Follow me.

Thirty minutes later, Randy and Adam are heading west on I-20 to make the first delivery.

Adam: You are about 20 minutes behind schedule. At some point, you will have to make up for this time. You have a required 75 deliveries today. FELIX likes for us to aim for 50 deliveries above the required number though. It is desired but not required. Sometimes deliveries go faster than expected and your time so far may not be a problem. You can evaluate it right before lunch time. If you're still behind, lunch may need to be 30 minutes instead of one hour.

Randy: Cool. I got it.

After a few deliveries, Randy turns the volume up on the radio. Adam also notices that he is driving at 70 miles per hour (mph) when the speed limit is 60. On his personal cell phone, Randy speaks to his mother. Adam notes his observations but does not say anything to Randy.

Randy: I need to stop to use the bathroom. I'm hungry, too.

Adam: It is your call today. I am observing, but there are a few drive-thrus at the next exit.

Randy: Nah, bro. I got another place in mind.

Randy exits I-20 and drives for another 10 minutes. He goes through a neighborhood and eventually stops and parks in front of a house.

Adam: Where are we? You really shouldn't be this far off your route.

Randy: Relax. This is my mom's place. She's at home. I'm just gonna use the bathroom, grab some grub, and be right back. Wanna join me?

Adam: No, thanks. Please hurry.

Twenty minutes later, Randy exits the house.

Randy: All right. Here we go. I'm better now since I had some coffee and breakfast.

As Randy speeds through the neighborhood trying to make up for lost time, he becomes distracted. He focuses on the radio while trying to find a station that he likes.

Adam: Watch out, Randy!

Randy hits on the breaks but still collides into a car. Randy and Adam are not injured. They exit the vehicle to examine the damage and to check on the other driver. Adam calls 911 after seeing the driver's bloody arm hanging out of the window. After the police arrive, they take statements from two witnesses and question Randy and Adam about the accident. The ambulance transports the other driver to the hospital. Meanwhile, Adam and Randy drive back to FELIX headquarters to file an accident report.

DISCUSSION QUESTIONS

1. Is the cellular phone section of the FELIX delivery policy fair and practical? How would you change this policy?
2. If you were to rate the professionalism of Randy and Adam, what score would you give them and why? Use the following scale: 10 for superior, 5 for average, and 1 for poor. What mistakes did Randy make on his first day of deliveries as a FELIX employee? Should Adam have addressed Randy's cavalier demeanor? If so, how?
3. Could Adam have done anything differently to avoid this incident? Should FELIX management reprimand Adam based on his lack of intervention during his observation? What types of parameters should be in place during an observation such as this? Explain.
4. Regarding tort law, would you consider Randy's actions equal to a frolic or a detour? Explain the difference between the terms in your answer. Did Adam act unethically by not correcting Randy as he was violating the FELIX delivery policy? Explain your answer.
5. Could FELIX be vicariously liable for the actions of Randy? What potential lawsuit(s) could be brought against FELIX? Against Adam? Against Randy? Who could bring the lawsuit(s)? If FELIX is sued by the injured party in the accident, should FELIX seek indemnification from Randy? From Adam? Explain.
6. Evaluate the pros and cons of retaining Randy as a FELIX delivery driver. What should be the final decision of management regarding Randy? Support your decision.

SELF-ASSESSMENT

Draft three policies and procedures that a business owner should establish to minimize employer liability due to employee actions.

APPLICATION ACTIVITIES

1. In small groups, research performance evaluation criteria for delivery drivers, and then create your own. From Adam's perspective, write a performance evaluation of Randy. Include Randy's strengths, weaknesses, and areas of improvement in your assessment.
2. You are Adam's supervisor, and support his actions during Randy's observation. However, FELIX management is considering suspending Adam for a week without pay. Compose a persuasive message detailing why Adam should not be disciplined in this manner. Include alternative disciplinary options in your message.
3. In small groups, research current company delivery policies that include cellular phone usage. Develop a new FELIX delivery policy, and share it with the class.

CASE STUDY 19

MEN HAVE ISSUES, TOO

OBJECTIVES

Students will be able to:

A. understand that all employees may have issues with balancing their personal and professional lives;
B. recognize the employer's role in identifying areas and creating policies that may help minimize employee anxiety; and
C. identify personal emotional triggers that could result in stress.

SUGGESTED CLASS TIME

2–3 class periods

TERMS TO KNOW

Define the following terms:

A. work-life balance;
B. competence;
C. character;
D. emotional trigger;
E. stress; and
F. flexible time.

PRELIMINARY ACTIVITY

Research and read four articles concerning work-life balance issues. Note any issues and solutions offered to assist men in achieving a balance between home and work life.

WHO'S IN THIS STORY?

Mary Kate Harrison, 49
FELIX Senior Attorney

© Shutterstock/kurhan

Daryl Peterson, 40
FELIX Attorney III

© Shutterstock/Charlotte Purdy

SETTING

Atlanta, FELIX Headquarters

CASE SCENARIO

Over the last several years, Daryl has been having a difficult time. He does not want to remember that his fiancée Mercedes left him a year after Nikki was born. He had heard the rumors about Mercedes being unfaithful but did not wish to believe them. When Daryl questioned her, she swore that Nikki was his child. Raised by a struggling single mother, Daryl promised to forgive Mercedes, take care of their baby, and move forward with their relationship.

After Nikki is born, Mercedes suffers from postpartum depression and does not want to bond with the baby. Daryl does all he can to help Mercedes adjust, but her attitude toward Nikki does not change. A year later, Mercedes states that motherhood and marriage are not for her. She packs her bags and leaves no forwarding address.

Daryl finds himself alone and a single father. When picking up Nikki from daycare after a long day at work, Daryl overhears the conversation of some mutual friends of Mercedes stating that the child is probably not his. Deeply hurt and succumbing to doubt, Daryl obtains a DNA test six months later and discovers that the nearly two-year-old Nikki is not his biological child. To him, it no longer matters. His name is on the birth certificate. She is his daughter, and he is the only father she will ever know.

Four years later, Daryl moves to Atlanta with Nikki to have a fresh start. Without any family, close friends, and significant other in Atlanta, Daryl is lonely and struggles to balance the demands of the job with fatherhood. He has to be intentional about spending more time with Nikki. Although she is only six, Daryl knows that he cannot afford to miss these precious years because she is growing up so fast. Being a single parent is tough, but he can do it. After all, he has seen women like his mother do it all the time. Why was it so difficult for him? Daryl believes that men are supposed to be the primary breadwinners in their families and the ones who can overcome challenges by finding the right solutions.

It has been over six months since Daryl and Destinie stopped dating. Daryl had hoped that the relationship would last, especially since he rarely has an opportunity to meet professional women outside of work. His recent promotion negatively impacted his personal life by making it more challenging to keep up with his daughter's schedule. His new role requires that he travel and work longer hours, which means that he also spends less time with Nikki.

He realizes that many of the men at FELIX have wives who manage their home lives. Because of this, the husbands can work excessive hours. But, this is not the case for him. He has to figure out how to balance his work and home life before he ends up failing at both. Nikki depends on him to keep it together.

Meeting with Mary Kate Harrison . . .

Daryl: Good morning, Mary Kate. May I speak with you for a moment?

Mary Kate: Sure, Daryl, but can you give me a minute? I need to make a phone call.

Daryl: Yes, not a problem.

Mary Kate: I will meet you in your office once I finish with this call.

Feeling anxious, Daryl returns to his office. He wants to discuss a flexible schedule with Mary Kate, knowing that this is uncommon for an attorney in a supervisory position. Although he does not want to appear incompetent to Mary Kate in his new position, he has to admit that work-life conflict does not only affect women. He realizes that he has to be careful in his approach but quietly hopes that Mary Kate will be sensitive toward his parental needs. Promotions do not come easily, especially in the fashion industry. They are given to those who can accomplish more while working long, demanding hours.

Mary Kate tends to be all business and does not believe people should have special treatment because they are experiencing issues in their personal lives. Even when she experienced marital problems and her husband moved out of the house, Mary Kate only confided in a select few. Through her personal challenges, she continues to handle all of her work relationships in a professional manner and expects the same in return. Mary Kate is no-nonsense and believes that there is a separation between one's personal life and professional life. Daryl needs to present a strong argument as to why he should be allowed to have flexible hours.

Ten minutes later . . .

Mary Kate (*lightly knocking on Daryl's office door prior to entering*): Good morning, Daryl. Thanks for waiting. What would you like to discuss?

Daryl: Well, as you know I'm a single father of a six-year-old. I have to take Nikki to the daycare by 5:45 a.m. to arrive here by 8:00 a.m. It's a struggle every morning to get up at 4:30 a.m., to get Nikki ready for school, and to navigate the traffic in downtown Atlanta. Luckily for me, Nikki's daycare transports her to and from the center to school. We live about an hour away so if I have to work past 5 p.m., I cannot pick her up on time. Because of my work schedule and the demands of the job, I have missed parent–teacher conferences, school plays, and invite-your-parent-to-school days. You name it, and I've either missed it or arrived so late that I missed whatever part my daughter played. Right now, it's a challenge to spend quality time with her. I need to find a balance between my work and home life. I wanted to ask you about working a flex schedule.

Mary Kate: Okay. I understand, but Daryl, you just accepted a promotion that will require you to travel and work longer hours. How do you plan to handle that?

Daryl: I know, and I am grateful for the promotion. I welcome the new challenge. Please don't get me wrong, but I've had to work about 40 hours of overtime during the last two weeks. As you know, I have to pick up Nikki by six o'clock, or the daycare will charge me extra fees. I have been tardy five days in a row and have had to pay in excess of $300 in late pickup fees. After so many incidents, the daycare will dismiss her, and I will have to make other arrangements for her care. I have searched and no other daycare will transport her to and from school.

Mary Kate: I hear what you are saying, Daryl. I can't begin to understand the challenges you face as a single parent. Exactly what do you want FELIX to do to help you through this situation? You accepted the position and were informed that it will require that you travel, work longer hours, increase your client workload, and assume more supervisory responsibilities. I don't see how you working from home or changing your hours is conducive to your new role. Besides, how will FELIX gauge whether you are productive? We have no way of monitoring your progress. I realize that other companies may offer flexible accommodations, but at this time, FELIX does not officially offer them.

Daryl (*becoming frustrated*): I understand that FELIX is concerned about how to manage or monitor employees who use workplace flexibility options. But what have I done to warrant that type of suspicion? I have been a very ethical employee. Why would I stay home and not work? I'm not only concerned about the well-being of my child, but I also want to be a good employee. I desire to do both well and I am requesting schedule modifications so that I can be successful. Will you consider my case on an individual basis?

Mary Kate (*noticing the concern in Daryl's voice*): Daryl, I see that you are a caring parent and desire what's best for Nikki. I will have to see what I can do. Are you sure there is no one you can depend on to help you with this situation? I mean, you are in a leadership role at one of the largest retail companies in the Southeastern region. Why don't you put your request in writing. In the meantime, I will check with HR.

Trying to obtain buy-in from Mary Kate one last time, Daryl offers her some additional information.

Daryl (*sighing heavily while maintaining his composure*): You know, Fortune 500 companies offer and encourage flexible work schedules all the time, Mary Kate. They work with their loyal employees. I looked on the internet just yesterday and discovered that flexible accommodations, even if temporary, enhance overall job satisfaction by improving employee retention, morale, work relationships, and engagement. Please consider these factors when you speak with HR.

Mary Kate leaves his office without assuring him of anything. As he watches her leave, Daryl wonders why she is so reluctant to work with him. He has always received stellar performance evaluations and has covered for co-workers when they attended to personal obligations. Why was his situation any different than DeAngelo and Tracy's when they adopted Craig? The company allowed D'Angelo paternity leave to bond with Craig and even gave him a hefty check to purchase new baby clothes. What could he do to convince FELIX they should do this for him?

DISCUSSION QUESTIONS

1. How should Mary Kate respond to Daryl's request? Should Mary Kate's decision be determined on a case-by-case basis or should all cases be decided in the same manner? Support your position.
2. Think about your communications class, and the guidelines for crafting a persuasive message. How did Daryl deliver his message to Mary Kate? Did he use the correct communication style? Explain.
3. Do you think Daryl was well-prepared for his response to Mary Kate's question about his accepting the promotion knowing that he had childcare issues? Did he demonstrate to Mary Kate that he was a highly productive employee? Explain.
4. Based on the case scenario, identify some emotional triggers that may have caused Daryl to become frustrated during his conversation with Mary Kate.
5. What would happen if Daryl discovers that Min allows Cameron to use a flexible schedule to care for April when FELIX does not officially offer one? Would Daryl have a legitimate claim against FELIX? If so, for what?
6. How important is it to fit into work culture? How can a person lose a sense of self in order to advance in a profession? Discuss the importance of setting boundaries to maintain a work-life balance.

SELF-ASSESSMENT

1. Complete the Communication Style Survey in Appendix J to obtain an understanding of how you respond to others in daily situations.
2. Locate the article "How to Ask for Flex Time" by Judi Ketteler and answer the questions located under Access Yourself and Your Job. These questions will help you identify your needs prior to negotiating flex time with your employer.

APPLICATION ACTIVITIES

1. Assess how Mary Kate communicated with Daryl. Does she demonstrate caring, competence, and character? Support your answer.
2. How could Daryl have been more effective in communicating his needs to Mary Kate? Separate into groups and create additional dialogue that Daryl could have used in this situation.
3. Draft a proposal to negotiate for flexible time. Determine what you need and include tangible benefits for the company in your proposal. Anticipate your audience's objections, address them, and provide alternative ideas.
4. Locate the Working Mother Report Sponsored by EY, Building a Better Working World titled "How Men Flex." Based on the statistics in the report concerning flexible work hours for men, deduce and write a one-page report on how the trend will either spiral up or down in years to come.
5. In three- to five-paragraphs, describe the emotional triggers that you would experience if you were in Daryl's situation? What would you do about his personal situation before speaking with Mary Kate?

CASE STUDY 20

WHY DID THEY HIRE YOU ANYWAY?

OBJECTIVES

Students will be able to:

A. understand employee rights under the *Pregnancy Discrimination Act of 1978* (*Pregnancy Act*);

B. identify ways in which pregnant employees may be treated differently; and

C. recognize the filing restrictions under the *Pregnancy Act* that may limit an employee's legal rights.

SUGGESTED CLASS TIME

2–3 class periods

TERMS TO KNOW

Define the following terms:

A. pregnancy discrimination;
B. unfair treatment;
C. legal claim;
D. systemic practices;
E. protected class; and
F. gender discrimination.

PRELIMINARY ACTIVITY

Visit the EEOC's website to learn more about the *Pregnancy Act*. Research EEOC cases that involve legal claims brought under *Title VII of the Civil Rights Act of 1964* because of systemic practices that perpetuated the unfair treatment of pregnant employees.

WHO'S IN THIS STORY?

Kasia Scottsdale, 30
FELIX HR Secretary
(New Hire)

Joshua Scottsdale, 33
Kasia's Husband

Aaron Bernstein, 33
FELIX Mid-Level
Finance Analyst

Joe Roberts, 37
FELIX Security Officer

Cameron Knox, 37
FELIX HR Supervisor

Min Kwon, 38
FELIX HR Director

SETTING

FELIX—New York City (NYC) Office and Atlanta Headquarters

CASE SCENARIO

Kasia Scottsdale has worked as a secretary in the Felix NYC office for two years. She and her husband Joshua, an electrical engineer, have had enough of the brutal cold weather and fast-paced life to which many New Yorkers are accustomed. Kasia and Joshua agree that, should an opportunity present itself, they will trade in their expensive small apartment for a spacious home, southern living, and warmer weather.

Meanwhile, in the Atlanta office, Min and Cameron are sharing the responsibilities of the secretarial position that once belonged to Stephanie Lane. After firing Stephanie over a month ago, Min has not been able to locate an acceptable replacement. This time, Min and Cameron plan to be even more intentional in the hiring process. Their previous secretary exemplified competent writing skills on her résumé but failed to do so on assigned tasks after she was hired. Future job candidates will have to demonstrate their abilities and pass four in-house exams consisting of writing, speaking, typing, and word processing. It is clear that Min and Cameron do not want to repeat past mistakes by hiring someone too quickly as they had done with Stephanie. Such hiring decisions lead to too many negative long-term consequences on the office.

In the NYC Office . . .

After noticing and inquiring about the job opening on FELIX's intranet, Kasia decides that it is the ideal time to make the move. She takes a break and calls Joshua to tell him about the opportunity.

Kasia: Joshua, hey! Are you on a job?

Joshua: No, what's up? Are you all right?

Kasia: Oh, yes. I'm fine. Listen, I just noticed on our corporate intranet that there's an opening in the Atlanta FELIX office!

Joshua: Really? You're kidding, right?

Kasia: No, I'm serious! Weren't we just talking about this the other night? You know, if I could find a job in the south that paid me what I made here and offered the same health benefits, we could move.

Joshua: Unh-huh! Yep, that's right!

Kasia: In this position in Atlanta, I would be working for the same company, so my benefits and pay wouldn't change. We would have health coverage while you start your business.

Joshua: That's sounds great, babe! But, how do you know you'll get the job?

Kasia: FELIX is like a family organization. The company prefers to promote from within. The last girl they hired as a secretary didn't work out. I haven't had a poor performance review since I've been here, and I just got a raise about six months ago. Why wouldn't I get it?

Joshua: Well, your co-workers do love you in your office. Also, I'm not so sure your boss is going to be happy to hear the news. You may want to talk to him first before applying. You don't want him to be upset with you for going around him.

Kasia: Yes, you're right. I'll talk to him and then contact Cameron, the HR person in the Atlanta office later on today. I'm so excited!

Joshua: Me too. Okay, babe, I gotta go.

Kasia: Okay, I'll see you tonight!

After speaking with her boss later on that day, Kasia contacts Cameron to inquire about the position. Cameron asks that she e-mail her résumé as soon as possible. Because Kasia is a current FELIX employee, Cameron schedules her telephone interview for the following Monday. Kasia thanks her for the opportunity and spends the rest of the week preparing for the interview.

At the end of the day in the Atlanta office . . .

Cameron receives Kasia's résumé and is quite impressed with her accomplishments. She also has a voice mail from John, Kasia's boss, stating how wonderful she is and how he would hate to see her go. He believes that Kasia will be a valuable asset in any of the FELIX's offices. In his opinion, she is professional and capable of working on multiple projects in a fast-paced environment. He goes on to say that Kasia has talked about relocating to the south for some time now but did not want to lose her benefits and salary in transition. He then closes by offering to call Min and give her the same recommendation. Cameron is surprised by John's premature phone call, but she is also relieved. After listening to the message, she secretly decides that Kasia will get the job even if new candidates apply.

A week later . . .

Cameron sees Min in the employee lounge and reminds her that they have a telephone interview with Kasia in 20 minutes. Min states that she needs to go to her office first but will come to the interview as soon as possible. Cameron retrieves the interview packets from the secretary's file cabinet and proceeds toward her office. She places the packets on the table and prepares to call Kasia. Cameron decides not to mention John's message to Min at this time. She wants to see how Kasia's interview goes first.

In NYC . . .

Meanwhile in the New York office, Kasia is anxiously watching the clock. At 12:50 p.m., she takes her lunch break and goes to sit in her car. It is the quietest place to compose herself before the telephone interview begins.

In Atlanta . . .

Cameron peruses Kasia's impressive résumé again and places a copy on top of Min's packet. She assumes that based on Kasia's credentials, it would be easy to convince Min that she is the right fit for the Atlanta office. At 1 p.m. sharp, Cameron calls Kasia's cell phone.

Kasia: Hello?

Cameron: Hello, Kasia. This is Cameron. How are you?

Kasia: I am well, thank you. How is your day going?

Cameron *(laughing lightly)***:** Busy! We have several product launches this week and a vital position to fill!

Kasia: Oh, I see. A typical day at a FELIX office.

Cameron: Exactly!

Both women laugh.

Cameron: Kasia, Min should be here any minute. Once she arrives, we can officially start the interview.

Kasia: That's fine. I understand.

Cameron hears a light knock, followed by a slow opening of the door. She sees Min and motions her to come inside and sit in the chair closest to the phone. Now, they are ready to conduct a more formal interview.

Cameron: Kasia, Min has just arrived.

Kasia: Hello, Min. Thank you for the opportunity to interview.

Min: Hello, and you're welcome, Kasia. To start, I see that you have worked for John Marshall for two years.

Kasia: Yes, that's correct.

Min: I must tell you that I have known John for many years. I interviewed him for the management position when FELIX launched its New York office. We also worked closely together when he staffed that office.

Kasia *(sounding surprised)***:** Oh, I didn't know that! John didn't tell me that he worked with you personally. He just said that he would call you and Cameron to provide a reference, if you all asked for one.

Cameron gives Min a quick look to see if she caught Kasia's last statement. It does not appear as though she noticed.

Min: Yes, he did. As a matter of fact, he almost made me late for this meeting. I just got off of the phone with John. He was prepared to place several of your co-workers, who were ready to sing your praises, on the line. They seem to really enjoy working with you

Kasia: Wow! That's great to hear.

Min: Yes, it is. I can't recall a time where this has happened before. John told me that you saved him on many occasions! He doesn't know how he's going to fair, should you leave. How do you feel about that?

Kasia *(laughing lightly)***:** John and I work very well together. I think he'll be fine. John is such a hands-on boss and team player. He has even worked the front desk while I was on vacation. I'm sure he will do the same with my replacement.

Cameron: Kasia, tell me about a time where you had to save John.

After an hour of chatting, in between formal and informal interview questions, Kasia is offered the job and given a month to relocate to the Atlanta area. She will have the same hours, pay, and benefits that she has in the New York office. She is even promised a raise after her six-month review if her performance review scores are above average.

A month later . . .

Although the move was stressful, Kasia is very excited about her first day. She enters the Atlanta office and goes through security . . .

Kasia: Good morning, sir. Where is the HR department located?

Joe: Ma'am, who are you here to see? Do you have any ID?

Kasia (*searching through her purse*)**:** Yes, I do. I have my old ID from when I worked for FELIX in the New York office. Here it is. I am here to see Cameron Knox or Min Kwon.

Joe: You must be Mrs. Scottsdale? Mrs. Knox told me that you'd be arriving today. I have your name on my list. Just take the elevators to the fourth floor, and go down a long hallway. Once you come to the end of that hallway, take a left. You'll pass the sales office, then hang a right. Once you go past the copiers in that little corridor, take a left at legal, and then a quick right. You'll see the HR office on your right.

Kasia: Okay. Thank you so much.

Joe: No problem. Welcome to Atlanta!

Kasia: I'm excited to be here.

Kasia takes the elevator to the fourth floor, but by the time the elevator stops, she forgets what the security guard told her. She is lost and ends up near the employee lounge where she accidentally bumps into Aaron.

Aaron: Whoa! Watch the coffee!

Kasia: Oh, my goodness! I'm so sorry. I was too busy trying to read the names on the doors. I think I'm lost.

Kasia laughs nervously.

Aaron: I would imagine so. How did you get up here, anyway? Well, never mind. Who are you looking for?

Kasia: I am trying to find the HR department. My name is Kasia Scottsdale. I'm the new HR secretary. I am here to meet with either Min or Cameron.

Aaron pauses and looks intently at Kasia. He's quiet for a few moments. Kasia steps back to create more personal space between them. He does not appear to have that southern hospitality, a trait that people up north typically associate with Southerners.

Aaron: You said that you're the new secretary?

Kasia: Yes, I am. Can you point me in the right direction? I am supposed to meet with them at 8 a.m.

Aaron: Wait a minute. My goodness! How far along are you?

Kasia: I'm sorry?

Aaron: You're pregnant, right? I mean you're just starting today, and by the looks of it, you'll be on leave in a few months! Why did they even hire you?

Kasia: Excuse me? Well, sir, I am qualified for . . .

Aaron abruptly cuts her off in mid-sentence.

Aaron: You won't be able to endure the long hours and handle the stress associated with the demands of this office in your condition. Besides, we can't afford to have you out on maternity leave in the middle of product launches. What were Min and Cameron thinking?! Whatever! Anyway, just follow me.

Aaron leads Kasia to the HR department, where he finds Cameron in her office. He walks in with Kasia trailing behind him.

Aaron: Cameron, this is your new secretary. She got lost on her way up here.

Kasia sidesteps Aaron and extends her hand to Cameron.

Kasia: Hi, Cameron. It's great to finally meet you. I'm so excited about my first day at work.

Cameron stands up and shakes Kasia's hand. Kasia then turns to Aaron and thanks him for leading her to HR.

Cameron: Nice to meet you, Kasia. Oh my word, how far along are you?

Kasia: I'm going into my sixth month.

Aaron (*chuckling):* Good luck with that, Cameron. I guess you and Min will be looking for help again in a few months.

Aaron sips his coffee, eyes Cameron, and exits the office quickly, leaving Cameron and Kasia in an uncomfortable silence.

Kasia (*holding her protruding belly*): Cameron, is this going to be a problem?

DISCUSSION QUESTIONS

1. Reflect on the employment hiring procedures in case scenarios one and eight. Do you think Cameron and Min followed proper protocol when interviewing Kasia? How do the hiring procedures in the previous case scenarios differ from this one? Explain.
2. Was Kasia obligated to reveal her pregnancy status to Cameron and Min during the interview process? As a transferring employee, should Kasia be subjected to the traditional 90-day probationary period associated with new employees? Explain.
3. Can Aaron's comments concerning Kasia's condition be grounds for a lawsuit if she is terminated during the orientation process? Should Kasia report the incident with Aaron and Cameron to the EEOC? Does she have a legitimate case against them even if she is not fired? Explain. Based on the case scenario, what procedures, if any, should FELIX take to protect itself from possible liability due to a pregnancy discrimination claim?
4. Do you believe it was appropriate for John to call Min and Cameron to provide a reference for Kasia without being asked to do so? How could this jeopardize the integrity of the interview selection process? Explain.
5. How could Aaron's comments impact FELIX? Explain. If you overheard these comments in your workplace, what is your obligation, if any, to bring it to the attention of HR?
6. If you were Kasia, what would be your response to Aaron in this situation? Write what you would say and why.
7. Present a summary of what employers are allowed to do in the event an employee is having a difficult time keeping up with the pace of the job. Now, factor in that this employee is pregnant. What should you consider and why?

SELF-ASSESSMENT

Interview three to five people who are members of a protected class. Ask them to describe incidents where they believed they were being discriminated against on the job. Inquire as to whether they reported the incident and took action. If they did not take action, ask them to elaborate as to why. Then ask, if they had known that the outcome would have been in their favor, would they have filed? Write a one-page report.

APPLICATION ACTIVITIES

1. Research cases where employers were sued because of pregnancy discrimination or for discriminatory practices during the hiring process. In the role of a manager, summarize these cases, and write a recommendation section. Describe how you would have mitigated these situations.
2. Research the steps in the EEOC enforcement process. Present your findings to the class.
3. Write a letter of reprimand to Aaron. Be sure to include any laws and/or training mandates in the letter. Consider how his comments could have impacted not only FELIX but also his career.

CASE STUDY 21

MY NAME IS MYNX*

OBJECTIVES

Students will be able to:

A. identify and consider the workplace challenges for lesbian, gay, bisexual, and transgender (LGBT) employees;
B. state and present the workplace protections for LGBT employees; and
C. summarize how employers should respond to unfair treatment of LGBT employees.

SUGGESTED CLASS TIME

2–3 class periods

TERMS TO KNOW

Define the following terms:

A. unfair treatment;
B. gender identity; and
C. hostile work environment.

PRELIMINARY ACTIVITY

Visit the EEOC website. Pinpoint and summarize information about workplace protections for LGBT employees. Share your information with the class.

WHO'S IN THIS STORY?

Parker Cobb, 27
FELIX HR Benefits Manager

Cameron Knox, 37
FELIX HR Supervisor

Kenny Hyde, 28
FELIX IT Specialist I

David (Mynx) Yang, 39
FELIX IT Specialist II

Aaron Bernstein, 33
FELIX Mid-Level Finance Analyst

DeAngelo Moore, 42
FELIX Accounting Supervisor II

Female Employee, 41

Joe Roberts, 37
FELIX Security Officer

SETTING

Atlanta, FELIX Headquarters

CASE SCENARIO

David Yang has been employed with FELIX as an IT Specialist for four years. Six months ago, he received a promotion based on his excellent interpersonal skills, IT certifications, and efficient task completion. As a part of his new job responsibilities, he must train those in the IT Specialist I position. Last week, David was notified about his nomination for IT Employee of the Year. As a finalist, he is preparing to submit a portfolio to the review committee.

Based on his previous performance reviews and superb IT skill set, David is optimistic that he will win and receive the plaque and cash award of $2,000. In fact, his co-workers have already begun to congratulate him. If pronounced the winner, David plans to allocate the cash award toward his long-desired gender reassignment surgery. Shortly after moving to Atlanta, he joined a local LGBT support group, which encourages him to start living his life as Ms. Mynx Yang. However, David is a very private person and remains apprehensive about revealing his true self at work. Nevertheless, following Thursday night's support group meeting, David feels ready to make the transition. Mynx will report to work on Monday morning.

Monday morning, 7:28 a.m.

After entering FELIX headquarters, Mynx scans her ID badge, which has the picture and name of David Yang. Mynx starts walking to the elevator when she hears the beep from the security scanner.

Joe: Excuse me, ma'am. Could you please return to the security area? I need to check your ID.

Mynx: Good morning. I work here. I arrive every morning at 7:30 a.m. Here's my badge.

Mynx presents her badge to Joe.

Joe: Ma'am, your badge belongs to Mr. David Yang. Who are you?

Mynx: I am Ms. Mynx Yang, formerly known as David Yang.

Joe: Ohhh. Well, ummm . . . Mr. Yang, I didn't recognize you. Forgive me for asking, but why are you wearing a wig, skirt, and heels this morning? Did I miss something? Is FELIX having some sort of special event today that I don't know about?

Mynx: No, there's not a special event. It's just that I'm no longer David. My name is now Mynx Yang. Have a good day, Joe.

Mynx begins to turn away from Joe.

Joe: Wait. Is this something that's permanent, or is it just for today? Because if it's permanent, then we'll need to get you a new ID badge for security purposes.

Mynx: Okay. I'll take a picture later on today. Does that work?

Joe: I guess so. I'll let you know if there are any problems.

Mynx turns, walks to the elevator, and goes to her floor. After getting settled at her cubicle, she checks her mailbox in the employee lounge and grabs a cup of coffee. Upon returning to her desk, Mynx notices a red blinking light on her office telephone, indicating that she has new voicemail. As she listens to the first message from DeAngelo, Mynx notates that he and Aaron are having computer issues. They are preparing for a meeting with Felix and need Kenny Hyde, an IT Specialist I, and David to assist them. Kenny has already reported to DeAngelo's office. David must report there as soon as he arrives. The second voicemail is from security. Joe informs Mynx that she must present a new state-issued driver's license with a name change in order to obtain a different ID badge. This updated information is needed as soon as possible.

More people are starting to arrive at work. Mynx notices a few co-workers are staring and questioning among themselves. Several of them are asking who the new person is working at David's cubicle. Mynx ignores them and proceeds to the finance department where DeAngelo and Aaron's offices are located. From the hallway, Mynx hears Kenny, DeAngelo, and Aaron talking. She stops at the doorway of DeAngelo's office. Everyone is hovering over his computer with their backs to the door.

Mynx (*knocking on DeAngelo's door*): Good morning. Help has arrived.

Turning, they all say good morning and then pause to stare at Mynx.

DeAngelo: David?

Kenny: What's up with you, dude? What you got on?!

Aaron simply stares and bursts out laughing.

Mynx (*shifting uncomfortably*): Good morning. I'm no longer David. I am living my life now as Mynx Yang. So please call me Mynx. Anyway, what kind of computer problems are you having?

Kenny: Hold up, man. What happened to David? Where's my bro? You can't just show up early on Monday morning with a wig, a skirt, and heels calling yourself Mynx! I mean, wassup with that? Why you calling yourself a cat?

Aaron continues to laugh while DeAngelo interrupts Kenny.

DeAngelo: A cat? What are you talking about?

Kenny: You know. A Mynx cat. A feline.

DeAngelo: I believe you mean a Manx, not a Mynx, cat, Kenny.

Kenny: Well, whatever. But for real, dude. Why you dressed like that? You're freaking me out!

Mynx: I'm still the same person, Kenny. I'm just your female friend now instead of being your bro or your dude.

Aaron starts laughing again.

Kenny: No way! You ain't no female friend of mine! I like *real* women! Just don't come around me dressed like that, dude. We'll talk once you return to David. And you can forget about me calling you Mynx or Manx or whatever it is. DeAngelo, I'm outta here. Aaron, I'll work on the computer in your office.

Kenny exits DeAngelo's office. Bothered by Kenny's behavior, Mynx excuses herself. She enters the ladies restroom and waits for an empty stall. Cameron exits a stall and looks at Mynx.

Cameron: Hello. How are you?

Mynx: Hi, Cameron.

Cameron: Oh, have we met?

Mynx: Yes, Cameron, we have.

Cameron: We have? What's your name again?

Mynx: My name is Mynx. Mynx Yang, but you know me as David.

Cameron: David? David Yang?

Mynx: Yes, but it's Mynx now.

At this time, another female employee exits a stall.

Female Employee: Why is there a man dressed like a woman in here?! Did I come inside the wrong restroom?

Cameron: No, this one is for ladies.

Female Employee: Well, why is *he* in here? This area is supposed to be for women only. This is totally inappropriate. I'm reporting this to my boss.

Cameron does not respond to the lady. Mynx turns and exits the restroom.

Returning to DeAngelo's office, Mynx reboots his computer. After the maintenance is completed, Mynx goes back to her cubicle. Kenny is working at his desk now. Mynx asks him a question, but he refuses to acknowledge her presence. This is when Mynx notices a Post-it note on her desk. It reads, "#nofreaksatfelix." She takes the note and discards it in the trash.

Throughout the day, Mynx carries out her assignments as usual despite the stares and laughs. As she walks the halls and works in her cubicle, she hears comments like "What is the world coming to?" and "There goes David's chances at getting that cash award." At the end of the day, Mynx feels emotionally and mentally worn. As she walks to her car in the garage, she hears laughter after someone yells, "Go home, you freak!" She turns and then hears the old 1980s Whodini song "The Freaks Come Out at Night" blasting from a cell phone. She recognizes them as FELIX employees; Kenny is one of the men in the group.

This behavior continues and even magnifies during the remainder of the week. Mynx receives a call from DeAngelo on Thursday. He informs Mynx that a lot of complaints about restroom use have been reported. Many of the female employees are uncomfortable when Mynx uses the same restroom. To make matters worse, the male employees definitely do not want her in their restroom either. DeAngelo states that he is not trying to cause a problem but merely is attempting to give Mynx some practical career advice. DeAngelo suggests that he rethink "this Mynx thing and return to being a man."

By Friday, Mynx is even more exhausted from dealing with the name calling and silent treatment. She is devastated that this abuse is coming from co-workers who she once thought were her friends. Relieved that it is lunch time, she goes to the cafeteria. Upon entering, she sees Kenny, Aaron, and two other male employees sitting at a table.

Kenny (*snickering*): David? Ohhhh, Daaavvviiiddd!

Irritated, Mynx walks toward Kenny.

Mynx: Of all the people, Kenny, that I thought would've been mean to me, I never imagined that it would be you! I'd appreciate it if you would stop taunting me. I've told you that my name is Mynx. Please address me by this name from now on.

Kenny: Well, you thought wrong, David. My friend is a man, not a freak. Help me, guys. This boy–girl here is being rude to me. Maybe I should report his . . . my bad, *her* behavior to HR.

Mynx: Report me?! I haven't done anything! You are the ones who have been harassing me all week.

Kenny (*smiling coyly*): Really? Where's your proof?

Mynx: The note that you left in my cubicle along with that awful song you played in the garage.

Kenny: What? You guys know anything about notes or a song?

Laughing, the guys shake their heads.

Kenny: I don't care what you say. Your name is David. Just like it says on your driver's license and your security badge. I'm surprised security didn't detain you for impersonating a woman!

The men at the table continue to laugh loudly.

Kenny: Hey, David. My niece is going to her school's Sadie Hawkins dance this weekend. You wanna ask Aaron to go with you?

In the midst of more laughter, Parker enters the cafeteria to meet Cameron for lunch. Parker initially walks toward the buffet area until he sees the angry look that Mynx is giving the four men. Moving to stand next to her, he wonders why she looks so upset. He has been wondering all week how her transition is going.

Parker: Is everything all right, Mynx? You look bothered.

Mynx: It's nothing I can't handle.

Parker (*looking at the four men*): Is everything all right, gentlemen?

Kenny: Yeah. Why wouldn't it be? We're just having a friendly conversation with our co-worker here.

Aaron: And we were just leaving.

Kenny: Yep. Let's go. You know Parker works for HR. You don't want him to get us all fired for just talking to a co-worker. You never know how stories can get twisted around.

The four men gather their lunches, leave the table, and exit the cafeteria.

Parker: Are you okay?

Mynx: No, but it's nothing I can't handle.

Parker: Don't let them get to you. Please let me know if there's anything that I can do.

Cameron enters the cafeteria to find Parker. Having lost her appetite, Mynx leaves and returns to her cubicle.

Over the next month, Mynx encounters the same treatment at work. She is disappointed that she does not win the IT Employee of the Year Award. After the awards banquet, she discovers a second Post-it note stating, "Freaks don't get awards" on her car in the garage. Kenny continues to ignore her even though she is still responsible for training him. He has been engaging in training with another IT Specialist II.

Although Mynx loves her job, she knows that she cannot continue working under the present conditions. She contemplates resigning from her position when she remembers that Parker offered to help. She visits him in HR.

Parker: Hi, Mynx. What brings you to my office today?

DISCUSSION QUESTIONS

1. Is Mynx being discriminated against and/or harassed? If so, what is the basis of the discrimination and/or harassment? Provide specific examples to support your answer.
2. What legal protection(s) does Mynx have if she is indeed being discriminated against and/or harassed? Could Mynx sue FELIX or any of its employees under civil law? If so, whom and for what?
3. Is Mynx being subjected to a hostile work environment? Explain your answer.
4. What actions is FELIX required to take to protect Mynx in the workplace? What course of action(s) does Mynx have if FELIX does not properly respond?
5. Under criminal law, could any of the actions against Mynx be considered hate crimes? If so, which ones and why?
6. Should Mynx be required to present new state-issued identification to obtain an updated FELIX security badge? Why or why not?
7. In the case scenario, DeAngelo suggested to Mynx that "he rethink this Mynx thing and return to being a man." Were DeAngelo's suggestions to Mynx appropriate? Explain.
8. At the end of the case scenario, Mynx speaks to Parker in the HR department. What information should she relay to Parker? Against whom would her allegations be if she decides to file a complaint? What proof does she have of these allegations?
9. Do female and male employees at FELIX have a legitimate legal concern about using the same restroom as Mynx? What accommodations may be applied to help resolve this situation? On the EEOC website, locate and read the *Macy v. Department of Justice, EEOC Appeal No. 0120120821, 2012 WL 1435995 (April 20, 2012)* to assist you with your answer.
10. If you were Cameron, what follow-up conversation should you have had with Mynx when she entered the restroom for the first time? Create a dialogue for this conversation.

SELF-ASSESSMENT

Visit the Diversity, Inc. website. Locate an article concerning diversity or LGBT issues. Write a one-page response. In your answer, discuss what tools you can use to effectively manage a diverse workforce.

APPLICATION ACTIVITIES

1. Research EEOC cases regarding LGBT workers. Consider the following cases: *Lusardi v. Department of the Army, EEOC Appeal No. 0120133395, 2015 WL 1607756 (Mar. 27, 2015)* and *Jameson v. U.S. Postal Service, EEOC Appeal No. 0120130992, 2013 WL 2368729 (May 21, 2013).*
   a. In small groups, create a presentation on current laws protecting LGBT employees in the workplace.
   b. What type of training may be beneficial to FELIX employees regarding LGBT issues? What topics should be covered in the training? Use this information to conduct your own class training session.

CASE STUDY 22
THE BIG C

OBJECTIVES

Students will be able to:

A. understand the requirements under the federal Family and Medical Leave Act (FMLA);
B. recognize employer responsibilities under FMLA; and
C. identify who is eligible to use leave under FMLA.

SUGGESTED CLASS TIME

2–3 class periods

TERMS TO KNOW

Define the following terms:

A. Family Medical Leave Act (FMLA);
B. medical leave;
C. serious health condition; and
D. sick bank.

PRELIMINARY ACTIVITY

Research the FMLA of 1993 and its amended versions of 2009. Report to the class what sections of the Act have been amended. Provide a rationale for the amendments in each section that is discussed.

WHO'S IN THIS STORY?

Destinie Taylor, 27
FELIX Attorney I

Parker Cobb, 27
FELIX HR Benefits Manager

Dr. Merriwether, 48
Destinie's Physician

Medical Receptionist, 25

Nurse, 31
Destinie's Nurse

SETTING

Atlanta, FELIX Headquarters and Dr. Merriwether's Office

CASE SCENARIO

Destinie is at the physician's office . . .

Medical Receptionist: Ms. Taylor?

Destinie: Yes?

Medical Receptionist: Please come to the front desk.

Trying to stifle a cough, Destinie walks to the front desk and smiles wryly at the receptionist.

Destinie: Excuse me, ma'am. I've been here before, and all of my information is still the same. I do have a $30 copay. Here's my visa card.

Medical Receptionist (*taking the card*): Thank you, Miss Taylor. I see that you're an old patient, but we haven't seen you in over a year.

Destinie: Are you serious? I thought I came for a physical last year.

Medical Receptionist: No, ma'am. The last time you visited the office was close to two years ago. Please complete these forms and update your medical history. Also, please sign the HIPPA form, which is the last page on this clipboard. This form authorizes us to disclose protected medical information to your physician and anyone you list in the event of an emergency. Please give me one moment to swipe your card.

After swiping the card, the receptionist extends her arm to Destinie.

Medical Receptionist: Here you go. Would you like a receipt?

Destinie: Yes, please.

Destinie returns to her seat and begins to fill out the forms. Ten minutes later, her name is called.

Nurse: Destinie Taylor?

Destinie: Yes. I'm coming.

Nurse: How are you today? Follow me, so that I can get your current weight. You can place your purse in the chair.

Destinie has a coughing spell and finds it difficult to catch her breath.

Nurse: Are you okay, Ms. Taylor?

Destinie: No, I have this cough I can't seem to get rid of, and now I'm feeling a little dizzy.

Maybe I'm coming down with a virus or something. I'm tired all of the time. I have been working a lot of overtime lately

Nurse: Let's see if the doctor can fix you right up then. Please get your purse, and follow me to room 209.

Destinie follows the nurse down the hall and into room 209.

Nurse: Please have a seat. I'm going to take two readings of your blood pressure. You'll feel a little tightness. Uncross your legs, and just relax.

Destinie: Okay.

Nurse: The doctor will be with you shortly.

The nurse exits the room. The physician comes in a few minutes later.

Dr. Merriwether: Good morning, Ms. Taylor. I see it's been a while since we've seen you. How are you doing?

Destinie: I'm tired, and I can't seem to stop coughing. I told your nurse that I think I may have contracted a virus.

Dr. Merriwether: Well, we are going to order some blood work. Don't worry. We do everything in-house now, so you don't need to leave the office. The nurse will come in and draw your blood right here. In the meantime, please sit on the table so that I can check your vitals.

Destinie: Sure.

Dr. Merriwether: When was your last menstrual cycle? How often do you conduct self-breast examinations? Are you a smoker?

Destinie: It was two weeks ago. I stopped smoking four years ago. But, I must admit that I don't do the self-examinations very often. I try to remember, but most of the time I forget.

Dr. Merriwether: I understand, but keep in mind that you do have a family history of breast cancer. So you need to remember to do your monthly breast exams. I suggest that you place it on your calendar so that you remember. Self-examinations are important because they can be the key to early detection.

Destinie: I will.

Dr. Merriwether: So, according to your chart, you've been coughing for a few days, and I notice that you sound a little hoarse.

Destinie: I thought it was because of the coughing.

Dr. Merriwether: I see. Let's check out this cough, and do a breast examination while we have you here. Please remove your top and bra, and put on the patient gown. I'll return in a few minutes.

The physician returns.

Dr. Merriwether: Take a few deep breaths. Open wide and say ahhhh. I feel a little nodule in your thyroid. It could be normal, but let's get that checked out. Lean back for me, please. Everything feels normal over here. Wait. I may have spoken too soon. Can you feel that?

Four weeks later and after several medical visits . . .

Destinie returns to the office after a visit with an oncologist carrying news that she has cancer. Although she is nervous and afraid, she refuses to tell anyone in the office other than Parker, the HR benefits manager. She needs to talk to him about requesting time off for personal reasons. She does not want her co-workers to know what is happening. Unwanted attention from sympathetic well-wishers would only cause her to wallow in self-pity. What she needs to do is muster up all of the energy she has to fight this disease. She plans to call her parents when her procedures are all done, and she is well again.

Destinie: Parker, are you busy? I need to ask you a few questions.

Parker: Can you come back in about an hour? I have to call the insurance company to negotiate our new health insurance rates. We are lucky; no one has a serious health issue here. That would only increase our rates. What did you need? Is it something that I can handle quickly?

Destinie pauses.

Destinie: Probably not. I can come back around 1 p.m. Will that work for you?

Parker: Sure. That'll be fine. Destinie, are you okay? You look tired.

Destinie: Yes, I'm fine. I'll see you at 1 p.m.

Destinie returns to her desk and conducts an online search on FMLA. She has been an employee at FELIX for eleven and one-half months. She is thinking about the time that she will need to combat this illness and how she will pay her bills and other living expenses. There is a knock at the door, and Destinie quickly switches tabs on her computer screen.

Destinie: Come in.

Parker: My phone call did not take as long as I thought it would. What did you need to talk to me about?

DISCUSSION QUESTIONS

1. Who is eligible to use FMLA? Explain the stipulations. What is a serious health condition as defined by FMLA?
2. What happens when an employer fails to inform employees about current FMLA requirements?
3. Do Destinie's recent diagnosis and health condition qualify her to use FMLA? If FELIX allows employees to donate medical leave time to a sick bank, can Destinie use or borrow leave from other employees in this case? According to the law, is she obligated to provide her employer with a reason for the leave? Explain.
4. Will employees still qualify for FMLA if their 12 months of service is not consecutive?
5. What are some common legal risks many employers face with FMLA certification?
6. If Destinie does not qualify for FMLA, what can she do to find the time she needs for treatments? How can FELIX help her through this process?
7. What should Parker do if Destinie asks for an extended leave for medical reasons?

SELF-ASSESSMENT

Take the *Test Your FMLA Knowledge* by completing the questions located in Appendix I.

APPLICATION ACTIVITIES

1. If you were Destinie, what can you do to ensure that you will have adequate time off for medical treatment? Compose a persuasive letter to your supervisor requesting the leave. In Destinie's request, consider that only a select few are privy to her personal situation. Offer the supervisor work alternatives that would provide Destinie with additional time to qualify for FMLA.
2. In small groups, research how cancer impacts the workplace. Develop a set of guidelines that employers can use to support cancer survivors who are returning to work. During your research, consider employees who suffer from fatigue due to cancer treatments. Include statistics on the impact that cancer and the financial obligations to treat cancer have on the employees' work and private lives. You may research other cancer-related diseases in addition to or other than breast cancer. Prepare a presentation, and present your findings.
3. Draft a memo from Parker to Min suggesting that FELIX implement a policy to address cancer and cancer-related issues in the workplace. Create the policy, and attach it to your memo.

CASE STUDY 23
PROFESSIONALISM—WHOSE BUSINESS IS IT ANYWAY?*

OBJECTIVES

Students will be able to:

A. define intentional infliction of emotional distress;
B. differentiate between professional and unprofessional behavior;
C. describe and demonstrate professional dress attire; and
D. engage in a mediation simulation.

SUGGESTED CLASS TIME

3–4 class periods

TERMS TO KNOW

Define the following terms:

A. intentional infliction of emotional distress;
B. mediation;
C. professionalism;
D. professional work attire;
E. due process of law;
F. ethics/ethical behavior;
G. political correctness;
H. professional image; and
I. workforce readiness.

PRELIMINARY ACTIVITY

Research codes of ethical behavior as well as standards of professional attitudes and dress in your respective career choices. Individually, make a list of ten words that describe professionalism. In small groups, compile your individual lists into one. From the compiled list, choose five words that you believe best reflect professionalism and explain why you selected them.

WHO'S IN THIS STORY?

Natalia Lopez, 22
FELIX Marketing
Intern

Cameron Knox, 37
FELIX HR
Supervisor

© Shutterstock/Maksim Shmeljov

Parker Cobb, 27
FELIX HR
Benefits Manager

© Shutterstock/vgstudio

Kenny Hyde, 28
FELIX IT
Specialist I

Min Kwon, 38
FELIX HR Director

© Shutterstock/Dragon Images

SETTING

Atlanta, FELIX Headquarters—HR Department and Employee Cafeteria

CASE SCENARIO

Upon consulting with Parker, Mynx chooses not to resign from her position as an IT Specialist II. Based on tenure, income, and job location, Mynx knows that FELIX is still the best place for her to work. Besides, she has friends and a support system in Atlanta.

Mynx also decides not to file a formal complaint with HR or meet with her supervisor because she discarded all of the evidence that would have upheld her claim. Not initially understanding the value of such evidence, she makes a mental note to always document and save it in the future. She recalls how, during the meeting, Parker stressed the importance of documenting the alleged harassment from Kenny and other FELIX employees. Parker informed her that such cases may be difficult to prove and that documentation is key to supporting her allegations. As he closed their meeting, Parker reminded her that all accused employees are subject to due process, meaning that they must receive notice of the allegations as well as have an opportunity to be heard and respond to the allegations in a hearing.

After his meeting with Mynx, Parker relays her statements and concerns to Cameron. She reiterates that Mynx will have to file an official complaint before HR can formally investigate. It has been over two weeks since Parker first spoke to Cameron about this matter.

Parker's Office, 9:17 a.m.

Parker: Cameron, how are we going to help Mynx?

Cameron: Parker, you already know the process. HR can't do anything until David . . . I mean, Mynx files an official complaint. I'm not sure what else you want me to do. You're obviously irritated with how Mynx says she's being treated, but you also seem to be taking this rather personally.

Parker: Personally?

Cameron: Yes, personally. You have mentioned this situation to me every day over the last two weeks. You've said, "I wonder if anything else has happened to Mynx? I wonder when she'll file an official complaint." You may not be aware of this, but you've done it.

Parker: I don't think it's personal. It's just that it's been over two weeks since Mynx and I had our meeting. Do you remember when I told you that I saw Kenny, Aaron, and the other guys bothering Mynx in the cafeteria? I only fully understood what was happening when she later came to my office to speak to me. No one should be treated like this at work or anywhere else for that matter. I want to know what's going on is all.

Cameron: Parker, think about it. If Mynx hasn't filed a formal complaint, is she really that concerned about this situation? Didn't she tell you that she could handle it herself?

Parker (*sighing heavily*): Yes, she did, but I know in my gut that something is going to happen. I can feel it.

Cameron: Wait a minute. What are you feeling? Why do you think something is going to happen? Remember this. Our job is to deal with only the facts. I've never seen you this preoccupied over a case. That's not like you at all. Just make sure that you're maintaining a professional distance and are not becoming personally involved. You're making me wonder what is really going on here.

Parker: I don't know what you mean. After all, you haven't been very professional lately, Cameron.

Cameron: Don't go there with me, Parker. You're the one who's always asking questions and running to everyone's rescue. Don't forget you work in HR. People should come to us. You could be unknowingly compromising yourself by being nosy.

Parker: We'll have to agree to disagree. What you call nosy, I call zealous HR representation. The actions of these men are extreme and outrageous. The notes. The songs. The taunting. According to Mynx, she's even started having difficulty concentrating at work, breathlessness, headaches, and nausea. She did not experience any of these symptoms before encountering these four men at FELIX. Until now, I have always felt comfortable here. Of late, that has been taken away from Mynx . . . and from me. She's being mistreated. Their behavior makes me wonder if they've treated anyone else this way. We have an important role in HR. If we can't help, who can?

Cameron: Wait, when did these symptoms start? I don't recall you mentioning this information before.

Parker (*pausing*): I didn't.

Cameron: Why not?

Parker: Well, I may have *innocently* checked to see how Mynx has been doing. She told me this information a few days ago.

Cameron (*rubbing her temples*): Parker, what are you doing? You know better than to go searching for information. See, this is what I mean about maintaining a professional distance. Do you have a personal agenda here?

Parker: Cameron, come on. You're being awfully politically correct. Really? Me? Have a personal agenda? I'm just trying to be helpful.

Cameron: Well, you're being awfully politically correct now. Using David's . . . oh my goodness, I've got to get this right. I mean Mynx's situation to encourage her to file a complaint is unethical and unprofessional. Your unsolicited helpfulness can get our department in hot water. Besides, Mynx didn't exactly prepare us for her transition. Did you ever consider that?

Parker: I can't believe you just said that. Also, if I'm being politically correct, then you're being hypocritical. You haven't been exactly professional lately yourself. Your home life has been impacting your work life for a while now.

Cameron: What?! I never expected any special consideration because of issues in my personal life and neither should Mynx. That's why I haven't left Brandon yet. I'm still carefully exploring the options that Cooper Jones gave me. Mynx needs to do her job and deal with it like the rest of us! Just like I'm trying to do!

Parker: Cam, I didn't mean to . . .

Cameron: No! This conversation is over! I'm leaving.

Cameron exits Parker's office. Frustrated and regretting that he offended Cameron, Parker tries to refocus and complete paperwork until lunch time.

In the cafeteria, 1:07 p.m.

Taking a late lunch, Parker is sitting alone in the cafeteria. At a nearby table, Kenny Hyde and Natalia Lopez are eating snacks during their afternoon break. Parker rises to purchase an orange and intentionally walks past their table to the counter.

Kenny: Hey, Parker. How's it going? How's David?

Kenny laughs quietly.

Parker (*turning red*): What did you just say?

A puzzled Natalia looks back and forth between Kenny and Parker.

Kenny: I just asked how you and David are doing. That's all. Is there a problem?

Parker: You knows there's a problem. You know what you're doing. I'm watching you, Kenny. If your behavior continues, then there will be consequences.

Kenny turns to Natalia.

Kenny (*looking serious*): Natalia, I believe that Parker may be threatening me. I just might have to file a grievance.

Parker: I am not threatening you. What you are doing is criminal. And you, Natalia. How can you sit there when you know what he's been doing? The way that everyone talks about how you dress like you're going to the club rather than to work . . . I would think that you would be more careful about the company that you keep.

Natalia: What? What are you talking about?

Kenny: Please leave us alone so we can finish our break, Parker. I believe that you're making Natalia uncomfortable.

Cameron enters the cafeteria looking for Parker so that she can apologize for how their conversation ended. Since they are friends as well as colleagues, she wants to resolve their dispute quickly and not allow it to linger. She has enough conflict with her husband; she does not want it with Parker as well. She sees him engaging in conversation with Kenny and Natalia. Cameron notices that Parker looks upset as she walks over to the group.

Cameron: Hi, everyone. Is everything okay?

Parker: No. Kenny is causing problems as usual.

Cameron: Kenny? Parker? What's going on?

Neither Kenny nor Parker respond to Cameron.

Cameron: Natalia, can you tell me what happened since neither of them will?

Natalia: I have no idea. Apparently, Parker has a problem with the way I dress.

Cameron: I beg your pardon? What's wrong with your outfit today?

Kenny: Nothing's wrong with her outfit. She looks greats like she always does. I thought we were having a friendly conversation with Parker until he started going off.

Parker: Whatever, Kenny. I don't have time for this.

Parker turns to walk away from the table. Cameron says good-bye to Kenny and Natalia and quickly walks to catch up with Parker.

Cameron: Parker, wait. Let's go to my office. Better yet, maybe we should talk to Min. We may need some assistance here.

Ten minutes later in Min's office . . .

Min: These are serious allegations, Parker. Are you sure that you want to file a grievance against Kenny?

Parker: Well, why wouldn't I?

Min: Have you done anything to bring these actions upon yourself? If you file a grievance, then he will respond.

Parker: What is the problem with everyone around here? Mynx is being bullied and harassed and no one seems to care. If I were a woman claiming sexual harassment, would you have said that to me?!

Cameron: Parker, calm down.

Min: Yes, Parker, calm yourself.

Parker: I'm filing a grievance today, and I expect this to be handled as soon as possible.

Parker abruptly stands up and leaves Min's office without saying another word.

The next day . . .

Natalia goes to HR to speak to Cameron regarding Parker's comments about her attire.

Natalia: Cameron, do you have a moment?

Cameron: Yes. Have a seat. How may I help you?

Natalia: Thanks. Listen, this is really awkward for me. I just wanted to tell you that I didn't know anything about the Kenny and Parker situation.

Cameron: Okay.

Natalia: I do have a question for you though. Parker mentioned yesterday that some people have been talking about how I dress? Is it true?

Cameron: Well, I won't discuss any rumors, but we can have a chat about professional dress in the workplace if you want.

Natalia: What do I need to know? I thought that I was dressing appropriately because this is a place of fashion. At DAF, we dressed like this all of the time.

Cameron: I understand, but you're in a professional environment now. You are no longer a student, and FELIX is not your runway. Let's review some do's and don'ts for appropriate corporate and business casual attire.

A few weeks later . . .

Min and Daryl from the legal department are holding a mediation session with Parker and Kenny.

DISCUSSION QUESTIONS

1. What is the due process procedure that HR must follow? When an employee is accused of violating a company policy that results in harm to another employee or the company, is this employee automatically guilty or liable for the violation? Explain your answer.
2. Who exhibits unprofessional behavior in this case scenario? Give examples to support your answer.
3. Are Parker's motives in helping Mynx purely professional? Should Parker be engaging in an investigation into Mynx's allegations without her filing a formal complaint? What ethical issues arise with how Parker has handled this situation? Explain your answer.
4. Does Mynx have a case against Kenny for intentional infliction of emotional distress? What does Mynx need to do to successfully prove this claim?
5. Review Parker and Kenny's interaction in the cafeteria. In a brief script, state how Parker and Kenny could have modified their conversation to be more professional toward one another.
6. What is professional work attire? What are the possible direct and indirect consequences of not dressing professionally in the workplace? How would unprofessional dress impact a client's view of the company? How would it impact your professional image?
7. Should Parker be reprimanded for addressing Natalia's attire without consulting with her immediate supervisor, Ernesto? Or, should Parker have addressed Natalia's attire with her in private? If so, how? How could Parker's outburst impact work relationships? Explain your answer.
8. What is the purpose of mediation between Parker and Kenny? Are Min and Daryl the best persons to mediate this session? Are there any possible conflicts of interest with Min mediating between Parker and Kenny? If so, how can the conflict(s) be resolved? What are some goals for this mediation session?

SELF-ASSESSMENT

How do you perceive those who dress professionally versus those who do not? How important are first impressions? Reflect on a time when you were or were not professionally dressed. Assess the response(s) that you received or felt.

APPLICATION ACTIVITIES

1. A co-worker confides in you and says that her supervisor informed her that she was dressed inappropriately. She asks you for advice on how to respond in writing. Assist her with a written response to her supervisor.
2. In small groups, conduct a mediation exercise with students acting as Min, Daryl, Parker, and Kenny. Research and follow the most recent standards of conduct for mediators.
3. Find articles that state how students are not prepared for the workforce. Identify areas in which your academic program is intentionally preparing you for the work environment. Based on your findings, what activities could your program require you to engage in to maximize workforce readiness?

CASE STUDY 24

WORKPLACE HORROR*

OBJECTIVES

Students will be able to:

A. define workplace violence;
B. develop a workplace domestic violence (DV) prevention policy; and
C. recognize how DV incidents impact the organization and its members.

SUGGESTED CLASS TIME

3–4 class periods

TERMS TO KNOW

Define the following terms:

A. workplace violence;
B. DV prevention; and
C. zero-tolerance policy.

PRELIMINARY ACTIVITY

Research the number of deaths that occur in the workplace as a result of DV. Locate the top five companies in your respective discipline. Research whether they have a formal workplace DV prevention policy in place. Share your results with the class.

WHO'S IN THIS STORY?

Min Kwon, 38
FELIX HR Director

© Shutterstock/Dragon Images

Parker Cobb, 27
FELIX HR Benefits Manager

© Shutterstock/vgstudio

Cameron Knox, 37
FELIX HR Supervisor

© Shutterstock/Maksim Shmeljov

Brandon Knox, 37
Cameron's Husband

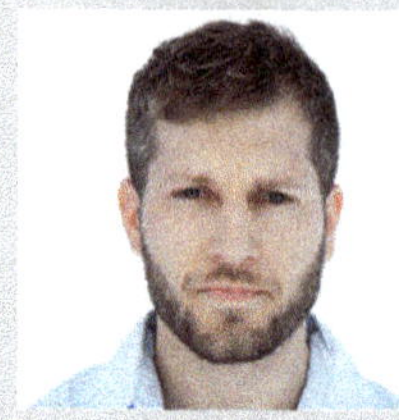

© Shutterstock/wavebreakmedia

April Knox, 7
Cameron's Daughter

SETTING

Atlanta, FELIX Headquarters; Cameron Knox's Home; and Parker Cobb's Home

CASE SCENARIO

Cameron Knox's Home, 7 a.m.

Cameron could sense that it was a matter of time before Brandon made good on his promises. If she ever told Brandon that she needed some space, he would become even more violent. The bruises she sees on her body are a constant reminder that he will do anything to obtain the stock information. Brandon, the husband she loves, has forced her to compromise her integrity. Now, she risks losing her beloved daughter April. Although her daughter is only seven years old, she is a smart child. April knows that her mommy is in trouble. She has witnessed the beatings and heard the arguments, which is why she no longer talks when her father is present. Toweling his hair after taking a shower, Brandon walks in the bedroom and sees Cameron packing.

Brandon: Where do you think you're going?

Cameron: Did you forget that I have to attend a conference in New York City for two days?

Brandon places the towel around his neck and grabs Cameron's arm and squeezes it tightly, causing her to wince.

Brandon: Well, I guess that's all right. Don't forget what we talked about Cameron. I need that information.

Cameron: I know. Please, Brandon, you're hurting me.

Brandon releases his grip slowly and pushes her away.

Brandon: Are you packed already? Why do you have two suitcases?

Cameron: My flight leaves at 8 p.m. I told you that April was going to stay with a friend so that she can remain in school. I know that you have a lot to do. If you have to take her to ballet and gymnastics after school, then you would have to leave work early. I asked Ginny's mom to watch her while I'm away. I'll be back on Saturday. She's going over there tonight so that your morning workout won't be interrupted.

Brandon *(watching Cameron closely for signs of deceit)*: Fine. You just make sure that both of you are back here on Saturday!

Cameron: Yes, of course, Brandon.

Cameron's escape is a well-crafted lie. She and April are going to stay with Parker tonight. Following Cooper Jones' lead, she is going to confess to the company about the insider trading offense and tell the authorities about the coercion and abuse. She is hoping for the best. Both Cameron and April live a life of fear and uncertainty. They know what roles to play in public, and they know how to keep silent. Cameron worries about her daughter's well-being and would never leave her alone with Brandon.

Later that evening, Cameron and April arrive at Parker's house . . .

Parker: Come on in, ladies. I have you both in the guest bedroom. Is that okay?

Cameron: Thanks so much, Parker, for being such a good friend. I appreciate you letting us stay here. I know the risk you're taking, and I'm sorry.

Parker grabs Cameron's hands and rubs them gently. He looks Cameron in the eyes and smiles slightly.

Parker: Don't be silly. We'll figure this out together. Well, hello there, Ms. April. How are you, honey?

April: I'm fine, thank you. Mom, I'm hungry.

Cameron: Oh goodness, I forgot we haven't had anything to eat. Parker . . .

Parker: I'm already on it. Do you like spaghetti?

April: Yes! I love it, Mr. Parker.

Parker makes April a plate of spaghetti and urges Cameron to eat something, but she refuses. After April eats, Cameron gets her ready for bed. The following day, Cameron prepares to take April to school and to meet with FELIX's senior executives.

April: Good morning, mom.

Cameron: Good morning, sweetheart. Do you have everything you need for school?

April: Yes. Is Mr. Parker coming with us to drop me off at school?

Cameron: Oh, no, honey. I'm going to take you to school and meet Mr. Parker at work. Let's go, okay? Do you remember what we talked about last night?

April: Yes, mom. I remember. See you later, Mr. Parker.

Parker: Have a great day, honey. I will see you later on.

April: Okay.

Cameron: Go on out to the car, sweetie. I'll be there in a minute.

Cameron turns to Parker and tells him about the lie that she told Brandon. Parker looks worried. He asks her about her plans should Brandon discover that she is still in town with April.

Parker: Cameron, what are you going to do if he drops by the school this morning to verify your story? He's a paranoid man! He knows you're afraid and would try to leave him. Please call the police before someone gets hurt!

Cameron: Parker, it will be fine. He hardly ever visits the school. I need to think about what I'm going to say this afternoon. Can I just focus on one thing at a time?

Parker: You're right. I'm sorry. I'll see you at work. You don't think he followed you here last night do you?

Cameron: Of course not. Why would he do that?

Parker: I don't know. I guess I'm being paranoid now. I'll see you in a few.

Cameron: I need to get April to school. I also need to contact Ginny to see if she can take

April to her afterschool activities. I'll see you soon.

Cameron leaves to take April to school and arrives just in time to speak with Ginny. Ginny agrees to take April to her afterschool activities. So far, everything is going as planned. When Cameron arrives at work, she hides from everyone for most of the day. The meeting that Parker scheduled with senior executives would come soon enough. She looks at her phone and discovers that it has been off since last night. She forgot to turn it on. Cameron begins to panic when she realizes that Brandon left her several messages. She forgot to call him when her imaginary plane landed. She needs to call him but does not know what to say, so she texts him instead.

Cameron: Sorry, I forgot to call you last night. I was so tired, I just went to bed. How are you this morning? ☺

Brandon: I called you several times! Didn't I tell you to call me when you landed?! You didn't even leave a number for April's friend's mother. What are you up to, Cameron? Are you trying to leave me?!

Cameron: I swear, I'm not up to anything. No! I am at a conference. Baby, I'm in a session now. I will call you later. I have some of the information you want. I will send it when I'm finished with this session.

Brandon: Good! I'll be waiting. What time are you returning on Saturday? I will pick up April after her gymnastics class. I'll keep her with me to make sure you do what you promised. Where is she? Give me the address and call her friend's mom and tell her that I'm coming. I don't want people questioning me when I get there.

Cameron: Okay . . . But are you sure? I wanted to make things easier for you while I was away. Brandon, honey, I can pick her up on Saturday. Try to relax. Just leave her where she is. She will have a great time with her friends and you can relax.

Brandon: Okay, fine. I'll call you later. Keep your phone on!!!!

Cameron: Okay, I will. I have to go!

Cameron panics and does an overhead page for Parker to come to her office.

Parker: What's wrong? Are you okay?

Cameron: No, Parker, I think he suspects something!

Parker: Why would you say that?

Cameron: I forgot to turn on my phone last night, and when I finally did, I had several voicemails from Brandon.

Parker: Did you play it off like you had forgotten to turn it on after you landed?

Cameron: Well, yes, but I'm not sure he bought that! Why are people leaving?

Parker: Cameron, it's close to 5 p.m. You haven't left your office all day. Have you eaten?

Cameron: I ate an apple and drank a cup of coffee. I'm not very hungry. I'm too stressed to eat. Are the senior executives in the conference room?

Parker: Yes, some of them are already speaking with Cooper Jones. Cameron, I need for you to come to my office and fill out some forms. Min told me to tell you to write down everything that happened. She knows that we're friends, so she figured it would be easier if I told you. Oh, the investigator needs a thorough account of the insider trading. Try to remember as much as you can, Cam. I know this is overwhelming for you.

Cameron: Okay, I'll be there in a minute.

Sitting at her desk, Cameron tries to mentally access the gaps in her story. She does not want to say or do anything that would trigger Brandon's rage. She needs to focus, but too many issues are competing for her attention. She says a silent prayer and prepares to leave her office when she hears her phone chime.

Brandon: How's the weather in NYC?

Cameron: I don't know. I'm inside the hotel in a meeting room. I haven't gone outside yet. Why?

Brandon: Because you're not in NYC, Cameron! You're such a liar! You are at the office. What are you up to, Cameron?! Don't do anything stupid!

Cameron: No, I'm not Brandon. I left the car at work. Parker took me to the airport. Please calm down!

Cameron is visibly shaken and upset. What if Brandon stops by the office and finds her there with the investigator? She rushes to Parker's office to tell him what happened. Most of the workers are gone for the day. The only light in the building comes from Parker's office and the conference room.

Cameron: Parker! He knows!

Parker: He knows what?

Cameron: He knows that I didn't go to New York City for a conference.

Parker: Why would he know that? There is a conference going on at the hotel, and you booked a room in your name. Do you think he would call to check up on you after he texted and you responded?

Cameron: Yes! I do! I mean . . . I don't know! Oh my goodness! I should have crafted a better lie. He's probably on his way! Should we alert Joe at the security office?

Parker: No. Calm down, Cameron. Let's think! The less people who know, the better. Text Brandon back to put his mind at ease.

As Cameron is texting, there is a light knock on the door. Parker glances nervously at Cameron and places his index fingers to his lips, signaling for her to keep quiet.

Parker: Yes?

No one answers. The light knocking continues. Parker motions Cameron to hide behind the door and swings it open.

Min: Hi, Parker.

Parker *(quickly exhaling and grabbing his chest)*: Oh, Min, hi!

Min: Are you feeling well, Parker? You look pale.

Parker (*breathing deeply*): Oh, no, I'm fine. What can I do for you?

Min: I just wanted to let you know that we'll be ready in about 15 minutes. Have you seen Cameron?

Parker (*clearing his throat*): Ah, she was in her office. Maybe she went to the restroom or something.

Min: Okay. Well, everyone is almost here. We are waiting for Phil to arrive. As soon as he gets here, we'll start the meeting. Please make sure that she's completed the paperwork you and I discussed. I'll be in my office until you guys are ready. We need to show our support for Cameron, so we will all walk over to the meeting together.

Parker: Sure thing!

Parker closes the door and releases another sigh of relief. He is just as nervous as Cameron.

Parker: Okay, Cameron, you need to finish this paperwork quickly. I'm a nervous wreck.

Cameron: Me, too. Where do you want me to start?

Ten minutes later, there is another light knock at the door. Assuming that it is Min again, Parker opens it wide. He is shocked to see who it is.

Brandon: Move!

Parker: Oh my goodness! Brandon, please put down the gun.

Brandon: Keep quiet, or I'll shoot you in the face! Sit down over there in the corner, and shut up. I'd better not hear you say another word!

Cameron (*screaming*)**:** Brandon, what . . .

Brandon: Shut up! Do you really think I'm that stupid, Cameron? I'm the mastermind behind this plan. I told you what to do! Remember? Don't patronize me and act like I haven't thought about this. You know me better than that!

Cameron: I'm not patronizing you! I just . . . I'm scared, Brandon. Parker found out about the illegal trading. If he found out, don't you think someone else in the office may have figured it out too? Please, think of April. You don't want to do this, not here. We can talk about it. Let's go home. Please!

Brandon: Shut your mouth, and stop all that crying. I warned you, Cameron, a hundred times over, that if you ever betrayed me, I was going to kill you. Did you think I was lying? I can show you better than I can tell you! You look surprised to see me. I guess you're wondering how I found you. I have a tracking device on your phone that is linked to one of my accounts. When you didn't pick up on my calls last night, I checked to make sure that you arrived in New York. Imagine my shock when I found out that you were nowhere near New York!

Parker: Please, Brandon. Put the gun down.

Brandon points the gun in Parker's direction.

Brandon *(viciously eyeing Parker)*: Parker, if you move one more time, I'm going to shoot you first! Don't test me. You should have minded your own business. All of this is your fault. I should put a bullet in you just to teach you a lesson. What were you writing there, Cameron? Let me see that! Are these dates of when you told me about the stock prices? Is this a confession?!

Cameron: No, I had to come down here to help Parker prepare for the meeting.

Brandon: Why you lyin' . . .

Shots fired.

DISCUSSION QUESTIONS

1. What can employers do to help protect employees from workplace violence? How can management and employees work together to minimize workplace violence incidents?
2. Did Parker have a legal responsibility to report Cameron's insider trading and DV incidents? What should Parker have done in this situation? Based on his behavior, can you deduce whether FELIX had a zero-tolerance policy toward workplace violence against or by their employees?
3. What is FELIX's responsibility following a workplace incident? If you were Min, what would be your first course of action?
4. Why do you think Cameron, an HR professional, did not report her husband's coercive tactics against her? What else could cause employees to not report violent incidents in the workplace?
5. If Cameron and Parker survive this ordeal, who should attend therapy and why? What resources do employers have to assist employees with traumatic experiences? Can an employer force an employee to seek mental health treatment? Explain.
6. Is there a difference between workplace violence and domestic violence? Explain.

SELF-ASSESSMENT

Reflect on what you have learned about domestic and workplace violence. As an employee, what would you do if you were in Cameron's situation? Would you report the incident to your employer, or would you try to hide it as Cameron did? Explain.

APPLICATION ACTIVITIES

1. Research the number of deaths that occur in the workplace from employee dissatisfaction in your particular industry. Compare your findings to those discovered in the Preliminary Activity. Create a mini-PowerPoint presentation. Present the information to the class.
2. Develop a policy on workplace violence using guidance from OSHA's Safety and Health Management Program Guidelines. Identify vital elements that should be a part of the development and implementation of a valuable safety and health management system.
3. Research the financial costs associated with DV and how those costs impact an organization.
4. Research organizations in your city that offer safe housing for DV survivors. Create a pamphlet or brochure that informs your peers of their options.

CASE STUDY 25

A WORKPLACE IN SHAMBLES*

OBJECTIVES

Students will be able to:

A. create internal and external bad news messages;
B. outline how an employee assistance program functions; and
C. analyze how workplace violence may impact a company.

SUGGESTED CLASS TIME

3–4 class periods

TERMS TO KNOW

Define the following terms:

A. employee assistance program;
B. duty-based ethics;
C. outcome-based ethics;
D. open-door policy; and
E. Violence Against Women Act (VAWA).

PRELIMINARY ACTIVITY

Conduct research on employee assistance programs. What kinds of services are offered and under what circumstances? Should there be a duty-based or an outcome-based ethical approach to services provided? Why or why not?

WHO'S IN THIS STORY?

Phil Fox, 64
FELIX CEO

© Shutterstock/Ruslan Guzov

Trish Fox, 38
FELIX Marketing Manager

© Shutterstock/DC Studio

Felix Fox, 40
FELIX CFO

© Shutterstock/doodko

Ernesto Diaz, 45
FELIX Marketing Supervisor

© Shutterstock/Andresr

Min Kwon, 38
FELIX HR Director

© Shutterstock/Dragon Images

Parker Cobb, 27
FELIX HR Benefits Manager

© Shutterstock/vgstudio

Mary Kate Harrison, 49
FELIX Senior Attorney

© Shutterstock/kurhan

DeAngelo Moore, 42
FELIX Accounting Supervisor II

© Shutterstock/Hugo Felix

Blake Golden, 51
FELIX PR Agent

© Shutterstock/pkchai

SETTING

Atlanta, FELIX Headquarters and Parker Cobb's Home

CASE SCENARIO

FELIX Headquarters, 11:27 p.m.

Phil: Thank you, detectives. If we remember anything else, we'll let you know once you return in the morning. We have a long night ahead of us. We're preparing to brief our employees about what happened tonight before everyone arrives tomorrow. By mid-morning, you should be able to speak with our employees.

Phil walks the homicide detectives to the elevator and then reenters the meeting room where Parker, Min, DeAngelo, Ernesto, Mary Kate, and Blake sit in silence. Everyone is thinking about what Min revealed to them earlier. At about 5 p.m., Min was in her office when she heard gunshots, which were immediately followed by loud screams. After calling FELIX security, Min locked herself in her office. Then, she telephoned both Cameron and Parker, but she only received their office voicemail. Min waited impatiently for security to hopefully tell her that everything was fine. Unfortunately, it was not. Joe discovered Cameron in her office gasping for breath from two gunshot wounds to the chest. Parker was unconscious on the floor next to her. He immediately called 911.

After paramedics arrived at the scene, Cameron was rushed to the hospital. She was pronounced dead on arrival. Parker was treated for an injury that he received upon hitting his head on Cameron's desk; he had fainted when Cameron was shot. After getting stitches for his head injury, Parker was questioned by homicide detectives and then released after spending hours in the hospital. The detectives suggested that he go home to rest, but Parker insisted on returning to FELIX headquarters. He did not want to be alone.

Blake: Everyone, I know that you're all still processing this tremendous loss. However, we must prepare a statement for tomorrow morning. It is imperative that we're prepared to inform FELIX employees of what happened tonight.

Parker: My goodness, do we really have to do this right now?! Cameron was just shot and killed by her husband! I heard her screaming! It was awful! And, then it just all went dark!

Min reaches over to Parker.

Min: Parker . . . I know you're hurting. Cameron and you are . . . were very close. Don't you think it's best that you go home?

Felix: Wait, Min. I hate to say this, but Parker may need to stay because he knows the most about what happened.

Min: I understand that, but no one except Parker was with Cameron when this happened. I only heard the gunshots. Cameron was my colleague, but she was Parker's colleague and friend. Let's not be insensitive.

Ernesto: He's already given his statement to the police and he told us what happened. Parker, go home. Get some rest. We'll see you in the morning.

Trish: Tomorrow morning? I think that Parker should take some time off to recuperate.

Parker: Please stop talking about me as if I'm not here! I'm fine! Cameron is not! She's dead! We need to focus on how to tell the employees tomorrow and catching her crazy husband who killed her.

Phil: Parker, I normally wouldn't tell you what to do, but I think it's best that you go home.

Parker gasps as he begins to sob.

Parker: I can't believe that this happened! I can't believe that Cameron's gone! And what about April? She's only seven years old. Who's going to break the news to her?

Phil: Parker, you've experienced unbelievable trauma today. You really need to rest. I'm sorry, but this isn't a suggestion. I'll have my driver take you home. Try to get some sleep.

As Parker rises to leave, everyone tells him good night. After he exits the room, Blake gets everyone's attention.

Blake: We need to prepare two external messages that relay bad news. The first one is for the media. We'll release a statement tomorrow. The second one is for FELIX employees. Delivering the bad news within a timely manner is essential. You must choose your channels of communication. Will you deliver the message in writing or in person? You want to acknowledge the situation by demonstrating concern, provide details and clarification for what happened if possible, describe the immediate effect this incident has on FELIX, and emphasize the company's responsive resolutions. Also, what kind of employee services can you offer to assist them in this situation?

Everyone looks around the table, but no one responds.

Blake: Anyone?

Blake looks around the table. After a few moments of silence, Min speaks.

Min: I understand that this is important, but do we have to do it tonight? This has been a horrible day.

Mary Kate: Yes, it has been. Yet, I don't suggest waiting to inform employees. Tomorrow's message will be hard enough. Being unprepared will not help.

DeAngelo: Phil. Felix. Maybe we need to close the office out of respect for Cameron. Then, we can take a few days to prepare the statements. We can email all of the employees and ask them to report to work on Monday.

Ernesto: What about the detectives? They need to speak with everyone tomorrow.

DeAngelo: Well, most FELIX employees don't know anything. They will probably only need to talk to Min and Parker. Plus, the yellow crime scene tape is bound to unnerve everybody. We don't need an office panic.

Ernesto: Speaking of a panic . . . Felix, are we going to increase office security?

Felix: I don't think that we should wait until Monday.

DeAngelo: Has anyone informed Cameron's parents? What is going to happen to her daughter April? There is so much to consider.

Mary Kate: We shouldn't make contact with her family. They may think about filing some type of lawsuit against FELIX.

Min: That's a bit harsh, Mary Kate. Her parents will be grieving terribly once they receive the news. I cannot imagine how they're going to feel.

Mary Kate: I know that, Min, but I'm thinking about what's best for the company. I'm not trying to be insensitive. Besides, the detectives told us that they would be in contact with Cameron's family.

Blake: Everyone, please listen. I know that it's hard, but you must focus on what you can handle within FELIX. I will give you a few minutes to discuss what you want to do.

Blake exits the room.

Felix: Dad, it's already after midnight. What do you think? Do we remain open tomorrow? When and how do we inform the media and employees? Do we contact Cameron's parents? What do you want us to do?

Standing, Phil begins to speak.

At Parker's home . . .

Parker lies on his bed looking at a picture that Cameron took at the last Christmas party. He blinks back the tears that threaten to fall. Maybe he should have called security when Cameron suggested it. He is unable to sleep because he continues to mentally replay the last moments of Cameron's life. He never had a chance to apologize to her.

DISCUSSION QUESTIONS

1. How has FELIX been negatively impacted by Cameron's murder? Despite the tragic situation, what can FELIX learn from this incident? In your answer, contemplate how FELIX's security measures, open-door policy, and training sessions can be improved and used to educate its workforce.
2. Is FELIX criminally and/or civilly liable because of Parker's decision not to reveal Cameron's physical abuse? If so, for what? Explain.
3. How can FELIX employees cope with the death of Cameron? How can the employee assistance program and VAWA benefit them? What services would you suggest?
4. How should management respond to employee questions regarding the safety of their workplace environment?
5. Revisit the comments made by Mary Kate. In the case scenario, Min believed that Mary Kate was being insensitive toward Parker. Was Mary Kate insensitive in her leadership role as a legal representative for FELIX or was she simply representing the interests of the company? Was Min making an emotional decision rather than a practical business decision? How can a balance of the two be established here in order to protect the company and show compassion for Cameron's death? Explain your answer.
6. Based on today's fast-paced business environment, what are the pros and cons of FELIX continuing with a regular business day after Cameron's murder? What is the best decision from a business perspective while acknowledging the emotional and mental needs of employees? Explain.
7. Reflect on the following ethical perspectives: duty-based (e.g., Kantian ethics) versus outcome-based (e.g., utilitarianism). Which perspective is better for FELIX? Which is more supportive of FELIX employees? Which do you prefer? Explain your answers.
8. From a managerial standpoint, what kind of support would you provide to Parker?

SELF-ASSESSMENT

Place yourself in Parker's position. What kind(s) of services would you need to recover from this traumatic experience? Based on these services, how would you assist the FELIX family in the healing process?

APPLICATION ACTIVITIES

1. In the case scenario, Blake informed FELIX management that two messages conveying bad news had to be created. Compose one or both of the following messages using the information that Blake relayed in the case scenario.
   a. Negative message to the media
   b. Negative message to FELIX employees
2. At the end of the case scenario, several questions were posed to Phil. Phil stands to provide his response to his employees. Write a one-page response stating how Phil should address these issues. Include strong support for your decisions.

BONUS ACTIVITIES

FAREWELL FELIX

As a class, discuss case studies 1-25, and complete the bonus activities. Acting as business managers, students should craft their own endings to the following prompts by referring to their knowledge, skills sets, and experiences. Use the facts provided in the case scenarios to determine the best solutions and outcomes. These bonus activities may be used for writing portfolios, additional projects, and/or parts of an exam.

Phil Fox sits in his office staring out of his window. The spectacular view of the city lights and skyline in the amazing downtown Atlanta area would normally bring him peace and tranquility. However today, this is not the case. Over the past year, FELIX has been embroiled in a number of negative incidents. As Phil reflects on how FELIX can improve to minimize future ethical, legal, and management issues, he wonders what else is happening in his company. To prepare for the final quarterly meeting, he asks his management team to create a compiled list of unresolved issues that require attention. His ultimate goal is to minimize these issues to foster a safer, healthier, and more diverse working environment.

The prompts below represent the management team's compiled list.

Prompt 1:

Adrienne Ray has been on paid leave for several weeks. She is inquiring as to whether she will return to FELIX. Conduct a negotiation and/or mediation simulation between Adrienne and FELIX representatives. Use the assignment sheet titled "FELIX v. Adrienne Ray Negotiation/Mediation Simulation Exercise" located in Appendix L. Your instructor may include additional facts as needed.

Prompt 2:

Based on your academic major(s), you have received a grant to open your own business. Considering all that you have learned in these case studies, create an employee handbook that addresses eight major ethical, legal, and/or management issues outlined in this text.

Prompt 3:

Choose one of the major ethical, legal, and/or management themes in the text. Compare the actions of the characters in the case scenarios to fictional characters or real people in a movie, TV show, or book. Citing at least three legal cases, predict the outcome of your favorite case scenario(s).

Prompt 4:

Select a workplace issue identified in the case studies. Design a newsletter to inform and educate your class on your chosen topic.

Prompt 5:

Mentally and physically exhausted from her treatment plan, Destinie finds it difficult to keep up with her work at FELIX. She is considering the recommendation of her best friend, Leila, to quit her job and focus on her health. Leila even offered to let Destinie stay with her free of charge until Destinie is better. Destinie could try to break her lease to move in with her friend while she recovers; however, mounting medical bills as well as her apartment rent, car note, and student loans are looming over her. Destinie's monthly credit card bill competes with her car note, and she just signed a new one-year lease two months ago. Distraught, Destinie wonders what her options are. Research bankruptcy and real estate law. Can Destinie break her lease? Is it advantageous for Destinie to file for bankruptcy? Will she be absolved of her student loans? Write a two-page plan detailing Destinie's best course of action. Present your findings to the class.

Prompt 6:

Before Cameron can even be buried, Brandon's mother begins a bitter custody battle with Cameron's parents for full custody of April. While April knows Brandon's mother much better because she lives less than an hour away, she once flew with her mother to Cameron's parents' home and lived with them for about three months during a particularly rocky point in Cameron's marriage. April sends cards for every occasion to Cameron's parents. Cameron's parents feel that Brandon's family has already taken their daughter from them. Now, they want to take the grandchild as well. Cameron's parents do not want Brandon's mother to have visitation rights. They do not want to talk to anyone in his family ever again. Research grandparents' rights in your state. Create a brochure that addresses the major considerations in custody cases. Who has a better chance of receiving custody of April? Will concessions have to be made? Create a presentation to share with the class.

Prompt 7

Kasia Scottsdale is performing well in her new position as HR secretary. Now eight months pregnant and only two months on the job, she is preparing to go on maternity leave. What preparations must she make at FELIX for her impending departure? Accordingly, how can the HR department prepare for her temporary absence? Devise a standard operations procedure (SOP) for what must be done in the event that an employee goes on temporary leave.

APPENDIX A

FOR THE INSTRUCTOR: KEY ISSUES TO CONSIDER IN THE CASE STUDIES

Review the following ethical, legal, and/or management issues included in each case study.

Case Study 1: An Addition to the FELIX Family

a. Application Process: Are the questions on the application and in the interview the best for an entry-level analyst in a finance department?

b. Interview Questions: Should Adrienne have asked or phrased her question (Would you feel comfortable speaking to your people on the corporate customer service line if a translator was needed?) to Andreas in this manner? Is this question discriminatory in nature?

c. Nepotism: Should Adrienne interview and influence hiring decisions when she has a preexisting relationship with Katherine? What consequences could her actions have?

d. Hiring Practices/Selection of Applicant: Was the best applicant selected in a fair and objective hiring process?

e. Conducting Background Checks: Is the FELIX background check policy overly broad? Consider the Equal Employment Opportunity Commission (EEOC) and its commentary on how employers should use background checks.

Case Study 2: Hiring Hodgepodge

a. Confidentiality: Is Adrienne violating confidentiality or being unethical by telling Katherine about FELIX hiring information? How could Adrienne's disclosure compromise FELIX?

b. Recording of a Conversation: Is it legal for Katherine to record the conversation without Adrienne's knowledge or consent? What collateral consequences could stem from the recording of the conversation?

c. Interview Questions: Based on Adrienne's interview questions, could Andreas sue FELIX for discrimination? If so, what type? If not, what other issues could arise from her questions?

d. Age Discrimination: Does Katherine have a valid age discrimination claim against FELIX?

Case Study 3: Incompetent Leadership—The Breeding Ground for Employee Sabotage

a. Leadership Style: Cite examples of incompetent leadership from the case scenario.
b. Competence: Is Felix a competent Chief Financial Officer? If not, how can he improve?
c. Nepotism: Does nepotism hurt the workplace when incompetent leaders are appointed/employees hired?
d. Professionalism: Do DeAngelo and Adrienne handle work pressures and stress professionally?

Case Study 4: Presenteeism—Weary, Worried, and Worn Out

a. Presenteeism: Dawali represents employees who have worked while being sick. Are they productive? Wasting company time and resources?
b. Worker Productivity: How is worker productivity impacted by health?
c. Employee Benefits: What types of benefits are available for sick employees at companies?
d. Health Concerns: What is the potential health impact on other employees when some are working in the office while they are sick?

Case Study 5: Friends, Where's the Money?

a. Pay Equity: Should Ernesto and DeAngelo be paid more than Min and Mary Kate? Is the pay difference based on fair standards like seniority or experience?
b. Social Media Use: Can Isabel, Ernesto's wife, cause problems for him at work by divulging information on social media that he revealed to her as his spouse?
c. Confidentiality: Does Ernesto violate confidentiality by discussing work issues with his wife?
d. Work-Life Balance: How can Ernesto establish more of a balance between his personal life and his work life?

Case Study 6: Friend, Colleagues, or Both?

a. Relationship Boundaries: Is the relationship between Cameron and Parker appropriate due to their supervisor–employee status at FELIX?
b. Domestic Violence: Is Cameron encountering domestic violence in her home life?
c. Balance of Home and Work: What are the challenges Cameron faces with balancing her personal and professional lives?
d. Insider Trading: Are Cameron and Brandon guilty of insider trading?

Case Study 7: No One's Bullied at Work, Right?

a. Workplace Bullying: Are Katherine and Parker being bullied at work?
b. Worker Dignity: In what ways should employees be respected in the workplace?
c. Leadership Style: Is Adrienne's leadership style commonplace or acceptable in the workplace? If so, should it be?

Case Study 8: The Ill-Prepared and Not-So-Focused Employee

a. Time Management: How can a rushed interview process cause problems with the hiring and selection process?
b. Worker Preparedness: Is Stephanie Lane prepared for the secretarial position at FELIX?
c. Employee Performance Review: How can employers conduct a proper performance review?
d. Alternative Options to Terminating Employment: When terminating an employee is not an option, how can an employer assist an employee in improving performance?
e. Communication Skills: Are verbal and written communication skills important at work? How can employees further develop these skills?

Case Study 9: Perceptions of Beauty

a. Professional Image/Hair/Grooming: What encompasses a professional image? Should weight be considered as a part of this image? Are there any hairstyles that would be unprofessional or inappropriate for the workplace? How does the employer determine the appropriateness of hairstyles?
b. Incivility in the Workplace: What constitutes workplace incivility? Should employees be disciplined because of inappropriate or offensive comments? Could incivility lead to legal action against the employer and/or employee?
c. The Impact of Obesity on the Workplace: Does obesity impact a company's insurance costs, worker productivity, and its corporate image?

Case Study 10: I'm Not Interested Anymore

a. Sexual Harassment: Is Daryl being sexually harassed by Destinie and two female employees? If so, is it hostile work environment or quid pro quo sexual harassment?
b. Workplace Dating: Is it appropriate for colleagues to date in the workplace? Should companies have a workplace dating/fraternization policy? What impact could dating a colleague have on one's career?

Case Study 11: Holiday Headlines

a. Business Etiquette: Is business etiquette required at after-hours business functions? What kinds of behavior are inappropriate at after-hours business functions?
b. Social Host Liability: Should businesses be liable for accidents that occur due to alcohol consumed at after-hours business functions?

Case Study 12: Competing in Style

a. Talent Pool/Employee Pipeline: How can companies develop a sustainable pipeline of quality talent?
b. Teamwork: How important are soft skills in working in teams?
c. First Impressions: Are first impressions significant in business? Can one recover from a negative first impression in an interview or competition?
d. Selection of Applicant/Hiring Criteria: For internship and employee selections, can companies legally consider appearance and physical attributes as a factor in hiring criteria?
e. Work Culture: How can applicants assess whether a potential place of employment has a suitable work culture for them?

Case Study 13: Employee Off-Duty Conduct

a. Business Client-Employee Personality Conflict: How should DeAngelo handle a personality conflict between Adrienne and a client?
b. Promotion Decision: What guiding factors are relevant in promotion decisions? Is seniority more important than worker productivity?
c. Gender Equality: What is gender bias? Is Adrienne treated differently by management because she is a woman?
d. Off-Duty Conduct: Should an employee be disciplined for conduct that is engaged in while off duty? How does employee off-duty conduct impact the employer?
e. Workplace Diversity Program: Should diversity programs be implemented in the workplace?

Case Study 14: A PR Nightmare

a. Public Relations: When does a company need to hire a public relations (PR) firm? For what can such a firm be used? How should PR messages be structured? Who should deliver these messages?
b. Agency Relationship: Who is the principal and who is the agent in the case scenario? Is the agent a special or general agent?
c. Crisis Communications: How should crisis communications be structured, and under what circumstances are they needed? When should a crisis communications plan be developed?

d. Employee Termination: Should Adrienne be terminated for making inappropriate statements in public when these statements are recorded and placed online? Is FELIX's reputation damaged based on Adrienne's statements? If so, how can FELIX's reputation be repaired?

Case Study 15: Crimes and Clauses

a. White Collar Crimes: Are Cameron, Brandon, and Brandon's brother guilty of insider trading, criminal fraud, wire fraud, and mail fraud?
b. Sarbanes-Oxley Act: What is the act? What does Section 406 require?
c. Contract: What is breach of contract? Who is liable in the scenario, and what are the resulting damages?
d. Morality Clause: Should morality clauses be included in contracts? Should FELIX have agreed to a morality clause with its supplier? What happens when a morality clause is violated?
e. Alternative Dispute Resolution (ADR): What are common ADR methods? What is the process for each method? Which may work best in employment and contract disputes?
f. Presenteeism: Does Cameron exemplify an example of presenteeism in the case scenario?

Case Study 16: The Battered and Bruised Insider

a. Friendships in the Workplace: Can friendships in the workplace lead to conflict between colleagues? How can these conflicts be effectively resolved?
b. Domestic Violence: Does FELIX have a responsibility to intervene and assist Cameron with the domestic abuse she is encountering?

Case Study 17: Ruffled Feathers—An Employee's Job Performance Reprimand

a. Employee Job Performance Review: How should Cameron and Min conduct Stephanie's subpar job performance review? How can management minimize conflict during the review?
b. Job Performance Feedback: When should a supervisor provide feedback to an employee? Should a supervisor wait until the formal performance review or correct an employee at the time of the improper action?
c. Cell Phone Usage at Work: When is it appropriate to use a cell phone during work hours? It is reasonable for an employer to restrict cell phone usage during work hours?
d. Supervisory Skills: Identify the strengths and weaknesses of Min and Cameron's supervisory skills.
e. Unfair Performance Evaluations: What legal recourse does an employee have upon receiving an unfair performance evaluation?

Case Study 18: Employee Conduct, Employer Liability

a. Employer Tort Liability: Can company delivery drivers like Randy make their employers liable for car accidents and injuries?

b. Cell Phone Usage While Driving: Is FELIX's cell phone usage policy too strict or overly broad?

c. Employee Retention: What factors should be considered when an employer must decide whether to retain an employee?

d. Professional Image: How can an employee's lack of professional image impact the company?

Case Study 19: Men Have Issues, Too

a. Work Accommodations for an Employee's Personal Life: Should Mary Kate change Daryl's work hours to accommodate his daughter's daycare schedule even though he recently received a promotion? Will she have to allow accommodations for other employees if she provides them for Daryl?

b. Human Resources (HR): Is Daryl required to report his former relationship with Destinie to HR since he is now in a supervisory position?

c. Emotional Hijacking: How does emotional hijacking occur in the workplace? How can an employee prevent it from happening?

d. Communication Styles: When does Daryl use direct and indirect messages with Mary Kate? How could he be more effective in his communication with her?

e. Harassment/Professionalism: Is Destinie's conversation with Daryl appropriate? Is she harassing Daryl? Are the two female workers harassing Daryl and his male colleague?

Case Study 20: Why Did They Hire You Anyway?

a. Pregnancy Discrimination: What is pregnancy discrimination, and how does it occur? Is Kasia experiencing this type of discrimination?

b. Hiring Process: Is the hiring process for Kasia fair?

Case Study 21: My Name is Mynx

a. Sexual Orientation/Workplace Bullying/Harassment: Is Mynx being harassed/bullied by Kenny, Aaron, and other employees due to being a transgender female? How should LGBT persons be treated at work by supervisors and other employees? Is she being subjected to a hostile work environment? If so, how should she respond?

b. Hate Crimes: Is Mynx the victim of a hate crime?

c. Restroom Accommodations: What restroom accommodations should be provided for Mynx and other male and female employees?

Case Study 22: The Big C

a. Family Medical Leave Act: What is the act, and who is eligible for it? How does the Act define a serious health condition? What employer responsibilities are required? What are the legal risks faced with employer certification mandates?
b. Extended Work Leave: What are the responsibilities of an employee and employer when extended leave is sought for medical reasons?

Case Study 23: Professionalism: Whose Business Is It Anyway?

a. Professionalism: What constitutes professional behavior and attire? Are Parker and Kenny acting professionally in the cafeteria? Does Natalia dress appropriately for work?
b. Due Process of Law: Are employees who are facing disciplinary action required to have notice and a hearing to respond to allegations?
c. Intentional Infliction of Emotional Distress: Are Kenny, Aaron, and the other two male employees liable for intentional infliction of emotional distress?
d. ADR: How can mediation help resolve employee conflicts? What can be gained through mediating such disputes?

Case Study 24: Workplace Horror

a. Workplace Violence: Are employers required to protect employees from internal and external sources of workplace violence? How should employers respond to incidents of workplace violence?
b. Employee Assistance Programs: What resources are available to employees? Under what circumstances may employees utilize these resources?

Case Study 25: A Workplace in Shambles

a. Impact of Workplace Violence: What impact could workplace violence have on FELIX? What additional security protocols should be implemented? How should FELIX management respond to concerned employees?
b. Employer Liability: Could FELIX be liable for Cameron's death?
c. Employee Assistance Program: How can employee assistance programs be used in response to workplace violence?
d. Ethics: Consider duty-based v. outcome-based ethical approaches in determining FELIX's ethical position.
e. Crisis Communication: How should FELIX management deliver bad news messages to employees and the media? What is the structure of these messages?

APPENDIX B

SAMPLE LESSON PLAN FOR CASE STUDY 1

FELIX Fashion Academy

Business Education Department

Course: *Contemporary* Legal Issues

Sample Lesson Plan for Case Study 1: An Addition to the FELIX Family

Instructor: Dr. Gonzalez

Title of Lesson: Unit 4—Employment Law and Business Practices

Topic: Interviewing and Hiring

Estimated Duration: 2 class sessions

Primary Learning Objective(s):

Students will:

- **a.** define the following terms: nepotism, outcome-based ethics, social contract ethics, and duty-based ethics;
- **b.** understand the interview process;
- **c.** distinguish between proper and improper interview questions;
- **d.** evaluate the fairness and objectivity of interviewing and selecting applicants; and
- **e.** create company background check and drug use policies.

Materials/Equipment/Technology Resources Needed:

1. *Training the Next Generation: Ethical, Legal, and Management Issues in the Workplace* case study text
2. Optional: Computer

Preliminary Preparation:

Students should complete the Preliminary Activity in Case Study 1.

Procedures/Activities:

Day One

- 10–15 minutes: As a class, create a list of all of the relevant interview questions for an entry-level analyst position that were compiled by students for the Preliminary Activity. Then students should select the top three to five most important questions and explain why.
- 20–25 minutes: Assign student roles based on the characters in Case Study 1. Students may read the case study as an entire class or in small groups. The instructor should guide students through the case content.
- 15–20 minutes: Answer the Discussion Questions.

Homework: Students should finish answering all of the Discussion Questions and review the definitions for duty-based, outcome-based, and social contract ethics. They should determine which ethical philosophy best fits them individually.

Day Two

- 10–15 minutes: Students will inform the class of their individual ethical philosophies selected during homework. As a class, engage in a discussion concerning the significance of ethical leadership.
- 25–30 minutes: Complete Application Activity 2. In pairs or in small groups, compose company background check and/or drug use policies.
- 10–15 minutes: Each student group should share the policies with the class.

Extension Activity: Case Study 1 Application Activities 1, 3, and/or 4 may be assigned as short- or long-term assignment.

APPENDIX C

PAPER TOWER EXERCISE

Goals

The goals of this exercise are

- to energize participants through an experience that relates to their work realities
- to allow participants to practice effective teamwork behaviors while accomplishing a task with an ambiguous goal
- to observe how participants react to change.

Materials

The materials needed for this exercise are

- newspapers (a 6-12-inch stack for each team)
- one roll of masking tape for each team
- one roll of string or twine for each team
- one pair of scissors for each team

Alternatively, this exercise can be done using firm tofu, food coloring, tooth-pics, plastic knives, and a few sheets of newspaper to protect the work areas. The food coloring is introduced when the "aesthetically appealing" criterion is added.

Time

- 45 minutes for set-up and exercise
- 30-60 minutes for debriefing

Instructions for Facilitators

1. Form groups of 10 or fewer participants (groups of five to seven people work best).
2. Each group should select and observer. Give observers instruction sheets.
3. Explain that the task is to build a free-standing tower, using only the material provided: newspapers, tape, string, and scissors.

4. Point out that the groups are in competition with each other. The criteria for the wining tower are height and structural soundness.
5. The groups have 25 minutes to complete their towers. After providing instructions, check for questions and begin timing.
6. Ten minutes into the exercise, add the criterion that the towers must also be aesthetically appealing. Let the groups know that the prize winner will be judged by a group voting process, and that each group gets one vote.
7. At 25 minutes, stop the activity. Direct the groups to clean up their areas. Give them five minutes to look at other towers and 10 to meet again as teams and decide for which tower to cast their votes.
8. Tally the votes, announce a winner, and award a prize.

Debrifing

Discuss the experience in teams. Instruct the observer to begin by sharing his or her comments, and then open up the discussion to the entire team. Each team should identify at least three things learned or three observation to share with the larger group. Take approximately 30 minutes for this part of the debriefing.

Bring the teams together for approximately 15 minutes to share what they have learned and observed with the larger group.

Key Points

In debriefing and discussion, be sure to discuss the following points. They may emerge spontaneously or the facilitator may raise them.

- What did the teams do well?
- What could the teams have done better?
- Did each team have a common vision at the start of implementation? At any time?
- Were everyone's ideas and inputs considered?
- Did the teams respond effectively to the change in criteria?
- How did the team handle time pressure?
- Were the team's tasks, resources, and roles clear to each team member?

Instructions for Observers

Instructions for observers can be found in Structured Experience 12-6. Located in the Appendix

Desired Outcome: Teams can use their experiences in the game to overcome work problems and relational issues.

"Adapted from materials found in *New Supervisor Training*, Published by the American Society for Training & Development (ASTD), 2002. All rights reserved."

APPENDIX D
NEPOTISM

Is hiring your nephew good for your company? What are the hidden costs and benefits? What policies should public companies follow?

BY RON PROKOSCH

The word "nepotism" in the business community originally referred to the hiring of relatives of the owner of the business. Today, this word has been extended to refer to the existence of employees within any organization that are related to each other either by blood or marriage. Is nepotism a cost or a benefit for an organization? How does it impact morale, loyalty, employee satisfaction, and a firm's ability to service their customers? These are critical questions that nearly every business must address. Researchers and business leaders agree that there are both costs and benefits to nepotism. However, there is disagreement on its overall impact on the bottom line of a business.

Research on the effects of nepotism has been opinion-based, rather than fact or incident based, and therefore views on the subject vary.

Nepotism pros and cons

The support for nepotism generally presents the following points:

- Lower recruiting costs: Nepotism allows firms to inexpensively identify a pool of candidates for positions (i.e. relatives of current employees). Firms that encourage hiring of relatives let their own employees do much of the recruiting for the company. However, where the objective is to hire the most qualified person for the job, limiting your market focus may not accomplish this objective.
- Lower training costs: Family members usually know a great deal about the company they are joining, and are more likely to be satisfied with what they find. It has been said that newly hired relatives are more dedicated to learning the job in order to "make their relatives proud".
- Lower employee turnover: It is suggested that family members are often the most dedicated employees. At several of the large businesses with whom we spoke, relatives of current employees are sought out because past experience has shown them to be the most motivated, conscientious workers. These firms have also found that related employees have significantly lower absenteeism.
- Higher level of commitment and a sense of ownership: Working on the same team with other relatives creates a greater sense of commitment and personal interest in the success of the company.

Employees who know that their family members may be impacted by their actions have an extra reason to want the company to grow and prosper.

- Higher level of loyalty: The opportunity to work with one's son, daughter or cousin is considered by most employees to be an intangible benefit of working for a company. However, in this day it would be very rare indeed, that a valued employee would stay with a company so that they might have an opportunity later to mentor their son or daughter as employees of the same firm.
- Higher level of morale: A "family-type" environment can boost the morale of all employees, and positively impact customer relations. Thomas Publishing, a large media company in New York City, views an employee's desire to bring another relative to the company as a great endorsement of the business. "It means that Thomas Publishing is a good, caring place." (Molofsky, 1999) However, for this to happen it is critical that such climates exist for all employees at all times, which requires strict guidelines.
- Higher trust levels: In organizations with a high degree of family involvement, there is often a higher level of commitment to "working through problems." As one executive stated, "at the end of the day they are all family, and they have to get along . . ."

In theory, this may support the case for employment of relatives. In practice though, there are many problems and difficulties with managing the trust factor so that it is consistent across all employees and the entire organization and not just reserved for the "inner circle."

Issues raised by nepotism

- Favouritism: Nepotism provides opportunities for favouritism in hiring, promoting and salary and bonus decisions. For this reason, companies with formal policies would generally not allow for family members to make such decisions.
- Discipline: Nepotism can create disciplinary problems for managers if they have to deal with a relative of another employee. Problems involving family members will often lead to a "polarization of perspectives" within the workplace, producing economic inefficiencies.
- Fraud: Nepotism can break down the system of "checks and balances" that are established in businesses. Some argue that this increases the likelihood of employee fraud. I recall one example from my own career where 19 employees had to be terminated. They worked in a large retail organization and would discount merchandise to a fellow employee/relative.
- Confidentiality: If is assumed that family members will be more likely to share confidential information with other family members which they might not otherwise do. This can result in suspicion, mistrust and paranoia or resentment and the general withdrawal of other employees in providing key information.
- Empowerment: Life as the "supervisor's son" can be difficult. Performance expectations are higher, and often nepots have a hard time determining if their success was due to their performance or because they are the boss' son.
- Personal issues: Firstly, not all family relationships are positive and mutually respectful. Personal issues and difficult relationships at home can make it difficult to work and interact effectively at work. Or, when workplace differences occur, inappropriate workplace behaviours such as shouting or pouting often arise and when such differences enter the home it can put a strain on the marriage or family relationships too. These behaviours are, of course, unprofessional and inappropriate and have a negative effect on the other employees who have to cope with this uncomfortable atmosphere.

Spouses in the workplace

One of the most challenging components of the nepotism debate is how to deal with spouses in the workplace.

Some large international corporations actively recruit married couples to work for the company as they believe it leads to happier marriages, healthier families, and ultimately, more motivated employees. But in these cases there are well-established and formal policies that are applied equally to all employees and which are often designed to address "conflict of interest" concerns.

Many more companies actively discourage spouses from working in the same company, as they believe it increases the opportunity for workplace tension and inefficiencies. This would be particularly so if the home relationship is under stress (i.e. pending separation or divorce).

Most intermediate and large organizations we researched have a written nepotism policy designed to avoid husbands and/or wives from supervising one another or being in a line of influence or the same chain-of-command. If employees choose to marry, one of the two in encouraged to transfer to a new department and out of the chain-of-command.

While it is illegal to terminate or otherwise discriminate on the basis of marital status, in the best interests of all concerned, most organizations draft their policies around an effort to avoid conflicts of interest.

Queens University, one of Canada's premier schools of industrial relations has a succinct policy on the employment of relatives. Their policy states:

"The University does not discourage, not prohibit the employment of more than one member of a family. However, due to the potential for conflicts of interest, the appointment of an immediate relative of a current employee to the same department is discouraged and requires prior declaration to the appropriate authority (usually the department head or director). This policy is in accordance with the 'Conflict of Interest and Conflict of Commitment' policy."

Procedure

Normally, such appointments should not occur in circumstances where one member of a family would exercise any form of supervision or direct influence over an immediate relative. For the purpose of this policy, an immediate relative is defined as spouse, common-law spouse, same sex partner, child, stepchild, sibling, parent, sister/brother-in-law, mother/father-in-law, grandparent and grandchild. This policy should also be applied in circumstances involving familial or intimate personal relationships.

Examples of conflicts of interest related to the employment of relatives include:

Hiring decisions
Promotions
Renewal of contracts
Performance evaluation
Disciplinary procedures
Salary considerations
Respect for confidentiality

In the event that this situation does occur, the supervisor in the relationship will not be the sole decision-making authority.

What is appropriate?

As dual-career couples become a larger part of the worldwide workforce, an increasing number of firms are forced to consider what should be an appropriate nepotism policy. If a policy is not in place, and enforced uniformly, legal issues, low morale and productivity and loss of staff can result.

The degree to which nepotism is an acceptable practice is based largely on what boundaries/guidelines are defined and applied consistently and equally across the entire organization and includes all employees. There are three "golden rules" regarding nepotism within an organization:

- The first is that the primary criteria when hiring or promoting must be finding the most qualified person for the job regardless of their relationship to members of the company.
- Second, every effort should be made to avoid potential conflict of interest situations. This is usually accomplished by ensuring that there is not direct line of influence or same chain-of-command of one relative over the other. BP Canada in their policy explicitly states, "Employment of relatives of employees in salary grades 17 and above is prohibited and is applicable to all categories of employment, including summer hiring."
- Third, policies and practices must be applied consistently and equally across the entire organization and be applicable to all employees.

Our literature research and survey of a variety of companies (beyond family-owned businesses) suggest that almost all have a policy or a least a practice that include these three principles.

A family-owned and operated business is nepotistic by nature, but even here owner-managers will testify to the difficulties of managing nepotism. However when the firm grows beyond the family or is held by multiple shareholders nepotism can lead to difficulties where the atmosphere is highly charged and suspicion and mistrust abound. It is extremely difficult to hold the talent required for a growing enterprise when by default (of a clear consistent policy) a climate of second-guessing, mistrust and concern for competence emerges.

Policies and practices around nepotism usually grow out of experience and the fact that most of Canada's top corporations have policies regarding nepotism would suggest that each must at some time have consumed a significant amount of management time to deal with issues of nepotism. So much so, that they found it necessary to have a policy to guide and pro-actively prevent nepotistic practices and potential conflict of interest situations.

(Ron Prokosch is President of Legacy Human Capital Group, which specializes in providing Human Resources Management services to small to medium size enterprises.)

APPENDIX E

UNDERLYING FACTORS CONTRIBUTING TO PRESENTEEISM AND ABSENTEEISM

By Tammy Prater and Kim Smith

INTRODUCTION

Modern workplaces must learn how to respond effectively to two trends which can cost employers billions of dollars each year in lost productivity: presenteeism and absenteeism. In 2010, the annual cost of presenteeism, $180 billion, surpassed the cost of absenteeism, $118 billion (Weaver, 2010). According to the ***American Heritage® Dictionary of the English Language*** (2006), presenteeism is defined as "the practice of coming to work despite illness, injury, anxiety, etc., often resulting in reduced productivity". According to *Dictionary.com Unabridged* (n.d.), absenteeism is defined as "habitual failure to appear, especially for work or other regular duty". In the past, the main attributable factor for presenteeism and absenteeism was workers being sick; however, this research uncovered other underlying causes for this phenomenon. In addition, this research expanded the existing research and found other ways employees cost employers in lost productivity, one of which included conducting personal business during working hours. The research concluded, through the use of Chi-Square tests for independence, there was dependency between some of the variables.

LITERATURE REVIEW

This section reviews research on medical conditions and other underlying causes that contribute to presenteeism. It also examines if these causes, such as stress, anxiety, financial status, and others, have a negative effect on both work productivity and employee health. Presenteeism, as indicated in previous research, is the antithesis of absenteeism. It is when an employee believes he/she "must show up for work, even if one is too sick, stressed, or distracted to be productive; the feeling that one needs to work extra hours, even if one has no extra work to do" (Middaugh, 2007, p.172). Employees choosing to attend work, while feeling debilitated because of an illness, have a tendency to put, otherwise, healthy employees at risk. An unhealthy workforce costs the company in the form of lost profits; as once exposed to contagious contaminants, "these newly infected employees will elect to deal with their illness through either absenteeism or presenteeism" (Weaver, 2010, para. 4).

MEDICAL CONDITION AND WORK PRODUCTIVITY

Prolonged exposure to stress, whether positive or negative, can cause health problems, such as severe headaches, stomach issues, chronic back pain, neck pain, and depression. For many employees, who suffer with emotional and physical stress, it is difficult to perform well on the job. If not managed properly, "stress creates pressure on individuals and families" causing an individual to become easily agitated and less likely to exhibit emotional control (Kim, Sorhaindo, & Garman, 2006, p. 460).

One survey, geared towards gauging the mental health of Americans, found depression to be significantly high among Americans ages 15 to 44 and adults 40–59 were inclined to experience the most depression (Rankin, 2010). According to Rankin (2010), "depression cost the United States $83 billion a year. Nearly two-thirds of this $83 billion is from lower productivity and workplace absenteeism" (para. 1). In a survey conducted by the Centers for Disease Control, it was reported that "more than 1 in 20 people in the United States are depressed, and of those, 80 percent say their depression interferes with their ability to work" (Rankin, 2010, para.4). Individuals suffering from depression have a difficult time staying focused and performing adequately on the job. This will inevitably translate into higher costs for employers (Rankin, 2010). Unfortunately, employers do not endorse depression screening programs "because of the uncertainty of the return-on-investment of such programs" (Miller, 2007, para. 1). Whether employees choose to suffer from depression in silence while at home, or come to work not functioning at their best, employers are reaping the costs of these non-productive patterns of behavior. Employers "spend about 17 percent of its employee compensation budget on costs related to employees not working" (Cyboran & Morrison, 2006, para. 1). Every year disability-related costs, for most organizations, according to a report by Thomas Reuters, are on average "$1,038 for depressed people and only $325 for non-depressed people" (Rankin, 2010, para.4).

Employers must become more familiar with their employees and the health conditions which deplete company resources and potential profits. Miller (2007) reported, "A new study published in the Journal of the American Medical Association (JAMA) finds that a cost-effective approach to identifying and treating depressed employees, through telephone counseling resulted in higher job retention, decreased sickness, lower work-absence and increased work productivity" (para. 2). Co-morbidites, employees who suffer habitually from a combination of illnesses, cause companies the most in productivity losses (Miller, 2009). The difference between the cost associated with male and female co-morbidites may vary slightly. For example, Duke University researchers examined data from two health related surveys, one in 2006 and the other in 2008, and determined that the costs per person of those who suffer from obesity are as much as $16,900 for women and $15,500 for men. In addition, presenteeism, among full-time obese workers, proved to be a major expense for employers with costs ranging up to $73.1 billion: 56 percent for women and 68 percent for men (Preidt, 2010, para. 10). Ann Wolf, an instructor at the University of Virginia's School of Medicine, whose specialty is in researching the financial impact of obesity, believes that there is an "independent effect of diabetes on employee productivity" (Preidt, 2009, para. 6). In 2009, the *American Journal of Health Promotion* surveyed 7,338 working adults and established that individuals suffering from "obesity and Type 2 diabetes lost 11 to 15 percent of work time or 5.9 hours of lost productivity per week" (Preidt, 2009, para.2). On the other hand, employees of normal weight had only "9 percent of work time or approximately 3.6 hours of lost productivity per week" (Preidt, 2009, para.2). In addition, the survey revealed obese people with Type 2 diabetes proclaimed that performing simple activities caused them to become weakened 20 to 30 percent of the time. Thus, it is in the employer's best interest to provide programs that curtail the negative effects of poor health within its workforce. According to a recent study by the Strategies to Overcome and Prevent Obesity Alliance, over 500 benefits managers and 1,352 employees agreed that it is appropriate for weight management issues to be addressed in the workplace and "80 percent of employees, regardless of weight, agree that healthy lifestyles and weight management programs belong in the workplace" (Wells, 2010, para. 3).

Over the years, research studies have confirmed that individuals coping with diabetes and obesity perform at a decreased efficiency. However, employees suffer from other debilitating health conditions, such as stress, anxiety, arthritis, menstrual cramps, and migraines, which can also financially drain employers' resources and result in lost productivity. The impact of illness can affect anyone in an organization. Miller (2009) noted, "Executives and managers seem to suffer high presenteeism productivity-loss related to specific health conditions along with those in non-managerial jobs" (p. 20).

Stress is ubiquitous and not only surfaces in one's personal life, but is indigenous in organizational life today. According to Greenberg (2011), over "90 percent of American workers report feeling stressed at least once per week, and 40 percent describe their jobs as very stressful most of the time" and "in fact, about half of all American workers report that stress has adversely affected their health" (p.155). As the jobless rate increases and corporations deliberately prolong the rehiring process; survivors of corporate massive layoffs are concerned about work pile up and fear being laid off. The effects of insurmountable stress are injurious to the individual and expensive for the organization (Greenberg, 2011, p.155). Such high levels of stress can cause workers to become mentally distracted and disengaged in work activities. Fear of job loss may preempt employees from taking much needed days off when they are feeling sick or emotionally overwhelmed. Thus, presenteeism evaluates the "decrease in productivity for the much larger group of employees whose health problems have not necessarily led to absenteeism and the decrease in productivity for the disabled group before and after the absence period" (Schultz, Chen, & Edington, 2009, p. 366).

The inability to function with clarity on the job, which is another form of presenteeism, may be customary for chronic migraine sufferers. Researchers believe that the true economic cost of migraines has not been fully assessed; since most people who suffer from migraines have not been clinically diagnosed. Two research studies presented at the 2009 International Headache Congress in Philadelphia revealed "that people with 15 or more migraine attacks per month lost approximately 4.5 hours of work productivity a week" (Boyles, 2009, para. 4). To explain this phenomenon further, researchers surveyed over 500 people to elucidate the impact of migraines on employee productivity and discovered most workers forced themselves to go to work in distressed conditions. The University of Tennessee's Medical School partnered with drug manufacturer GlaxoSmithKline to conduct a survey of 509 migraine sufferers. "The patients stated that 11 percent of workday migraines resulted in a full day of work lost, while only 5 percent led to late arrivals to work and 12 percent led to early work days" (Boyles, 2009, para. 12). Unfortunately, 62 percent of the time, employees suffering from intense migraine pain opted to remain at work at a decreased productivity rate of possibly 25 percent during these times (Boyles, 2009). Migraines, according to Fred Sheftell, MD, president of the American Headache Society, cost American businesses over $24 billion annually in medical bills and poor productivity (Boyles, 2009).

Managers that create a competitive culture, where employees are expected to work long hours and assume projects, which require constant attention, may be unaware of the underlying pressures that force employees to come to work not feeling well. According to a survey conducted by the staffing service Office Team, there appeared to be a disconnection between employees and their managers when it came to defining what constitutes "not feeling well". Out of the 522 American workers surveyed, 45 percent said they "very frequently" go to work when they are sick; however, only 17 percent of their bosses actually thought they did so. Likewise, even when 30 percent of employees attended work "somewhat frequently" feeling ill, more than half of the executives failed to recognize they did (Gurchiek, 2009).

UNDERLYING CAUSES FOR PRESENTEEISM NOT RELATED TO MEDICAL CONDITIONS

As employees fear job loss and reprimands for excessive time off, they are more than likely to conduct personal business while at work. A survey conducted for Cigna in May 2008 found that there was an average of approximately seven days of presenteeism per employee during that month, even though employees were present, they were more focused on personal business rather than job-related tasks (Gurchiek, 2009). For example, even during the height of the swine flu epidemic, 71% of American workers were more likely to go to work because they feared job loss or did not want to miss a deadline at work (Immen, 2009). Thus, presenteeism can affect healthy employees when they are more focused on personal issues, such as their talking with teachers concerning a child's school performance, setting up doctor's appointments for family members or themselves, and solidifying quality care for an aging parent. These non-related medical issues can consume 2.4 hours per week of an employee's work time (Gurchiek, 2009).

UNDERLYING CAUSES FOR STRESSOR AND ANXIETY

Americans push themselves to attain the "American Dream" despite the financial crisis, even when concerns of obtaining economic stability are overwhelming. Kim et al. (2006) discovered "60 percent of working Americans, who are employed by a company that offers a retirement plan, indicated that they were experiencing moderate to high levels of financial stress" (p.460). Most workers living in the current devitalized economy experience challenges making, the smallest, monetary obligations. Many Americans, affluent and poor, have felt the strain of financial stress. Stressors related to long hours spent on the job, surmounting expenses piling up pursuant to job losses, increased credit card debt, fierce local and global competition, and the desire for work-life balances can be manifest into incapacitating diseases and lost work productivity.

Based on an interview by Office Team in 2009, a group of office workers over the age of 18 and 150 senior executives were polled, more employees are feeling pressured to come to work in the current economy, because they do not want to be "out-of-sight, out-of-mind" (Gurchiek, 2009, para.6). This is especially prevalent among women working full-time who, despite years of progress, "only earn 80 cents to every dollar earned by the average full-time working man" (U.S. Congress Joint Economic Committee, 2010, p.1). For most women, keeping their jobs during a recession is problematic. Lean workforces affect women, whom typically lead single family households, more as they may be terminated first. In 2009, women were heads-of-households for approximately 9.8 million families and were the primary caregivers of children, ages 18 and under (U.S. Congress Joint Economic Committee, 2010). Further, over the past four years, "female workers have lost 298,000 jobs" and "unemployment for them rose from 4.1 percent in 2000 (the yearly average at the time) to 5.2 percent in July 2008" (Gurchiek, 2008, para. 3). As evidenced in health insurer Bupa's report, women suffer sleepless nights over "financial fears and anxiety over their personal and family's health" and "almost 50 percent said they were stressed in their everyday lives compared with 4 out of 10 men" (Paton, 2008, p.5).

Bupa's poll also discovered "that among those worried about their job security, 40 percent felt their stress levels had increased at work since the financial crisis began, while almost 25 percent claim now to be working longer hours to ward off the risk of losing their job" (Paton, 2008, p. 5). Years of ostentatious spending may have caught up with Americans in general. A national survey confirmed that "52 percent of employees manage their finances by living paycheck-to-paycheck" (Kim et al., 2006, p. 460). Family obligations, limited financial resources, and the dependency on each paycheck, strongly influences many Americans to trudge to work sick; which, not only jeopardizes recovery time, but puts their fellow coworkers at risk ("Sick time means a healthier," 2009).

Despite Congress' endeavors to provide universal healthcare, many corporations do not share in its enthusiasm. According to "Sick Time Means a Healthier Economy" (2009), more than 50 percent of all private sector workers and 79 percent of all low-wage earners are not offered paid sick time off by their employers. In the November 24, 2010, issue of *What's Working in Human Resources*, several large firms would rather pay the government penalties than offer "worker health insurance under the new reform laws" that to them "doesn't make financial sense" ("One-third of firms to cut healthcare costs," 2010, p.1). Furthermore, a national survey, conducted by Grant Thornton, LLP, discovered that 30 percent of U.S. CFOs and senior comptrollers plan to decrease the number of health care benefits offered to their workforces. Twenty-three percent of them will slice bonuses, and another 18 percent agreed to eliminate some stock options/equity based compensation ("National Survey of U.S. CFOs," 2010). Without decent health insurance and living in economic distress, employees, particularly low-wage earners, are more likely to determine if the effects of an illness can be tolerated, and based on how sick they feel, will go to work. However, many in the field believe "Being able to take a day off when sick should not be a luxury reserved for those who work in shops with a beneficient employer. Paid sick days serve the public health, the bottom line and promote decent working conditions" ("Sick time means a healthier economy," 2009, p. 2).

For some employees, attending work ill may have more to do with a sense of duty than because of financial strain or lack of personal or sick leave. Several employees attend work because they do not want to disappoint their team members. According to Gurchiek (2009) "two-fifths of workers attributed their work ethic, dedication or a belief their company/co-workers needed them for going to work despite feeling ill or having other issues while only one in four did so because they needed the money" (para. 14). Managers must be cognizant of the hidden messages sent to employees with regard to workplace norms and expectations. Office Team's Britton observed that when employees watch their managers work sick; they are less likely to take sick leave when they are not well. Managers, can attempt to create a healthy work environment by encouraging employees to take leave and remain home when they are not feeling well. This can be done by "setting an example" and "communicating expectations that they prefer employees stay home when sick to ensure a quicker recovery and lessen the likelihood of spreading contagious illnesses, such as colds and flu" (Gurchiek, 2009, para. 18).

Economic pressures, coupled with expanding workloads, compel managers to place extraordinary pressures on their staff to perform. In a recent interview at the "Tulsa Business Forum: An Interview with Jack Welch," sponsored by Oklahoma State University's Spears School of Business on February 23, 2011, Mr. Welch admonished corporations to remain focused on profits by stating, "If it doesn't turn green into green, it doesn't turn out to be a helluva good business," Welch said. "The whole idea is to grow jobs. The main social responsibility for a company is to win" (Walton, 2011, para. 24). In the current corporate climate, employees are constantly reminded to do much more with less. Even Mr. Welch believes that underperforming workers, who are unable to adapt to highly competitive environments, should be fired. In his interview, Welch stated, "We played business like it was a sport," and "You make a game of it, you field the best team and weed out the weakest" (Walton, 2011, para. 8). "The weeds you've got to pull out if you're going to build a beautiful garden" (Walton, 2011, para. 9).

Results from surveys by Friends Provident Insurance Firm and the National Stress Awareness Day, revealed that 25 percent of adults are prepared to work longer hours over the next 6 months and 12.5 percent expected to take on another job (Paton, 2008). As stress and anxiety become the standard attribute of what used to be characterized as a "normal work environment", 66 percent of employees "said they felt more stressed, run down, and prone to illness than they did three years ago, with 10 percent, specifically, blaming their work, bosses, and colleagues" (Paton, 2008, p. 5). Oftentimes, the effects of stress can be seen by others; however, according to Bruce Tyson (2010), managers should be more concerned about how stress can affect worker attitudes as poor attitudes "fundamentally undermine any positive aspects of the work environment and generally results in hostility" (para. 9). Employees feeling overwhelmed by stress will often develop negative feelings about almost anything associated with their employer (Tyson, 2010). These feelings are also apparent in global corporations. A Workplace Stress Survey of Britons, working for the government, showed, "a disproportionately high 90% of respondents felt stress was a workplace problem, 63% said they did not feel their staff trusted the people at the top, compared with the overall survey average (28%), and only 35% said their people 'have a lot of laughs at work' compared with the average of 42%" (Clements, 2008, para.19).

Thus, the creation of a healthy work-life balance has become a universal problem for employees. "In the current economic environment, work-life balance now ranks as one of the most important workplace attributes—second only to compensation, according to research conducted by the Corporate Executive Board (2009) among more than 50,000 global workers. And employees who feel they have a better work-life balance tend to work 21% harder than those that don't" (para. 2). Unfortunately, many employers avoid fulfilling this need as they strive to remain competitive. The Corporate Executive Board (2009) also reported, "In 2006, 53% of employees felt they had a good work-life balance; that number fell to 30% in the first quarter of 2009" (para.3). Despite favorable reports from health care experts who indicate companies which have "implemented wellness programs are starting to see the first real ROI on their investments—mainly in the form of decreased healthcare costs"; many employers are not willing to wait 18 months to see the benefit of such programs (Bilski, 2008, para.3).

In an attempt to uncover an assortment of workplace issues from the employees' perspective, the Society for Human Resource Management (2009) asked U.S. employees in an Omnibus Employee Survey to answer several questions concerning the pressure they feel, whether perceived or real, within the past year to stay "connected" to the workplace, even when they are not obligated to work. The employees' selection of the "frequent" response showed that 25 percent checked e-mail while on vacation, 26 percent checked e-mail while taking sick leave, and 36 percent checked work e-mail after hours. After hours is considered work beyond scheduled time during the week or the weekends. The survey also segregated responses by differences in employee level. This showed "executive level and middle-management employees disclosed that they had a greater average frequency compared with non-management employees for 1) working after hours, 2) checking work e-mail after hours, 3) checking e-mail while on vacation, 4) checking e-mail while taking sick leave and 5) working through their lunch break" (p. 4).

Interestingly, the response to the question "In your current job, which of the following are the main sources of pressure to work after hours" showed the top three reasons were 1) self-imposed pressure, 2) meeting project or performance goals, and 3) pressure from immediate supervisor or/manager. Furthermore, 62 percent of middle-management employees versus 44 percent of non-management employees report self-imposed pressure; whereas, 23 percent of executive-level employees versus 6 percent non-management employees report pressure due to demands from people who support or invest in the organization and only 12 percent of non-management employees versus 3 percent of middle-management employees report other pressures (Society for Human Resource Management, 2009, p. 9).

As managers aim to meet shareholders' expectations during these economic times, the ability to disconnect mentally from the job is becoming exceedingly difficult. In a recent survey by CareerBuilder, even healthy employees have a tendency to call in sick when they are actually well. The survey revealed that more than 25 percent of firms asserted workers "call out sick with fake excuses because they are stressed or burned out by the economy" ("More workers call out sick when they're well," 2010, p.6). As a result, companies are developing health and wellness programs to be proactive in helping employees manage the life stressors that have become customary in U.S. workplaces. It is for this reason, that "most employers (68%) have four or more programs in place to help workers deal with stress, and 22% of companies offer eight or more stress-relief programs for workers" (Bilski, 2010, para. 2). Workers must learn to identify job stressors that cause them to become physically sick or mentally drained. EAPs (Employment Assistance Programs) are the primary resource that companies use to provide support to its employees and 78 percent of those surveyed stated that they had it in place (Bilski, 2010). Companies are acknowledging their role and responsibility towards the mitigation of stress among its workers. Thus, "63 percent of companies provide flexible work schedules, 46 percent offer work-life balance support programs, and 45 percent make leadership training available on worker stress" (Bilski, 2010, para.6).

Like the United States, England also faces challenges controlling employee stress. Stress and mental health issues account for 40 percent of absenteeism. Managers, who fail to offer mental health programs that support distressed employees when they return to work, may lose them, "as they often turn into the long-term 'unworkable' population" (Clements, 2008, para. 2). Ingolve Urnes, CEO of Active Health Partners (AHP), attempts to address stress incidents more quickly by establishing a process of intervention for employees who fail to contact the nursing center following a sickness absence (Clements, 2008). In addition, resilience to stress has become a major factor in how employees react to and manage stress. Drew Fobbester of MyVitality.com, an online resilience profiling company stated that, "The more healthy a person is, the more resilient to stress they will be" (Clements, 2008, para. 17). My Vitality's corporate clients were able to achieve a 10 percent 'vitality rating', based on a thorough questionnaire that assessed quality-of-life and productivity, and retention rates rose to 80–85 percent (Clements, 2008).

Physicians have long been advocates of eating well and engaging in daily exercise as possible combatants to stress, anxiety, diabetes, high blood pressure, and early signs of depression. In January 2008, Let's Get Healthy conducted an analysis of 327 office workers and discovered a significant difference between those who became easily stressed from those who felt they could cope. The results showed that people who were quickly stressed had higher levels of absenteeism than those who possessed hardy personalities (Clements, 2008). However, in another study, 68 percent of employers polled said that work-life balance was a significant producer of stress and only 38 percent of them said they were engaging in activities that would help them combat the effects of stress (Wojcik, 2009). Manhattan psychologist Dr. Joseph Cilona believes that employees can recover from stress and regain a sense of normalcy if they are willing to acknowledge that have a problem. Cilona suggests that employees use the following steps: 1) educate themselves about stress and use tactics that work for them, whether it involves a change in routine, counseling, or holistic treatment, 2) ask others if they have noticed a change in one's behavior, 3) avoid being ashamed by the stigma and seek the assistance of mental health professionals, who are trained to assist employees with their fluctuating moods and stress levels, 4) take a proactive approach to dealing with mental health needs and welcome different approaches that can solve one's problems (Goodman, 2010, para. 7).

PERSONAL BUSINESS CONDUCTED DURING OFFICE HOURS AND ABSENTEEISM

According to Middaugh (2007), "a report in *Risk & Insurance* indicated that the root causes of presenteeism are not always medical. They frequently include issues of childcare, financial worries, addiction, divorce, or family problems. *Boston.com* recently reported that many women are one sick child away from losing their jobs" (Middaugh, 2007, p.172). Family obligations also cause employees to miss work and employers should allow flexible scheduling as an option. In 2010, claims related to FMLA (Family Medial Leave Act) increased by more than 10 percent because of personal illness/injury, caring for a child and/or elderly relative ("FMLA claims rise by more than 10% in 2010," 2010, p.6).

Absenteeism, according to the article "Introduction to Attendance Management" (2010), "is the failure of employees to report for work when they are scheduled to work" ("Introduction to Attendance", 2010, para. 5). This would exclude "employees who are away from work on recognized holidays, vacations, or approved leaves of absence" ("Introduction to Attendance", 2010, p.1). In Canada, each time an employee is absent, the employer loses "an average of $2,500, which includes both direct and indirect costs (based on 9 days absent out of 250 working days and an average payroll of $35,000)" ("Introduction to Attendance", 2010, para. 3). The cost of absenteeism, according to Middaugh (2007), "is easy to calculate: 100 percent of the worker's productivity is lost each day that the worker is not on the job" (p.172). Therefore, companies need to be able to track both direct and indirect costs associated with absenteeism. According to Hall (2010), employers can use tracking programs to limit unscheduled time away from the job and objectively manage work productivity. The systems may be used as a prevention tool that not only "helps keep employees on the job, but it keeps them connected to the right support resources" (Hall, 2010, para. 8). Since the cost of absenteeism exceeds the "payment of wages and benefits paid during the absence", employers must consider the "indirect costs of staffing, scheduling, re-training, lost productivity, diminished moral, turnover, and opportunity cost. The indirect costs often exceed the direct cost of absenteeism" ("Introduction to Attendance", 2010, para. 2).

FACTORS AFFECTING PRODUCTIVITY

Loyalty, engagement, and trust continue to decline despite employer efforts to help employees cope with the economic meltdown and internal changes. According to a report by Watson Wyatt Worldwide and the National Business Group on Health, although health and productivity management programs have been able to minimize health care cost and decrease absenteeism, most employers have failed to develop procedures that will assuage the stress of mandatory long hours, lack of work-life balance, and fear of job loss. Consequently, management's failure to acknowledge employees' fear of job loss may cause problems as the economy slowly recovers as these stressors are factors that negatively affect productivity. In a recent survey, 67 percent of employers admit that fear of job loss is a leading cause of employee stress, yet only 41 percent of employers said they are addressing the issue (Wojcik, 2009).

In a [video interview with Sylvia Ann Hewlett, founder of The Center for Work-Life Policy's], Susan Berfield, associate editor of *Business Week*, discussed the anxiety felt by employees after the recession. Hewlett's book "Keeping performance up when businesses are down" researched seven Wall Street and seven Main Street Companies. She discovered that the office climates had changed and there was a rapid decline in trust and engagement among the remaining employees. According to Hewlett, 73 percent of employees stated they felt managers gave them little or no attention. She also stated that "in the wake of massive layoffs, 35 percent of survivors walk out the door", which means the top performers are leaving companies as soon as an opportunity presents itself.

The problem, according to Hewlett, is that CEOs are more concerned about clients than retaining his or her best performers. During the interview, Hewlett shared that one employee stated that "I have left the job, but I haven't quit". Thus, managerial neglect may also be a determining factor of employee presenteeism. Prior to the recession, 95 percent of the people Hewlett interviewed said they were very loyal to their employer, in 2008; that number had plummeted to 53 percent. Trust was also negatively affected after the recession, as it went from 79 percent to 37 percent. Employees who were forced to witness the laying off of top performers believed that the rules were no longer valid, thus engagement—the willingness to work and perform beyond what is required—decreased by 20 percent. In the wake of a dilatory economy, Hewlett suggested that managers intervene and become more accessible by building camaraderie with team members. She also warns of high voluntary attrition and how companies may suffer because of them. Similarly, a center for Work-Life Policy survey shows that between June 2008 and January 2009, 14 percent of college graduates lost their jobs—of these, 32 percent were fired; however, 68 percent voluntarily quit (Berfield, n.d.).

METHODOLOGY

After an initial review of the literature pertaining to absenteeism and presenteeism, an anonymous survey was given to students and faculty members at a historically black university. The participants were asked to answer questions pertaining to their full or part-time job. For this research, there were 138 useable surveys. The participants were asked to answer a series of "yes" and "no" questions, categorical questions, and ranking questions.

The questionaire was divided into six different sections. The first section of the questionaire collected demographic information. The participants were asked questions pertaining to gender, age, race, marital status, number of children, level of education, employment status, annual income, type of employment, and number of employees at the firm. Statistical analysis will be used to determine if there were any differences based on gender, age, or education level in the response rate as it pertains to absenteeism/presenteeism. The statistical analysis will reveal if there were any relationships between annual incomes, the number of employees at the firm, whether the person was self-employed and how often they had occurrences of presenteeism.

The questionnaire also covered areas pertaining to the overall health status of those being surveyed. The participants were given a list of common medical conditions, such as diabetes, depression, obesity, migraines, and anxiety/stress, and asked to respond if they had that condition. Next, the respondents were asked if their medical condition affected their productivity levels, how often they went to work sick, were they contagious, did they disinfect their work area, and had they caught an illness from another worker. Statistical analysis will be used to determine if there is a pattern between overall health status and their loss of productivity at work.

Respondents were asked to cite the causes for going to work "Not at Their Peak Level". The participant was given a list of 19 common causes and asked to check all that applied. Some of the reasons listed were: not that sick, needed money, sense of duty, fear of losing job, and did not want to use sick leave. Also, covered in this section were reasons the participant may be experiencing stress and/or anxiety. Since exercising has been shown to reduce stress levels, the questionnaire asked how often the worker engaged in exercise.

Another section addressed conducting personal business during working hours. Workers come to work and spend their workday sending personal e-mails, handling childcare/eldercare problems, scheduling doctor's appointments, handling vehicle purchase/repairs or handling debit/credit problems. Each participant was asked how often they conducted personal business at work, how many hours per day they spent doing these personal items, and last, which type of personal items they handled during business hours. Statistical analysis will be conducted on these categories to see if there is a relationship between gender and each of the above categories. Also, a means test will be conducted to compare the average number of hours per day spent on personal business by each gender.

Sick leave was also studied. The participants were asked how many days per month they miss work and their reasons for missing work. The survey listed ten typical reasons for missing work and the worker was asked to check all that applied. Some of the common reasons listed were: actually sick, going to doctor's appointments, childcare, home repair, and vehicle repair. Statistical analysis will be used to calculate the average number of days missed per month, and to determine the most common reasons workers cite for missing them. A means test will be used to determine if there is a difference in the number of days missed per month based on gender.

The last section of the survey covers other areas that may affect worker productivity and work-life balance. The participant is given a list of seven items that may decrease their productivity. The items included: poor management, organizational changes, lack of defined goals in the job, no longer motivated by the work, and lack of accountability. The participants were also asked "would they turn down a promotion if it required a significant increase in the number of hours" and "if they were willing to work fewer hours for less money." Last, the workers were asked if all of their vacation time was used. The researchers wanted to gauge if the workers were causing themselves undue stress and a shift in their work-life balance by not using all of their available vacation time.

RESULTS

SPSS was used to conduct the statistical analyses. The means were calculated for all ratio data, frequency charts were constructed for all categorical data, and pivot tables were constructed to run the Chi-Square tests for independence. This particular study involved over 150 variables.

Of the 138 completed surveys, 59 percent of the respondents were male and 41 percent were female. The average age for the participants was 23, of which, 86 percent were African-American, 7 percent were Caucasian, 2 percent were Hispanic, and 4 percent were other. Ninety-four percent of those surveyed reported they were single, two percent were married, two percent were divorced, and two percent were other. Of the 85 percent that reported having children, 7 percent were the sole provider, 13 percent were partial providers for their children, either living at home or out on their own, and on a surprising note, 10 percent stated they were the sole provider for terminally ill children. Concerning education, 83 percent graduated from high school and are currently attending college, 16 percent had either an Associate's Degree or Bachelor's Degree, and 1 percent held a Doctoral Degree.

Concerning employment, 92 percent were employed by someone else and 8 percent were self-employed. Of those employed, 51 percent were part-time employees, 22 percent were full-time employees, 5 percent were temporary, and 22 percent checked the "other" category. Concerning the type of work the respondents performed, 10 percent were professionals, 9 percent were managers, 6 percent were clerical, 5 percent were in operations, 4 percent were in a technical field, 2 percent were teachers, and last,

64 percent listed other. This "other" category needs to be examined to determine the type of work not covered by those already listed. An explanation could be they were working in a sales or service business.

Annual income was requested of the participants. Seventy-six percent reported making less than $20,000, 20 percent reported making between $20,000 and $40,000, 3 percent made between $40,000 and $60,000, and 1 percent made over $80,000, annually.

One of the items viewed as a contributing factor to presenteeism was the number of employees at the firm. The theory was, the smaller the firm, the more pressure placed on each worker to show up for work because there were not any replacement workers to perform extra duties. Forty-nine percent worked with less than 20 employees, 25 percent worked with between 20 and 100 employees, 8 percent worked with between 100 and 500 employees, and 18 percent worked at a firm employing more than 500 employees.

The next set of results addresses overall health status, common medical conditions, and medical conditions effecting productivity. Thirty percent stated their health status over the last twelve months was "Excellent", 57 percent had "Good" health, 12 percent had "Fair" health and last, 1 percent chose "Poor" health.

The respondents were then given a list of common medical conditions and asked to check all that applied. Twenty percent reported experiencing migraines, 12 percent had back and/or neck pain, 10 percent had anxiety/stress, 10 percent suffered from asthma, and 9 percent had severe menstrual cramps. Arthritis was reported by seven percent, depression was listed by five percent, two percent were obese, and heart disease and diabetes were listed for less than one percent each. When asked whether their medical condition affected their work, 91 percent said no and only 9 percent admitted that it did indeed affect their productivity while at work.

When asked how often they went to work sick and why, 12 percent reported "Never" going to work sick, 28 percent "Rarely" go to work sick, 50 percent "Sometimes" go to work sick, and 10 percent "Often" go to work sick. When asked if they were contagious when they went to work sick, 18 percent reported knowing they were contagious and still went to work. Forty percent reported catching an illness from another co-worker. Studies indicate a great source of contamination comes from eating at one's desk. Twenty-six percent reported eating at their desk and a surprising 52 percent, disinfect their work area.

The main initiative behind the survey was to determine some of the underlying causes for presenteeism and/or absenteeism so business leaders could address these areas. If workers continue to go to work sick, their production levels will not only be negatively affected, but they will spread their diseases and affect the total firm's production level. To help discover the rationale behind this phenomenon, participants were given a list of 19 reasons for going to work sick and asked to check all that applied. The number one reason the employees listed, at 42 percent, was that they were not sick enough to use a sick day and an additional 17 percent did not want to use their available sick days. However, 11 percent did cite they did not have any sick days left to use. Forty-one percent went to work because they needed money or had some financial obligations to meet. As to the reasons for showing up to work sick, some workers cited a sense of duty (29 percent), not burdening their colleagues (12 percent), and being in a management position and having others report to them (4 percent). Others cited work related reasons, such as to prevent work pile up (16 percent), looming deadlines (9 percent), and having meetings already scheduled with clients (5 percent). Retaliation was prevalent in some of the next set of responses. Twenty-one percent feared losing their job, 18 percent thought they would be viewed as a slacker if they stayed home, 12 percent would be penalized if they stayed home, and 2 percent were still on probationary status. Some workers thought they could not be replaced. They cited responses, such as nobody can do my job (8 percent), could not find a replacement worker (17 percent), and 8 percent stated they were self-employed. The last group of responses suggested it was the corporate culture to come to work sick (1 percent) and others said they must work 50–60 hours per week to be promoted (1 percent).

Since stress can be such a debilitating factor and lead to lost productivity, the survey asked participants to report the underlying causes for their stress and/or anxiety. Work-life balance and overworked accounted for 33 percent and 22 percent, respectively. In this economic time, all employers are trying to get each worker to do more with fewer resources. Twenty-two percent acknowledged family problems, 15 percent had work-related problems, and 17 percent had debit and/or credit problems. The last area, health problems, accounted for seven percent of the respondents. These numbers are especially interesting since only 10 percent cited they had stress and/or anxiety issues and five of the six categories had percentages above the previously stated 10 percent.

Some additional questions were asked to gauge the work-life balance phenomenon. Around 28 percent of the respondents stated they would turn down a promotion if it involved a significant increase in the number of hours worked. However, only nine percent said they were willing to work fewer hours than they currently work. When asked about their use of their vacation time, 38 percent stated they "Never" use all of their vacation time, 20 percent "Rarely" use their vacation, and 19 percent "Sometimes" use all of their vacation time. It is surprising that only 23 percent "Often" use all of their vacation time.

Studies have shown that exercising can be a great stress reliever. So, the participants were asked how many times per week they engage in exercise. Thirty-two percent stated they "Never" exercise, 31 percent exercise once per week, 30 percent exercise 3 times per week, and 7 percent recorded exercising 5 or more times per week.

Since most research on presenteeism has been related to workers going to work not at a peak production level, the researchers wanted to explore other forms of presenteeism. One area of interest was employees working on their personal business during company hours. When asked "How often do you conduct personal business at work", only 39 percent stated they "Never" conduct personal business at work. In contrast, 61 percent of the workers did work on personal business during company hours. Of that 61 percent, 15 percent "Often" work on personal business, 27 percent "Sometimes" work on personal business and 19 percent "Rarely" work on personal business during company hours.

The researchers were curious as to the approximate number of hours per day each respondent spent on personal business. The average number of hours reported spent on personal business was 2.17, with a standard deviation of 1.14 hours. The minimum was zero and the maximum number of hours reported was four. However, men reported an average of 2.33 hours per day, with a standard deviation of 4.64 hours and women reported an average of 1.13 hours per day, with a standard deviation of 2.25 hours. The researchers wanted to ascertain if there was a difference between the number of hours spent on personal business by men and by women. The researchers were very surprised to see that men were spending 1.2 hours more than women per day on personal business ($p = .05$).

The researchers were curious as to what type of personal business these workers were conducting at work. Surprisingly, 25 percent reported scheduling doctor's appointments during working hours. The next areas were debit/credit problems (19 percent), vehicle purchase or vehicle repairs (17 percent), childcare (7 percent), teacher conferences (7 percent), and home purchase or home repairs (5 percent). Around one percent cited eldercare, foreclosure, or personal relationships as their reason for using company time for personal business.

The researchers went on to ask the participants as to other causes that might affect their productivity levels. The number one cited cause was "Poor Management", at 51 percent, and an additional 17 percent cited organizational changes as to the cause of their lost productivity. Lack of motivation, defined goals, and accountability accounted for 34 percent, 23 percent, and 18 percent, respectively. Seventeen percent were ready to leave the organization. Surprisingly, eight percent said they felt pressure from management to show up to put in some "Face Time".

Absenteeism has been previously defined as "habitual failure to appear, especially for work or other regular duty" (*Dictionary.com*, n.d.). The survey participants reported an average number of days missed per month was .94, with a standard deviation of 1.47 days. The minimum number of days reported was zero, but the maximum number was an astonishingly seven days. However, men reported an average of .82 days, with a standard deviation of 1.4 days and women reported an average of 1.12 days, with a standard deviation of 1.57 days. There was not a statistical difference on the number of days missed per month based on gender.

In order to measure the causes for absenteeism, the participants were given a list of ten reasons for being absent from work and asked to check all that applied. The most common reason, at 51 percent, was actually being sick and right behind it, at 22 percent, was doctor's appointments. Eleven percent of the workers cited personal relationships and 10 percent cited vehicle purchase or repairs. Four percent of the workers were in teacher conferences. Last, around three percent of the workers cited debit problems, eldercare, childcare, home purchase, repairs or foreclosure.

Chi-Square tests of independence were constructed to see if any of variables were dependent upon another variable. In other words, did men typically report to work sick or were women reporting to work sick more often? Below describes the Chi-Square analysis results for the tests that resulted in a dependency with a p-value of less than 10 percent.

Concerning the males, it was confirmed they reported more often than women as being the one financially responsible for the children (.09). They reported their health status for the last 12 months as being "good" (.005). However, they went on to report they either "sometimes or often" go to work sick (.04). The rationale men used for reporting to work "Not at their Peak Level", was one of four reasons: because people reported to them, their sense of duty, to prevent work pile up, and because they were self-employed (.06, .01, .06, and .01, respectively).

Concerning the females, they reported their health status as being either "excellent or fair" (.005). Contrary to the above statement, more females reported having health problems than their male counterparts (.002). Females reported they either "never or rarely" go to work sick (.04). However, when females did go to work sick, they were contagious (.08). Females complained of having migraine headaches more often than men (.028). The rationale women used for reporting to work "Not at their Peak Levels", was one of two reasons: because everybody else in the office reported to work sick, or they did not want to use their sick leave (.08 and .04, respectively).

The last set of Chi-Square tests dealt with dependency and income levels. Respondents in the annual salary range of $40,000 and $59,000 reported the reason for coming to work sick was because they did not have any sick leave left (.08). This was surprising since the researchers assumed the respondents in the lower salary ranges would be the ones without any sick time left. The respondents in the annual salary range of $20,000 –$39,000 and $40,000 –$59,000 reported the reason for coming to work sick was either because they perceived nobody could do their job or because of a sense of duty (.002 and .007, respectively).

This was also surprising since the researchers assumed the lower salaried workers would not think anyone could replace them. However, it was confirmed that the higher salaried workers thought they could not be replaced.

FUTURE AREAS OF RESEARCH

It should be understood that this research does not cover every possible area. It is a starting point. Work is being continued in this area by many authors. The researchers would like to administer the survey instrument to a larger population. The larger group would need to include participants from an an older population and workers employed at larger firms. Some of the health problems listed are not typical for a younger population group and more information may be gathered as to how these health problems effect productivity levels. Also, workers at larger firms would have access to larger benefit packages. Employee benefits that would be of importance would be availability of sick leave, paid time off, replacement personnel, and health club memberships. Forty-one percent cited they went to work because they needed the money. However, if the firm offered adequate sick leave, the worker's salary would not be affected by missing days. Also, the researchers discovered other areas not included on the original survey instrument that would have had an impact on productivity levels. These areas are sleep deprivation, pregnancy, lupus, dental, smoking, endometriosis, and allergies.

CONCLUSIONS

Studies have shown that presenteeism and absenteeism costs employers $180 billion and $118 billion, respectively (Weaver, 2010). The survey results confirmed that employees are showing up to work consistently sick, stressed, and overworked. In fact, not only were the employees showing up sick; they were doing something far worse. They were contagious and knowingly infected other healthy workers. In addition, employees listed multiple medical conditions that increased the loss of productivity to the firm. The survey also confirmed some of the suspected underlying reasons why the workers came to work not at their peak performance level, such as, did not want to use sick days, looming deadlines, self-employed, and retaliation. Coupled with the above effects, workers were conducting a variety of personal businesses during company hours. An interesting finding was that men conducted personal business 1.2 hours more per day than women. Last, some of the underlying reasons for absenteeism were discovered such as: actually being sick, doctor's appointments, home repairs, and vehicle repairs.

AUTHOR INFORMATION

Dr. Tammy Prater, Professor of Management, has been a faculty member at Alabama State University since 1997. She has degrees from the University of Alabama (BS—MIS 1989, MA—Production Management 1981, Ph.D. —Production Management 1997). Prior to joining Alabama State University, she taught at the University of Alabama and Auburn University Montgomery. She has numerous articles and presentations on work force planning, personnel management, service section planning and published articles in the *S.A.M. Advanced Management Journal, CIIMA*, and *Journal of Contemporary Business Issues.*

Kim F. Smith is an Instructor of Management at Alabama State University. She joined the Alabama State's Business faculty in 2006 as an adjunct instructor and later as a non-tenured faculty member in 2008. Kim has 20 years of Human Resource experience and 15 years as an Executive Assistant. Kim graduated from Governor's State University in 1997 with a B.A. in business administration with a concentration in human resources. In 2007, she earned a MBA from Wesley College. Kim Smith's teaching experience at Alabama State includes: marketing, human resources, organizational behavior, and business communication.

REFERENCES

1. Absenteeism. (2006). *American Heritage® Dictionary of the English Language*. Retrieved from http://www.answers.com/topic/absenteeism#ixzz1EZ01Pgqc
2. Berfield, S. (n.d.). Interview by S. Berfield [Video recording]. Unmotivated, Anxious, and in Limbo: Suffering from Great Recession anxiety. Retrieved from http://feedroom.businessweek.com/index.jsp?fr_story=3466ab6f5e2c2b314df5a96740bdd70549eb5740
3. Bilski, J. (2010, July 23). Most firms have multiple stress-relief programs: How many does yours offer? Retrieved from http://www.cfodailynews.com
4. Bilski, J. (2008, November 11). Do wellness programs work? Let the numbers answer that. Retrieved from http://www.cfodailynews.com
5. Boyles, S. (2009, September 11). Migraines reduce workplace productivity. *WebMD Health News*. Retrieved from http://www.medicinenet.com/script/main/art.asp?articlekey=105524
6. Clements, A. (2008, April 1). Stress Survey 2008—Get a grip on your stressed out staff workers workplace. Retrieved from http://www.humanresourcesmagazine.com/news/796383/Workplace-Stress-Survey-2008—grip-stressed-out-staff-workers-workplace/
7. Corporate Executive Board. (2009, March 27). The increasing call for work-life balance. *Bloomberg Businessweek*. Retrieved from http://www.businessweek.com/managing/content/mar2009/ca20090327_734197.htm
8. Cyboran, S. & Morrison, T.M. (2006, November 12). Paid time off: Giving employees more control over leave. SHRM.org. Retrieved from http://www.shrm.org/hrdisciplines/benefits/Articles/Pages/CMS_018373.aspx
9. FMLA claims rise by more than 10% in 2010. (2010, November 24). *What's Working in Human Resources*, 6.
10. Goodman, M. (2010, February 18). Work overload brings panic, anxiety, stress: The more demanding recession-crunched jobs become, the more health problems ensue. Retrieved from http://abcnews.go.com/Business/work-overload-brings-panic-anxiety-stress/story?id9868689&page=1
11. Greenberg, J. (2011). Coping with Organizational Life: Emotions and Stress. In *Behavior in Organizations*. (pp. 142–175). Upper Saddle River, NJ: Prentice Hall.
12. Gurchiek, K. (2009, February 2). Managers, employees view presenteeism differently. *HR News*. Retrieved from http://www.shrm.org/Publications/HRNews/Pages/ViewPresenteeismDifferently.aspx
13. Gurchiek, K. (2008, August 15). Economic woes hit female workers particularly hard. *HR News*. Retrieved from http://www.allbusiness.com/government/government-bodies-offices-legislative/11658007-1.html
14. Hall, C. (2010, October 6). The hidden cost of absenteeism: New workplace options absence tracking helps businesses mitigate missed work. Retrieved from http://www.workplaceoptions.com
15. Immen, W. (2009, June 12). Feeling sick? Booking off is better for your career. *The Globe and Mail*, p. B15. Retrieved from: http://proquest.umi.com/pqdweb?index

16. Introduction to Attendance Management. (2010, March). *Attendance Management—working together. Retrieved from: http://www.benefits.org/interface/cost/absent.htm*
17. Kim, J., Sorhaindo, B., & Garman, E. T. (2006, June 20). Relationship between financial stress and workplace absenteeism of credit counseling clients. *Journal of Family and Economic Issues*, 27(3), 458–478. DOI:10.1007/s10834-006-90024-9.
18. Middaugh, D.J. (2007, April 1). Presenteeism: Sick and tired at work. *Dermatology Nursing*; 19(2), 172–185.
19. Miller, S. (2009, June). Most employers underestimate health impact on productivity. *HR Magazine, 54*(6). p. 20. Retrieved from http://www.shrm.org/hrdisciplines/benefits/Articles/Pages/Impacton-Productivity.aspx
20. Miller, S. (2007, October) Depression intervention: Telephone counseling increases worker productivity. SHRM.org Retrieved from http://shrm.org/hrdisciplines/benefits/Articles/Pages/CMS_023215.aspx
21. More workers call out sick when they're well. (2010, November 24) *What's Working in Human Resources*, 6.
22. National Survey of U.S. CFOs finds nearly one-third targeting healthcare cutbacks for their workforce. *Greatest pricing pressure is employee benefits relating to healthcare and pensions.* (2010, November 1). Retrieved from http://www.grantthornton.com/portal/site/gtcom/menuitem.550794734a67d883a5f2ba40633841ca/?vgnextoid=96820b6d7bdfb210VgnVCM1000003a8314acRCRD&vgnextchannel=f51ecbbdad9c4010VgnVCM100000368314acRCRD
23. One-third of firms to cut healthcare costs: Employee benefits top lists of pricing pressure points. (2010, November 24). *What's Working in Human Resources*, 1.
24. Paton, N. (2008, December). Economic downturn continues to put employee health at risk. *Occupational Health.* Sutton. 60(12), 5.
25. Presenteeism. (n.d.). *Dictionary.com Unabridged.* Retrieved from Dictionary.com website: http://dictionary.reference.com/browse/presenteeism
26. Preidt, R. (2010, October 8). Obesity among U.S. workers has hefty price tag: Study. *Bloomberg Businessweek.* Retrieved from http://www.businessweek.com/lifestyle/content/healthday/644073.html
27. Preidt, R. (2009, May 13). Productivity takes a hit from obesity, diabetes. *Bloomberg Businessweek.* Retrieved from http://www.businessweek.com/lifestyle/content/healthday/626770.html
28. Rankin, D. (2010, August 23). Lower costs and raise productivity in your business by improving employees' mental health. Retrieved from http://ezinearticles.com
29. Schultz, A. B., Chen, C., & Edington, D.W. (2009). The cost and impact of health conditions on presenteeism to employers: a review of the literature. *Pharmacoeconomics*, 27(5). 365–378.
30. Sick Time Means a Healthier Economy. (2009, June 7). St. *Petersburg Times.* p.2.
31. Society for Human Resource Management. (2009, January 12). Omnibus Employee Survey. [PowerPoint Presentation] Retrieved from: www.shrm.org/Research/SurveyFindings/Articles/Documents/OE%20-%20econ%20data.ppt · PPT file.
32. Tyson, B. (2010, October 30). How Does Stress Affect Attitudes and Behavior in Work Settings? Retrieved from http://www.brighthub.com/office/career-planning/articles/93650.aspx#ixzz1F8QVfFGN

33. U.S. Congress Joint Economic Committee. (2010, August). Women and the Economy 2010: 25 Years of Progress But Challenges Remain [Report]. Retrieved from http://jec.senate.gov/public/?a=Files.Serve&File_id=8be22cb0-8ed0-4a1a-841b-aa91dc55fa81
34. Walton, R. (2011, February 23). Jack Welch talks up innovation at Mabee Center forum Original Print Headline: Welch offers advice. Retrieved from http://www.tulsaworld.com/business/article.aspx?subjectid=49&articleid=20110223_49_E1_ULNSom672498
35. Weaver, R. (2010, June 8). Cost of presenteeism surpasses absenteeism. Retrieved from http://www.examiner.com/human-capital-in-detroit/cost-of-presenteeism-surpasses-absenteeism
36. Wells, S. J. (2010, October 1). Obesity in the workplace: Employers' concern runs high. HRMagazine, 55(10). Retrieved from http://www.shrm.org/Publications/hrmagazine/EditorialContent/2010/1010/Pages/1010wells1.aspx
37. Wojcik, J. (2009, December). Most employers aren't combating workplace stress. Retrieved from http://www.workforce.com/archive/feature/benefits-compensation/most-employers-arent-combating-workplace-stress/index.php

APPENDIX F

STRESS QUESTIONNAIRE

No one reacts to stress in the same manner, and tests designed to access stress levels rarely provide an accurate diagnosis. The following stress test is designed to provide general feedback only.

It is not an instrument that should substitute a legitimate diagnosis by a Stress Management Consultant or physician.

Answer all of the questions by selecting either yes or no. If only a part of the question applies to you, respond in the affirmative. Be honest with your answers.

	Answer the following questions:	YES	NO
1	I respond to emails after the work day is finished.		
2	I answer phone calls from those I work with after the work day is finished.		
3	I bring work home most nights.		
4	I complete tasks by myself and rarely ask for help.		
5	I tend to procrastinate and underestimate how long tasks will take.		
6	I suffer from sleep deprivation or take medications to sleep at night.		
7	I feel uncomfortable when I do not have something to do.		
8	While listening to others, my mind tends to wander.		
9	I am highly competitive and get upset when I do not win.		
10	I do not like conflict and I tend to keep my feelings inside.		
11	I have headaches each week and am prone to bouts of colds and other infections.		
12	I feel lethargic and call out sick from work.		
13	I have to wear a mouth guard at night because I grind my teeth resulting in jaw pain.		
14	I am constantly irritated and experience frustration with other drivers on the road.		
15	I finish other people's sentences when in conversation because I am in a hurry to do something else.		
16	I experience pain in my back, neck, and shoulders.		
17	I have trouble relaxing and think about work issues even when I should be enjoying personal time.		

	Answer the following questions:	YES	NO
18	I give people compliments when they do a good job, but secretly envy their success.		
19	I have had to push my hobbies aside because work tends to consume my life.		
20	I have no interest in being intimate and I am easily irritated with family and friends.		
	YES answers equals one point (1); NO answers equals zero points (0).		

Your score:

Although, stress is inevitable and most people have learned to adjust and manage the amount of stress they experience, too much stress can wreak havoc, both physically and emotionally.

0-4 points: Indicate that you will probably not suffer from a stress-related illness.

5-15 points: Reveal that you are stressed either emotionally, physically, or both.

16-20 points: Suggest that you are experiencing extreme emotional and physical pressure. These pressures may cause you to become prone to depression, asthma, diabetes, high blood pressure, migraines and other stress-related illnesses. If you have scored in this section, you should explore stress eliminating techniques such as exercising, dieting, counseling, and consulting your personal physician.

Techniques to help improve your quality of life:

In each area in which you responded yes:

1. Make a conscious effort to reduce your level of stress.
2. Engage in hobbies and other activities that bring you pleasure.
3. Be intentional in addressing each area you responded with a yes.
4. Solicit the help of others when things become too overwhelming for you.
5. Consult with a professional to help you minimize your stress level.

APPENDIX G

7 EASY WAYS TO MEASURE EMPLOYEE PERFORMANCE

By Kurt Rakos

Productive employees are the lifeblood of every recruiting business, but how do you assess their performance levels? Do they understand your goals and expectations? Are they meeting their personal objectives?

Every company should continually monitor and evaluate their employees; here are seven easy ways to quickly gauge performance and ensure your firm is on the right track:

Punctuality: Employees who regularly arrive late for work or are frequently absent from the office are unlikely to be meeting their performance objectives. The underlying issue needs to be addressed here – have they received adequate training? Do they get along with their co-workers and manager? Issues with punctuality mean an employee is not doing their job to their full potential and a negative attitude may also be affecting their colleagues.

Quality of work: The timely completion of projects to the desired standard is a key indicator in measuring employee performance. Is the work being carried out average or outstanding? Are they committing maximum effort to projects? Is their attitude affecting their ability to meet your expectations? Do they understand their personal performance objectives? The answers to those questions will help you to understand the root causes of any problems.

Observe personal habits: Perpetual bad habits can detract from employee performance. This may include indulging in office gossip, taking unauthorized breaks, disruptive behavior and the use of computers for personal reasons (such as social media, online shopping). In order to prevent these habits from being adopted by their co-workers, you must be clear on what is acceptable in your business and issue an appropriate behavioral code.

Check their attitude: A bad attitude will often manifest itself in insubordinate behavior. Again, this is indicative of an individual who is unlikely to be meeting their performance objectives. Typically, these employees will not comply with company policies and are likely to display disrespect for your company and co-workers.

Review personal presentation: Most firms have a professional dress code appropriate to the job and company culture. Employees who disregard your expectations and present a disheveled or careless appearance reflect badly on your image. It's likely that their performance will be failing to meet your expectations too.

Carry out a client survey: The consequences of poor employee performance will ultimately manifest themselves in customer service. A client survey can quickly identify issues with individuals. A positive response means your employee performance is meeting or exceeding expectations. What is the overall customer service experience of your recruiters and representatives?

Carry out random checks: Depending on the nature of your business consider implementing random checks against quality standards. This may include reviewing telephone calls and checking records. While your employees may be aware of this policy, the random nature of the checks can motivate staff to put in a consistent performance.

Evaluating employee performance should be carried out on an on-going basis and encompass all areas of their work ethic and individual achievements. Remember too, that poor performance or negative behaviors can also be symptomatic of an underlying problem with your organization's culture, so have a plan in place to address any issues you discover.

APPENDIX H

WORKPLACE BULLYING: A REVIEW OF ITS IMPACT ON BUSINESSES, EMPLOYEES, AND THE LAW

By D.N. McDonald, Edward D. Brown, and Kim F. Smith

1. INTRODUCTION

Workplace bullying is not a novel issue in the employment arena. The term denotes a topic that was conceived when Heinz Leymann conducted a pioneer study on challenges in work environments in Sweden in the 1980s. Other nations, such as England, have been researching this theory and evaluating the impact of workplace bullying since the 1980s and the beginning of the 1990s. In the mid to late 1990s, Drs. Gary and Ruth Namie began research on this concept (Yamada, 2010, p. 252–254). Committed to helping employees targeted by workplace bullying, they established the Workplace Bullying Institute. Pursuant to their research, the Namies defined workplace bullying as "the repeated, malicious, health-endangering mistreatment of one employee . . . by one or more employees" (Yamada, 2008, p. 49). Targets of workplace bullying may also experience a range of destructive behaviors that are abusive and promote the use of power from those who bully. Some of the most widespread behaviors include "yelling, shouting, and screaming; false accusations of mistakes and errors; hostile glares and other intimidating non-verbal behaviors; covert criticism, sabotage, and undermining of one's reputation . . . use of put downs, insults, . . . and unreasonably heavy work demands" (Yamada, 2008, p. 51).

Careful analysis of workplace bullying incidents has revealed significant commonalities among them. Generally, workplace bullying consists of three essential components: 1. regularity of incidents; 2. consequences to employee health and morale; and 3. business standards for the treatment of personnel (Martin and LaVan, 2010, p. 178). Even though research on workplace bullying has expanded since the 1990s, state laws and employer policies are not largely available to counter such behaviors or to adequately address resolutions for them. Furthermore, the lack of federal or state workplace bullying laws leave targeted employees without applicable legal recourse that is intentionally designed to prosecute offending parties and their employers. The purpose of this paper entails considering the importance of healthy work environments and the negative consequences of workplace bullying, fostering greater awareness of workplace bullying and the employer-employee roles in combating it, and exploring current and potential legal options for workplace bullying claims.

2. EMPLOYEE HEALTH CONCERNS IN THE WORKPLACE

2.1 Employer Preventive Health Measures

It is a well settled issue that employers have a vested interest in the overall physical and psychological health of their employees. In order to address employee health concerns, some U.S. businesses have implemented preventive health measures for employee wellness by providing medical services at their respective places of employment. These progressive employers proceed in part with the hope of offsetting rising health care employee costs (Suk, 2011, p. 1091). Serving as a model for other businesses, Mitsubishi Polyester Film, Inc. in Greer, South Carolina has an onsite family medical center created precisely to meet employee health demands. Accordingly, Michelin also instituted the Michelin Family Health Center in support of its employee wellness program (Livengood, 2011).

2.2 WORKPLACE HEALTH MODEL OF THE CENTERS FOR DISEASE CONTROL AND PREVENTION

Employee wellness programs receive further promotion from the Centers for Disease Control and Prevention (CDC), the U.S. Department of Health and Human Services, and other U.S. government entities. In fact, the CDC asserts that if employers sustain a health-conscious work environment, their actions may not only reduce worker compensation suits and insurance-related costs but also increase employee attendance and production. Businesses that are alarmed about the impact of healthcare, wellness expenses, and compensation on their bottom line profits may be extremely interested in workplace health programs like the CDC's Workplace Health Model ("Workplace Health," 2014). The Workplace Health Model includes four principal steps, namely assessment, planning, implementation, and evaluation, for both small and large businesses to execute. This model deals with a host of health-related issues, including depression, blood pressure, and alcohol and substance misuse, thereby encompassing common stress-related health concerns ("Workplace Health," 2014).

3. THE IMPACT OF WORKPLACE BULLYING

3.1 Workplace Bullying Incidents

Employment research analyses have revealed personal employee perspectives on workplace bullying. In the context of the Workplace Bullying Institute's 2014 U.S. Workplace Bullying Report, respondent data in part is as follows: 27% have previously and are still undergoing incidents of workplace bullying; 72% of businesses minimize workplace bullying; and 93% advocate for the implementation of workplace bullying laws like the Healthy Workplace Bill. Similarly, *Parade Magazine, Career Builder*, and *Yahoo* have accumulated workplace bullying statistics via nationwide surveys and other research; *New York Times* and *Wall Street Journal* set forth accounts of applicable workplace incidents (Yamada, 2008, p. 51). In fact, a 2014 *TIME Magazine* article commented on the gender demographics of workplace bullying, most notably that approximately two-thirds of men are workplace bullies while about two-thirds of women are targeted (White, 2014). The accumulated research exposes the breadth of employee apprehension over workplace bullying incidents, ineffective employer responses, and legal options for filing suits.

3.2 The Physical and Psychological Impact of Employee Health

Regardless of the preventive health measures instituted at the workplace, employers must fairly assess whether the culture of their work environments may lead to various health issues that would negatively impact their employees and businesses. "A growing body of empirical evidence demonstrates that workplace bullying has deleterious health effects both physically and psychologically" (Martin and LaVan, 2010, p. 178). Health professionals also indicate medical concern regarding work environments and employee health. When employees are bullied, they often feel depressed and hopeless, suffer from loss of appetite, and generally receive poor nutrition (Ingram, 2005, p. 70–74). Dr. Ingram (2005), in his book entitled *How to Eat Right and Live Longer*, discusses that a poor diet is a primary cause of heart disease, stroke, heart attack, hardening of the arteries, high blood pressure, cancer, diabetes, and arthritis as well as other numerous diseases (p. 70–74). Equally as wide-ranging, the psychological effects of abusive workplace environments on employees contrast greatly but are commonly detrimental to mental health. Employees may become fearful and less innovative, undergo mood swings, have emotional distress, and experience difficulty concentrating (Cortina, 2008, p. 56).

3.3 The Financial Impact on the Employer

Employers, as a result of workplace bullying and related malfeasance, may suffer financially. First, employers may bear direct expenses in the defense of lawsuits as well as additional worker's compensation and health-related complaints filed by employees. Second, indirect expenses may be expended in association with increased employee turnover, internal sabotage, and absenteeism because of conflict, a reduction in worker motivation, and health problems (Yamada, 2008, p. 53).

In consequence, if a culture of permissive workplace bullying exists, then the financial costs of utilizing a work preventive health program to address employee health problems may indeed be ineffective when employees work within this type of stressful environment. Within an internal management assessment, employers must initially determine that if workplace bullying is intentionally or unintentionally permitted and could lead to a number of health issues, then they may also conclude that by inadequately addressing these situations, designated preventive health measures may be offset and render health-related funding of minimal effect.

3.4 The Impact on Employee Behavior

Workplace bullying could foster further undesirable work environment situations, such as violence and severe incivility. In particular, deviant behavior is a potential result when employees perceive injustice or a lack of resolution in their employment circumstances. Furthermore, studies reveal that anger may be a collective workplace emotion, and thus, link anger to a host of unproductive workplace experiences that create a hostile work environment (Fitness, 2000, p. 149). Researchers connect these harmful experiences to negative employee actions.

> [R]esearch suggests that although workers who feel unjustly treated may not take direct or confrontational action to remedy the situation, they may take covert retaliatory action, such as theft or sabotage, in an attempt to 'get even' or to balance an apparently inequitable situation (Fitness, 2000, p. 149).

Likewise, Penney and Spector (2005), in a research study on work-related stress and incivility, discovered a strong correlation between workplace incivility and job satisfaction and performance (p. 789–791). These results support the premise that workplace bullying may lead to reduced employee productivity. With countless workplace cultural concerns, employers must seriously consider executing internal organizational policies to combat bullying within their businesses.

4. WORKPLACE BULLYING LEGAL CONSIDERATIONS

4.1 State Legislative Efforts

In the face of widespread research detailing the destructive effects of unhealthy work environments, state workplace bullying laws still remain mostly nonexistent, rendering the majority of targeted employees without appropriate legal recourse. Over the last several years, supporters of the proposed Healthy Workplace Bill, which was authored by law professor David Yamada, have spearheaded efforts to spread awareness and to enact state legislation of anti-workplace bullying statutes. For instance, in 2010, advocates in New York and Illinois introduced the Healthy Workplace Bill into their corresponding state legislatures; both state senate bodies approved it, but the bills did not pass other voting mandates (Yamada, 2010, p. 255–257). Notwithstanding these setbacks, the Healthy Workplace Bill and other anti-workplace bullying legislation gained national notice and support. In 2014, California and Tennessee passed state laws prohibiting abusive conduct at work. As of 2015, the Healthy Workplace Bill has been presented in variable forms in twenty-nine U.S. states and territories ("Healthy Workplace Bill", 2015). See Table 1.1.

Currently, modest progression is found in North Dakota and Connecticut via House Bill 1428 and Senate Bill 432 respectively. House Bill 1428 asserts anti-harassment language to protect public sector employees while the focus of Senate Bill 432 mandates additional employee safeguards against workplace bullying. Utah progresses even further in House Bill 216, requiring training for employees on workplace bullying, its impact on health, and available damages for successful claims. New York makes a strong anti-bullying stand through Assembly Bill 3250, which mimics the Healthy Workplace Bill in its entirety. ("Healthy Workplace Bill", 2015).

4.2 The Healthy Workplace Bill

In general, the Healthy Workplace Bill aims to serve as the leading status-blind legislation that would provide a legal means for employees to sue in state trial courts for legitimate, damaging workplace bullying that is conducted with malice. State trial court petitions are desirable in lieu of filing with government administrative agencies due in part to case volumes and potential backlog (Yamada, 2013, p. 337). For those asserting claims of workplace bullying, this bill proposes that:

> [I]t shall be an unlawful employment practice . . . to subject an employee to an abusive work environment . . . [An abusive work environment] exists when the defendant, acting with malice, subjects an employee to abusive conduct so severe that it causes tangible harm to the employee. [While malice is] . . . the desire to cause pain, injury, or distress to another (Yamada, 2010, p. 257).

Purposefully omitting a definition for workplace bullying and electing to define an abusive work environment, the Healthy Workplace Bill moves to separate simple incivility or unprofessional workplace behavior from abusive conduct and practices that create a hostile work environment. Due to its framework, the bill parallels with the meaning of an hostile work environment in discrimination suits under Title VII of the Civil Rights Act of 1964 (Title VII) as well as various tort laws (Yamada, 2010, p. 259–265).

Under the Healthy Workplace Bill, the aggrieved employees must successfully demonstrate that they have sustained tangible harm, meaning psychological or physical harm. Employers may assert affirmative defenses alleging that they exercised reasonable care in preventive and corrective measures in which the plaintiff did not utilize. If the plaintiff wins the case, then, as the injured party, the plaintiff may receive compensatory and punitive damages, injunctive relief, and attorney's fees. In certain circumstances, injunctive relief may require that the defendant, as the workplace harassing party, be barred from the plaintiff's employment area (Yamada, 2010, p. 259–265).

4.3 Discrimination and Tort Suits against Workplace Bullying

The success of abusive work conduct laws passed in 2014 in California and Tennessee is presently undetermined. Since workplace bullying claims began, targeted employees have generally filed actions against employers through existing tort and discrimination laws, such as intentional infliction of emotional distress (IIED), intentional interference with the employment relationship (IIER), disability discrimination and harassment laws, and the Occupational Safety and Health Law (OSHL). Each of these legal assertions maintains individual challenges in winning claims for bullied employees (Yamada, 2010, p. 259–265).

First, consider IIED. This tort occurs when one is "intentionally doing an outrageous act toward another which goes outside the bounds of common decency and causes the victim severe emotional distress" (Bennett-Alexander and Harrison, 2012, p. 137). From the court's perspective, the key difficulty with basing workplace bullying suits using IIED lies with inadequate proof of the extreme and outrageous standard, which requires an exceptionally indecent act that leads to a reasonable person undergoing severe emotional distress. Second, under IIER, if circumstances permit an employee to sue a co-worker, the state court in which the suit is filed may not acknowledge that a co-worker can be classified as a legitimate third-party. This must be done to meet the requirements for the suit (Bennett-Alexander and Harrison, 2012, p. 137–141).

Next, and potentially more successful, are those workplace bullying lawsuits firmly connected to protected class discrimination concerning race, color, national origin, religion, and gender under Title VII, a recognized disability classified in the Americans with Disabilities Act of 1990 (ADA), age under the Age Discrimination in Employment Act, or state anti-discrimination laws. These discrimination-based suits could yield damages for plaintiffs on both federal and state levels. (Yamada, 2010, p. 259–265).

> Based on a sample of 45 litigated cases spanning 5 years, . . . it was discovered that Title VII race discrimination occurred in one-third (35.6%) of the cases; Title VII gender discrimination in nearly one-third (28.9%) of the cases; Title VII national origin discrimination in less than one-tenth (6.7%) of the cases tied with Title VII age discrimination; . . . and Title VII religious discrimination in 2.2% of the cases . . . The effects of the workplace bullying . . . were stress (53.3%), retaliation (17.8%), reduced productivity (13.3%), Post Traumatic Stress Disorder (4.4%), and violence (4.4%). The organizational effects of workplace bullying ... were reduced morale (31.1%), decreased productivity (13.3%), safety (6.7%), and voluntary turnover (2.2%) (Martin and LaVan, 2010, p. 186).

Then similar to Title VII and ADA, other federal and state regulations, like the OSHL, may also afford potential success for workplace bullying claims. However, one major drawback is that "the absence of direct compensation to injured parties makes" this law "a less than ideal frontline weapon in the legal struggle against workplace bullying" (Yamada, 2010, p. 259). Finally, one additional option that has not yet been tested is a governor-issued executive order, which could mandate state organizations to abide by anti-workplace bullying policies (Yamada, 2010, p. 256–265). In spite of the diverse set of laws presently used to prosecute workplace bullying actions, the majority of plaintiffs have not experienced notable success in court holdings for these cases.

5. RESPONSES TO WORKPLACE BULLYING

5.1 Organizational Responses

Business leadership and management set the cultural climate for actions fostering worker dignity, respect, and civility in the work environment. To formulate such a cultural climate, organizations must design and create internal policies that promote these desired goals. Places of employment should aim to have annual training on workplace bullying, its impact, and the potential consequences for bullies and their targets through the human resources and/or legal departments. Once implemented, it is incumbent upon management to indorse and encourage appropriate workplace behavior through modeling appropriate actions and reinforcement of such policies. Furthermore, employers have the option of implementing and enforcing more stringent workplace rules and bylaws in efforts to combat workplace bullying. Workplace bullying expert Dr. Gary Namie strongly suggests that employers incorporate and follow a four-tier model, categorized as the "values-driven policy, credible enforcement processes, restorative interventions . . ., and general and specialized education," (Yamada, 2008, p. 55–56) to assist with the beginning stages of this process. When leadership and management entities do not implement and/or follow employment policies for the protection of its employees and its business, opportunities exist for employee conflict and employer apathy.

5.2 Individual Responses

According to workplace bullying consultants, employees must be diligent in their responses to workplace bullying. Possibly the most important suggestion for targets who encounter bullying is to maintain detailed documentation of an incident in close proximity to its occurrence. Other suggestions are to avoid being overly accommodating or friendly and to find and sustain a solid support system that is not affiliated with the workplace. Lastly, employees should address workplace bullying concerns with management with a focus on how these incidents impede productivity in the workplace. In total, targets of workplace bullying are encouraged to be proactive in their own defense (White, 2014).

6. CONCLUSION

Within the management assessment framework, the reasons for the continuation of workplace bullying must be evaluated. Although none are conclusive, a few interesting points regarding this dilemma are worthy of consideration. One reason may be the perception that adults can not be bullied. This perception dilutes the reality of workplace bullying and tends to cause business managers to handle it in a nonchalant manner or to equate it as a lesser workplace issue. This is a critical point, especially if management does not take action or appropriately address workplace incivility or behaviors that are described as excessively assertive, autocratic behavioral styles, pushy attitudes, rude demeanor, and brash, tactless engagements. In fact, these behaviors may often be considered as personality or managerial style differences (Yamada, 2008, p. 51–56).

Another major area of concern centers on gender bias. Prior to reporting incidents of workplace bullying, employees will likely ponder the internal workplace consequences of such actions. A male employee who complains about being bullied may be viewed as weak or lacking the fortitude to spearhead a solid leadership base at work. On the other hand, a female who files a workplace bullying complaint might be labeled as being too emotional or sensitive. Contrastingly, if a woman is in fact the workplace bully, she may be dismissed as being bossy or assertive while the actions of a male counterpart may be ignored and discounted completely (Yamada, 2008, p. 51–54).

Since most of the existing administrative and legal options for those subjected to workplace bullying are not specifically tailored to meet relevant bullying cases, they still do not provide the most favorable outcomes. Consequently, targeted employees may remain in undesirable employment conditions.

Empirical research data strongly suggests that stress, depression, feelings of injustice, and anger may be the result for not only the targets of workplace bullying but also their co-workers and families (Cortina, 2008, p. 56). More far-reaching consequences are those in which the community is negatively affected by bullied employees who may engage in violent actions to deal with unfair workplace situations. Ultimately, whether an advocate or opponent of the Healthy Workplace Bill, one must acknowledge that historically and civilly the law has been an avenue through which societal issues are eventually mediated. It appears that the rising tide of workplace bullying concerns will not peak and fall. A plausible means of properly handling such matters must be designed for the benefit of all stakeholders in this growing societal challenge.

Table 1.1 — U.S. States and Territories with Anti-Workplace Bullying Legislative Action

California*	Maine	Nevada	Oklahoma	Washington
Connecticut**	Maryland	New Hampshire	Oregon	West Virginia
Florida	Massachusetts	New Jersey	Pennsylvania	Wisconsin
Hawaii	Minnesota	New Mexico	Tennessee*	Puerto Rico
Illinois	Missouri	New York**	Utah**	US Virgin Islands
Kansas	Montana	North Dakota**	Vermont	

Note: * indicates states that created laws against abusive work conduct in 2014 and ** are states with 2015 bills before their state legislatures ("Healthy Workplace Bill", 2015).

REFERENCES

Bennett Alexander, D. and Harrison, L. (2012). Torts. In L. Kueter (Special Edition.), The Legal, Ethical, and Regulatory Environment of Business in a Diverse Society (pp.137–141). Boston: McGraw-Hill Companies.

Cortina, L. (2008). Unseen Injustice: Incivility as Modern Discrimination in Organizations. The Academy of Management Review, 33, 55–75.

Fitness, J. (2000). Anger in the workplace: an emotion script approach to anger episodes between workers and their superiors, co-workers and subordinates. Journal of Organizational Behavior, 21, 147–162.

Healthy Workplace Bill. (2015, February 10). [State of the Union: State Activity]. Retrieved from http://www.healthyworkplacebill.org/index.php

Ingram, C. (2005). How to Eat Right and Live Longer. Buffalo Grove: Knowledge House Publishers.

Livengood, Nichole. (2011). Employers Turn to Preventive Health. Greenville Business Magazine.

Martin, W. and H. LaVan. (2010). Workplace Bullying: A Review of Litigated Cases. Employee Responsibilities and Rights Journal, 22(3), 175–194.

Penney, L. and P. Spector. (2005). Job Stress, Incivility, and Counterproductive Work Behavior (CWB): The Moderating Role of Negative Affectivity. Journal of Organizational Behavior, 26(7), 777–796.

Suk, J. (2011). Preventive Health at Work: A Comparative Approach. The American Journal of Comparative Law, 59, 1089–1134.

White, M. (2014, March). Bullying at Work: How to Make It Stop. Time, 183(9). Retrieved from http://time.com/17168/bullying-at-work-how-to-make-it-stop/

Workplace Bullying Institute. (2014, October 1). 2014 WBI U.S. Workplace Bullying Survey. Retrieved from http://www.workplacebullying.org/wbiresearch/wbi-2014-us- survey/

Workplace Health Promotion: Making a Business Case. (2014, October 23). Centers for Disease Control and Prevention. Retrieved from http://www.cdc.gov/workplacehealthpromotion/businesscase/index.html

Yamada, D. (2013). Emerging American Legal Responses to Workplace Bullying. Temple Political and Civil Rights Law Review, 22(2), 329–354.

Yamada, D. (2010). Workplace Bullying and American Employment Law: A Ten-Year Progress Report and Assessment. Comparative Labor Law and Policy Journal, 32(1), 251–284.

Yamada, D. (2008). Workplace Bullying and Ethical Leadership. Journal of Values-Based Leadership, I(2), 49–62.

APPENDIX I

TEST YOUR FMLA KNOWLEDGE

Published August 2010

Please choose the best answer. The correct answers are listed at the bottom of this quiz.

Quiz Questions:

1. **True or False: An employee can take FMLA leave for a common cold or flu.**
   A) False, under the new definitions it is unlikely that the conditions of a cold, flu, etc. apply as a serious medical condition.
   B) True, common colds and the flu are considered a serious health condition under the FMLA.

2. **How many hours and/or months must an employee work to be eligible for FMLA leave?**
   A) Employees must have worked at least 625 hours over the course of the last 6 months to be eligible for FMLA leave.
   B) Employees must have worked at least 1,250 hours over the course of the last 12 months to be eligible for FMLA leave.
   C) Employees must have been employed for at least 6 months in the last 7 years by their employer to be eligible for FMLA leave.

3. **How much leave is an eligible employee entitled to under FMLA?**
   A) The employee is entitled to 12 weeks of leave during a 12-month period. The maximum combined leave time is 26 weeks if care is for a wounded military veteran.
   B) The employee is entitled to 16 weeks of leave during a 12-month period regardless of who the care is for.
   C) The employee is entitled to 16 weeks of leave during a 12-month period. The maximum combined leave time is 32 weeks if care is for a wounded military veteran.
   D) The employee is entitled to 26 weeks of leave during a 12-month period.

4. **Do the 12 months of service with the employer have to be continuous or consecutive?**
   A) Yes, the 12 months of service have to be both continuous and consecutive.
   B) No, the 12 months of service must only be consecutive.
   C) No, the 12 months of service must only be continuous.
   D) No, all time worked during the past 7 years is counted. The work time does not have to be continuous.

5. **Do the 1,250 hours include paid leave time or other absences from work?**
   A) No, only paid leave time is included when computing the 1,250 hours minimum.
   B) No, the 1,250 hours include only those hours actually worked during the most recent past 12 months for the employer. Paid leave and unpaid leave, including FMLA leave, are not included.
   C) Yes, paid leave and unpaid leave including FMLA leave time are included when computing the 1,250 hour minimum.
   D) Yes, paid leave and unpaid leave, excluding FMLA leave time are included when computing the 1,250 hour minimum.

6. **How many employees must a company have for the FMLA to apply to them?**
   A) 20 or more employees.
   B) 50 or more employees.
   C) 75 or more employees.
   D) 100 or more employees.

7. **Does it make a difference if the employee is full time or part time?**
   A) No, all persons on your payroll disregarding their FLSA status are covered under the FMLA and all of its provisions.
   B) Yes, employees must be full time to be covered under the FMLA and all of its provisions.

8. **True or False: When requesting FMLA for a serious health condition for him/herself, it is required that an employee sees a health care provider.**
   A) False, it is not necessary for the employee to visit a doctor to complete the medical certification and request leave for a serious health condition.
   B) True, for most cases, the employee must see a HCP, Physician Assistant (PA) or other recognized provider during the first 7 days of the potentially qualifying event and again within 30 days (2 visits—may be HCP required or waived) or during the first 7 days of the occurrence and be under the HCP's care requiring at least 2 visits per year.

9. **Is the 12 week FMLA leave considered to be 12 weeks × 40 hours per week = 480 hours? So if an employee is working 50 hours work weeks, is the FMLA period 9.5 weeks?**
   A) No, you must calculate actual work replacement. This means that an employee who works 50 hours per week will have up to 600 hours of intermittent leave available. If the employee works 32 hours per week, then the calculation is 32 hours per week × 12 weeks = 384 hours.
   B) Yes, the employee is allowed 480 hours of FMLA leave only.

10. **What if you provide someone an FMLA leave but they do not have one full year of service yet?**
    A) You must accept the error and allow the claim to continue. You should then re-establish your FMLA program by informing the employees as of this date the following provisions of the FMLA and company policy will be enforced without exception or consideration of previous action.
    B) You may cancel any employee's FMLA leave at any time if you discover you made a mistake and the employee was not eligible for FMLA leave.

Correct Answers:

1) **A**; 2) **B**; 3) **A**; 4) **D**; 5) **B**; 6) **B**; 7) **A**; 8) **B**; 9) **A**; 10) **A**

APPENDIX J

COMMUNICATIONS STYLE INVENTORY

This is an informal survey, designed to determine how you usually act in everyday related situations. The idea is to get a clear description of how you see yourself. On the answer sheet, circle A or B in each pair of statements below, which shows the one that MOST, describes you.

1. **A)** I'm usually open to getting to know people personally and establishing relationships with them.
   B) I'm not usually open to getting to know people personally and establishing relationships with them.

2. **A)** I usually react slowly and deliberately.
   B) I usually react quickly and spontaneously.

3. **A)** I'm usually guarded about other people's use of my time.
   B) I'm usually open to other people's use of my time.

4. **A)** I usually introduce myself at social gatherings.
   B) I usually wait for others to introduce themselves to me at social gatherings.

5. **A)** I usually focus my conversations on the interests of the people involved, even if that means straying from the business or subject at hand.
   B) I usually focus my conversations on the tasks, issues, business, or subject at hand.

6. **A)** I'm usually not assertive, and I can be patient with a slow pace.
   B) I'm usually assertive, and at times I can be impatient with a slow pace.

7. **A)** I usually make decisions based on facts or evidence.
   B) I usually make decisions based on feelings, experiences or relationships.

8. **A)** I usually contribute frequently to group conversations.
   B) I usually contribute infrequently to group conversations.

9. **A)** I usually prefer to work with and through others, providing support when possible.
   B) I usually prefer to work independently or dictate the conditions in terms of how others are involved.

10. A) I usually ask questions or speak tentatively and indirectly.
B) I usually make empathic statements or directly expressed opinions.

11. A) I usually focus primarily on ideas, concepts, or results.
B) I usually focus primarily on persons, interactions, and feelings.

12. A) I usually use gestures, facial expression, and voice intonations to emphasize points.
B) I usually do not use gestures, facial expressions, and voice intonations to emphasize points

13. A) I usually accept others' points of view (ideas, feelings, and concerns).
B) I usually don't accept others' points of view (ideas, feelings, and concerns)

14. A) I usually respond to risk and change in a cautious or predictable manner.
B) I usually respond to risk and change in dynamic or unpredictable manner.

15. A) I usually prefer to keep personal feelings and thoughts private, sharing only when I wish to do to.
B) I usually find it natural and easy to share and discuss my feelings with others.

16. A) I usually seek out new or different experiences and situations.
B) I usually choose known or similar situations and relationships.

17. A) I'm usually responsive to others' agendas, interests, and concerns.
B) I'm usually directed toward my own agendas, interests and concerns.

18. A) I usually respond to conflict slowly and indirectly.
B) I usually respond to conflict quickly and directly.

ANSWER SHEET

O	G	D	I
1A	1B	2B	2A
3B	3A	4A	4B
5A	5B	6B	6A
7B	7A	8A	8B
9A	9B	10B	10A
11B	11A	12A	12B
13A	13B	14B	14A
15B	15A	16A	16B
17A	17B	18B	18A

TOTALS _____ _____ _____ _____

Total the numbers of items circled in each column and write it on the spaces above.

Now, compare the "O" column with the "G" column and circle the letter that has the highest total.

O or G

Then compare the "D" column with the "I" column and circle the letter that has the highest total.

D or I

SO WHAT'S THE VERDICT?

If you circled the G and D, you tend toward being a *Controller/Director.*

If you circled the O and D, you show many qualities of a *Promoter/Socializer.*

If you circled the O and I, you're predominantly a *Supporter/Relater.*

If you circled the G and I, you have lots of *Analyzer/Thinker* characteristics.

SUPPORTER/RELATER

- Harmonizer
- Values acceptance and stability in circumstances
- Slow with big decisions; dislikes change
- Builds networks of friends to help do work
- Good listener; timid about voicing contrary opinions; concerned for others' feelings
- Easy-going; likes slow, steady pace
- Friendly & sensitive; no person in unlovable
- Relationship Oriented

ANALYZER/THINKER

- Assessor
- Values accuracy in details & being right
- Plans thoroughly before deciding to act
- Prefers to work alone
- Introverted; quick to think and slow to speak; closed about personal matters
- Highly organized; even plans spontaneity!
- Cautious, logical, thrifty approach
- Thoughtful; no problem is too big to ponder
- Idea Oriented

PROMOTER/SOCIALIZER

- Entertainer
- Values enjoyment and helping others with the same
- Full of ideas and impulsive in trying them
- Wants to work to be fun for everyone
- Talkative and open about self; asks others' opinions; loves to brainstorm
- Flexible; easily bored with routine
- Intuitive, creative, spontaneous, flamboyant approach
- Optimist; nothing is beyond hope
- Celebration Oriented

CONTROLLER/DIRECTOR

- Commander
- Values getting the job done
- Decisive risk taker
- Good at delegating work to others
- Not shy but private about personal matters; comes on strong in conversation
- Likes to be where the action is
- Take charge, enterprising, competitive, efficient approach
- Fearless; no obstacle is too big to tackle
- Results Oriented

COMMUNICATION STYLES EXERCISE

Identify the communication style of each person described below. Simply use a letter **S** (Supporter/Relator); **C** (Controller/Director); **P** (Promoter/Socializer); **A** (Analyzer/Thinker).

1. _____George can quickly tell what's going on in any situation and is not afraid to speak out about what should be done. He doesn't follow the latest fad, but wears clothes that are practical. When you first meet George, you notice he is friendly. Later you realize he hasn't told you much about his personal life. You go out to lunch with George. He orders steak medium rare, but the meat is served nearly raw. George shouts for the waiter, and complains loudly. The waiter apologizes and takes the steak back to be cooked longer, but George doesn't want to wait. He demands to see the manager and tells her in the future he'll eat elsewhere. You both grab a lunch at a drive-through and are back at the office in time for George's next meeting.

2. _____Dave is really a nice guy. He's open and always willing to listen. On his desk are lots of photos with family and friends, many of them taken at Disneyland, the "happiest place on earth." Dave usually dresses in soft, warm colors, and hates to wear a coat and tie. You go out to lunch with Dave and he orders steak, well done. When he cuts into it, however, it's overdone and tough. He doesn't say a thing to you, and continues to eat. The waiter comes by and asks, "How is your steak?" Dave hesitantly replies he's sorry to say he likes his steak a little more tender. "Would you like me to take it back?" Dave answers, "Only if it's not too much trouble."

3. _____Jean is a rather complicated person. She cares a lot about what others think of her, but she is sometimes callous about the feelings of others. So she's both sensitive and insensitive. It can be confusing! There is no confusion about one thing-Jean is an excellent planner. She gathers all the data and can foresee potential problems. She researches ways to avoid them, at little cost to the company. At her desk, Jean displays her college diploma, framed, and a list of company policies. You go out to lunch with Jean, who orders steak medium well. It's a shade too pink for her, so she requests the waiter to have the chef cook it for exactly 2 and a half minutes more.

4. _____Caroline is a popular person with a big ego. She gets into many circumstances where she is the one to confront problems, because she knows how she thinks and feels about may issues. Caroline speaks her mind, but doesn't like to alienate others in the process. So she tries to make them feel good, about themselves and her. Caroline has a large closet full of clothes with lots of color, texture and bold designs. At her desk is a blown-up photo of her and the company president having fun at last year's Christmas party. You go out to lunch with Caroline and the steak is not cooked to her liking at all. She calls the waiter over immediately and asks for another plate. She quickly decided to try something else. "Bring me the sword fish special instead!"

APPENDIX K
FELIX EMPLOYMENT PERFORMANCE REVIEW

Employee: Stephanie Lane   Position: Administrative Assistant I

Date of Hire:_________   Department: HR__________   Supervisor: Min Kwon/Cameron Knox

Performance Review Period: ____

FELIX Performance Benchmarks: FELIX has four benchmarks for its 90-day FELIX Employment Performance Review.

Superior = SU	High Competence = HC	Satisfactory = SA	Requires Improvement = RI
Maintains superior work quality with minimal supervision and error	Maintains high level of work quality with need of some supervision and a few errors	Maintains satisfactory work quality with moderate supervision and errors	Maintains low level of work quality with high supervision and errors

Using the FELIX Performance Benchmarks rating chart, evaluate the employee's performance in the following areas:

1. Punctuality and Attendance

   ____

   ____

2. Content/Company Knowledge

   ____

   ____

3. Quality of Work and Productivity

   ____

   ____

4. Leadership Qualities

   ____

   ____

5. Team Work

____

____

6. Individual Work

____

____

7. Honors/Accomplishments/Special Notes

____

____

8. Overall Level of Performance

____

____

Signature of Supervisor: ______________________ Date: ______________

Signature of Employee: ______________________ Date: ______________

Notes (For the Evaluator Only)

____

____

____

____

____

____

____

____

____

____

____

____

____

____

APPENDIX L
FELIX V. ADRIENNE RAY NEGOTIATION/ MEDIATION SIMULATION EXERCISE

Adrienne Ray has been on paid leave for several weeks. She is inquiring as to whether she may return to FELIX. Conduct a negotiation and/or mediation simulation between Adrienne and FELIX representatives. The instructor may include additional facts and issues as needed.

FACTS ABOUT ADRIENNE RAY

- Is 58 years old
- Has 35 hours of annual leave and 52 hours of sick leave
- Has 16 days of vacation time
- Has $160,000 in 401k
- Pays $60/month for full health benefits

ISSUES TO CONSIDER

1. Should DeAngelo have exercised his power to remove the client from Adrienne?

____

____

____

____

____

2. What disciplinary action(s) should occur, if any, regarding Adrienne?

____

____

____

____

____

3. What actions must occur to minimize the damage, if any, to FELIX's reputation?

____

____

____

____

____

REFERENCES

Alan Purton v. Marriott International, Inc. (Find Law 2013). Retrieved from http://caselaw.findlaw.com/ca-court-of-appeal/1640784.html.

Almay, S. (2014, April 27). *Will the NBA make Donald Sterling the first owner to give up team?* Retrieved from CNN website: http://www.cnn.com/2014/04/27/us/nba-clippers-donald-sterling-next/index.html.

Basic HR Solutions Come Full Circle (2010, August). *Test Your FMLA Knowledge* [Survey]. Retrieved from https://www.basiconline.com/news_posts/test-your-fmla-knowledge/.

Bennett-Alexander, D. & Harrison, L. (2012). Torts. In L. Kueter (Special Edition.), *The* Legal, Ethical, and Regulatory Environment of Business in a Diverse Society. Boston:McGraw Hill Irwin.

Bidwell, Allie. (2015, August 31). Racist Fraternity Chant Learned During Leadership Cruise. U.S. News and World Report. Retrieved from http://www.usnews.com/news/articles/2015/03/27/university-of-oklahoma-racist-chant-learned-during-leadership-cruise.

Cardon, P.W. (2014). Crisis Communications and Public Relations Messages. *Business Communication Developing Leaders for a Networked World* (pp. 300–332). New York, NY: McGraw-Hill Irwin.

Cheeseman, Henry. (2016). *Business Law: Legal Environment, Online Commerce, Business Ethics, and International Issues.* Boston: Pearson.

Creative Communications Group, Divorce Online 2015. Domestic Violence Definition. Retrieved from http://www.domesticviolence.org/definition/.

Department of Labor (2002). OSHA Fact Sheet, Workplace Violence. Retrieved from https://www.osha.gov/OshDoc/data_General_Facts/factsheet-workplace-violence.pdf.

Department of Labor (2008). The Family and Medical Leave Act of 1993 67934 29 CFR Part 825). Federal Register *73*(222) Rules and Regulations.

Donald Sterling loses appeal to reverse sale of LA Clippers. (2015, November 29). Retrieved from http://www.cbsnews.com/news/donald-sterling-loses-appeal-to-reverse-sale-of-la-clippers/.

HBO Documentary Films (Producer). (2012). *Overweight in the Workplace (HBO: The Weight of the Nation)* [Documentary] retrieved from https://www.youtube.com/watch?v=BWI08ddBlno.

Healthy Workplace Bill. (2015, November 10). [State of the Union: State Activity]. Retrieved from 2016 Workplace Bullying Institute website: http://www.healthyworkplacebill.org/index.php.

Heathfield, S.M. (2015, October). What Is at *Will Employment*? See an at Will Policy for Your Employee Handbook. Retrieved from About.com website: http://humanresources.about.com/od/dictionarya/g/at_wll.htm.

Farlex, Inc. The Free Dictionary website: http://legal-dictionary.thefreedictionary.com/Due+Process+of+Law.

Fordyce Letter. (2014, June). *7 Ways to Measure Employee Performance*. Retrieved from http://www.eremedia.com/fordyce/7-easy-ways-to-measure-employee-performance/.

Jameson v. U.S. Postal Service, EEOC Appeal No. 0120130992, 2013 WL 2368729 (EEOC 2013). Retrieved from http://www.eeoc.gov/federal/reports/lgbt_cases.cfm.

Ketteler, J. (n.d.). How to *Ask for Flex Time*. Retrieved from Parents.com: http://www.parents.com/parenting/work/life-balance/flex-time/.

Levy, J. (2015). U.S. Obesity Rate Inches Up to 27.7% in 2014. Retrieved from Gallup: file:///E:/PCD/Lesson%20Plan/Permission%20Source%20Info%20Form/11_Perceptions%20of%20Beauty/U.S.%20Obesity%20Rate%20Inches%20Up%20to%2027_Gallup%20Obesity%20Rate.pdf

Lewicki, R., Barry, B., & Saunders, D. (2015). *Negotiation: Readings, Exercises, and Cases* (7th ed.). Boston: McGraw-Hill Irwin.

Lusardi v. Department of the Army, EEOC Appeal No. 0120133395, 2015 WL 1607756 (EEOC 2015) Retrieved from http://www.eeoc.gov/federal/reports/lgbt_cases.cfm.

Macy v. Department of Justice, EEOC Appeal No. 0120120821, 2012 WL 1435995 (EEOC 2012) *Retrieved from http://www.eeoc.gov/federal/reports/lgbt_cases.cfm.*

Martin, W., & LaVan, H. (2010). Workplace Bullying: A Review of Litigated Cases. *Employee Responsibilities and Rights Journal, 22*(3), 175–194.

Mathis, R., & Jackson, J. (2011). *Human Resource Management* (13th ed.). Mason, OH: South-Western Cengage Learning.

McDonald, D., Brown, E., & Smith K. (2015). Workplace Bullying: A Review of Its Impact on Business, Employees, and the Law. *International Journal of Business and Social Science, 6*(2), 27–31.

Nolo's Plain-English Law Dictionary. Retrieved from http://www.nolo.com/dictionary.

Penney, L., & Spector, P. (2005). Job stress, incivility, and counterproductive work behavior (CWB): The moderating role of negative affectivity. *Journal of Organizational Behavior, 26*(7), 777–796.

Plous, S. (2003). *The psychology of prejudice, stereotyping, and discrimination: An overview*. In S. Plous (Ed.), Understanding Prejudice and Discrimination (pp. 3–48). New York, NY: McGraw-Hill. Retrieved from: http://www.understandingprejudice.org/anthol.htm.

Plous, S. (2003). *The psychology of prejudice: An overview*. (pp. 3–48). New York, NY: McGraw-Hill. Retrieved in abbreviated form from http://www.tolerance.org/bias-self-assessment.

Prater, T., & Smith, K. (2011). Underlying factors contributing to presenteeism and absenteeism. *Journal of Business & Economics Research, 9*(6), 1–14.

Prokosch, Ron. (2011, September 22). Nepotism. Retrieved from file:///E:/PCD/Lesson%20Plan/Permission%20Source%20Info%20Form/03_Incompetent%20Leadership/NEPOTISM_Article_Case.IncompLeadrshp-02.pdf

Reynolds Lewis, K. (2015, July). *How Men Flex: The Working Mother Report.* Retrieved from the EY-Working Mother Report website: http://www.wmmsurveys.com/How_Men_Flex_Report_WMRI.pdf.

Reporters Committee for Freedom of the Press. (2012). State-by-State Guide. Retrieved from Reporters Committee for Freedom of the Press website: http://www.rcfp.org/reporters-recording-guide/state-state-guide.

SHRM Knowledge. Society for human resource management. *The Business Literacy Glossary of Terms.* Retrieved from: http://www.shrm.org/templatestools/glossaries/hrterms/pages/default.aspx.

The Counseling Team International. (2000–2016). Stress Indicators Questionnaire. [Survey]. Retrieved from file:///C:/Users/ksmith/Downloads/05%20Stress%20Indicators.pdf

The Southern Poverty Law Center (2016). Test Yourself for Hidden Bias. Retrieved from http://www.tolerance.org/bias-self-assessment.

Title VII of the Civil Rights Act of 1964. Retrieved from http://www.eeoc.gov/laws/statutes/titlevii.cfm.

Tony, A., & O'Connor, M. (1996). Communications Style Inventory [Survey]. The Platinum Rule. New York, NY: Warner Brooks. Retrieved from http://occonline.occ.cccd.edu/online/klee/CommunicationsStyleInventory.pdf.

U.S. Equal Employment Opportunity Commission. (n.d.). *Age Discrimination in Employment Act of 1967.* Retrieved from http://www.eeoc.gov/laws/statutes/adea.cfm.

U.S. Equal Employment Opportunity Commission. (n.d.). *Facts about Pregnancy Discrimination.* Retrieved from http://www1.eeoc.gov//laws/types/pregnancy.cfm?renderforprint=1

U.S. Equal Employment Opportunity Commission. (2014). *Pregnancy Discrimination Act.* Retrieved from http://www1.eeoc.gov//laws/types/pregnancy.cfm?renderforprint=1.

U.S. Equal Employment Opportunity Commission. (2015, December). *What You Should Know About EEOC and the Enforcement Protections for LGBT Workers.* Retrieved from http://www.eeoc.gov/eeoc/newsroom/wysk/enforcement_protections_lgbt_workers.cm.

U.S. Equal Employment Opportunity Commission. (2016, January). *Title VII of Civil Rights Act of 1964.* Retrieved from *http://www.eeoc.gov/laws/statutes/titlevii.cfm.*

U.S. Government Publishing Office. (2016). *Violence Against Women Reauthorization Act of 2013.* Retrieved from

U.S. Securities and Exchange Commission. (2015). *The Laws That Govern the Securities Industry.* Retrieved from https://www.sec.gov/about/laws.shtml.

Voluntary Safety and Health Program Management Guidelines. U.S. Department of Labor website: http://ehs.okstate.edu/training/oshaprog.htm

Wilkie, D. (2016, March). Where the bullies are: Why bad behavior is more prevalent in certain fields and what you can do about it. *HR Magazine SHRM.org*, 56, 51–54.

Workplace Bullying Institute. (2015, October 1). 2014 WBI U.S. Workplace Bullying [Survey]. Retrieved from http://www.workplacebullying.org/wbiresearch/wbi-2014-us- survey/.

Workplace Health Promotion (2013, October 23): Making a Business Case. Centers for Disease Control and Prevention website. Retrieved from http://www.cdc.gov/workplacehealthpromotion/businesscase/index.html.

Yamada, D. (2008). Workplace bullying and ethical leadership. *Journal of Values-Based Leadership, 1*(2), 49–62.

Yamada, D. (2010). Workplace Bullying and American Employment Law: A Ten-Year Progress Report and Assessment. *Comparative Labor Law and Policy Journal, 32*(1), 251–284.

Yamada, D. (2013). Emerging American legal responses to workplace bullying. Temple Political and Civil Rights Law *Review, 22*(2), 329–354.

www.ingramcontent.com/pod-product-compliance
Ingram Content Group UK Ltd.
Pitfield, Milton Keynes, MK11 3LW, UK
UKHW052008041026
15590UKWH00008B/2213

9 781465 275172